The Behavioral Investor

Educated at Brigham Young and Emory Universities, Dr Daniel Crosby is a psychologist, behavioral finance expert and asset manager who applies his study of market psychology to everything from financial product design to security selection. He is co-author of the *New York Times* bestseller *Personal Benchmark: Integrating Behavioral Finance and Investment Management* and founder of Nocturne Capital. He is at the forefront of behavioralizing finance. His ideas have appeared in the *Huffington Post* and *Risk Management Magazine*, as well as his monthly columns for WealthManagement.com and *Investment News*.

Daniel was named one of the "12 Thinkers to Watch" by Monster.com, a "Financial Blogger You Should Be Reading" by AARP and in the "Top 40 Under 40" by *Investment News*.

When he is not consulting around market psychology, Daniel enjoys independent films, fanatically following St. Louis Cardinals baseball, and spending time with his wife and three children.

Also by Daniel Crosby

Everyone You Love Will Die

You're Not That Great

Personal Benchmark: Integrating Behavioral Finance and Investment Management (with Chuck Widger)

The Laws of Wealth: Psychology and the secret to investing success

Dr Daniel Crosby

The
Behavioral
Investor

Hh

Hh Harriman House

HARRIMAN HOUSE LTD
18 College Street
Petersfield
Hampshire
GU31 4AD
GREAT BRITAIN
Tel: +44 (0)1730 233870
Email: enquiries@harriman-house.com
Website: www.harriman-house.com

First published in Great Britain in 2018
Copyright © Daniel Crosby

The right of Daniel Crosby to be identified as the Author has been asserted in accordance with the Copyright, Design and Patents Act 1988.

Print ISBN: 978-0-85719-686-6
eBook ISBN: 978-0-85719-687-3

British Library Cataloguing in Publication Data
A CIP catalogue record for this book can be obtained from the British Library.

For Katrina, the Why that guides my every How

For Charlotte, Liam and Lola, my light

Every owner of a physical copy of this edition of

The Behavioral Investor

can download the eBook for free direct from us at Harriman House, in a format that can be read on any eReader, tablet or smartphone.

Simply head to:

ebooks.harriman-house.com/behavioralinvestor

to get your free eBook now.

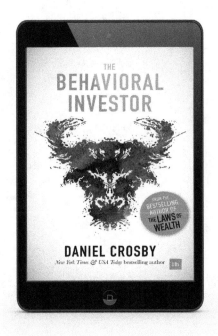

Contents

Foreword by Noreen D. Beaman

I HAVE WORKED WITH financial advisors and investors for the better part of 30 years. During that time, I have seen bubbles and busts, manias and meltdowns, and am now a firm believer that behavioral mastery is what separates successful from unsuccessful investors. Having now worked with and for some of the brightest minds on Wall Street, I can say with a confidence borne of a three-decade long career that the greatest financial intellect in the world is nothing if it is not paired with a self-understanding to match. All exceptional investing is, at its core, behavioral investing.

My adventure with Dr Daniel Crosby began in 2012 when he began to assist our firm in creating a framework to help financial advisors capture the elusive "behavioral alpha," or the outperformance that accrues to clients receiving sound behavioral coaching. Based on the success of this effort, we further deepened our commitment to behavioral finance by partnering with Daniel to create The Center for Outcomes, an educational initiative designed to combat the 50% non-compliance among clients receiving formal financial advice. After all, the only advice that works is advice that is followed through.

The ideas set forth in this book represent the coming together of years of applied work combined with a comprehensive review of the literature on psychologically informed investing. It is only through this blend of theory and praxis that we can begin to protect individuals from their greatest enemy: themselves.

My favorite part of beginning a new read is taking a step into the unknown. What new things will I learn? How might I begin to question some of my cherished beliefs? Will I walk away with information that changes the way that I live my life? While many investment books are a tepid rehashing of old ideas, *The Behavioral Investor* sets forth a vision for an entirely new planning and investing paradigm.

The journey that Daniel takes us on is by turns surprising, far ranging, sometimes downright weird, but always informative. Whether by drawing comparisons between monkeys and financial markets or ugly German towns and our penchant for the status quo, *The Behavioral Investor* has a knack for making the complex easily understandable. The reader will leave with a deep belief that there is no understanding markets without first understanding people and Daniel is a skilled guide through the labyrinthine maze of human behavior.

Daniel clearly demonstrates through effective sharing of the science and history that our brains, while unrivaled in sophistication, are still woefully ill-suited for the task of long-term investing. We are simultaneously the most evolved species on the planet and wholly unprepared for the demands of modern life. But this book is ultimately hopeful, and our shortcomings are only presented with an eye to setting forth solutions for the psychological traps to which we so easily succumb.

With humor, wisdom and, above all, passion, *The Behavioral Investor* sets forth a series of ideas that have done as much to enrich my life as they have my wallet. The best investment books understand that there is no growing of wealth without knowledge of self and *The Behavioral Investor* is a model of this new, more enlightened understanding of the financial world.

It is a rare finance book that can cause you to think, question and even laugh, but *The Behavioral Investor* is just such a work. I am confident that you will find it as enjoyable and impactful as I have.

Noreen D. Beaman
CEO, Brinker Capital

Preface

Gentle reader, the aim of this book is to be the most comprehensive guide to the psychology of asset management ever written. This goal is admittedly audacious, but I am a believer that only an impertinent dream such as this ought to give rise to so irrational an undertaking as writing a book.

In order to meet the full measure of its creation, *The Behavioral Investor* takes a sweeping tour of human nature before arriving at the specifics of portfolio construction. It is only as we come to a deep understanding of *why* humans make decisions in the way we do that we are left with any clue as to *how* we ought to invest.

This book is comprised of four parts. They are as follows:

- **Part One** – An explication of the sociological, neurological and physiological impediments to sound investment decision-making. Readers will leave with an improved understanding of how externalities impact choices and may also suffer a bout of existential malaise owing to an altered belief in free will.

- **Part Two** – Coverage of the four primary psychological tendencies that impact investment behavior. Although human behavior is undoubtedly complex, in an investment context our choices are largely driven by one of these four factors. Readers will emerge with an improved understanding of their own actions, increased humility and a deepened desire to do good in the world.

- **Part Three** – Illuminates the "so what" of Parts One and Two and provides practical exercises for overcoming the problems unearthed in previous chapters. Readers will complete Part Three with a greatly diminished belief in self and an uneasy awareness of the unpredictability of the world around them. No worries, though, it'll help in the end. I promise.

• **Part Four** – Provides a "third way" of investing that is distinct from popular passive and active approaches, as well as a framework for managing wealth in a manner consistent with the realities of our contextual and behavioral shortcomings. Readers will leave with a deeper understanding of the psychological underpinnings of popular investment approaches such as value and momentum and appreciate why all types of successful investing have psychology at their core. Those completing this section may feel an urge to wholly upend their current approach to investing, which in many cases will be exactly the right thing to do.

Wealth, truly considered, has at least as much to do with psychological as financial wellbeing. It is my hope that this book will leave you enriched in the most holistic sense of that word and that you will emerge with knowledge that will both improve your returns and make you more interesting at parties.

To greater things.

C. Daniel Crosby, Ph.D.

PART ONE.
THE BEHAVIORAL INVESTOR

Chapter 1.
Sociology

"Why, sometimes I've believed as many as six impossible things before breakfast."

— LEWIS CARROLL, *ALICE IN WONDERLAND*

IMAGINE FOR A moment that you are seated in the first class cabin of a luxury airliner, soon to wing your way toward Hawaii on a long overdue vacation. You have been working nonstop of late and you can actually feel the tension melting from your neck and shoulders as you settle in to your seat and accept the flight attendant's offer of a celebratory glass of bubbly. Better still, you are seated next to an attractive individual who bypasses the usual airplane banter and immediately engages you in a conversation that makes the first part of the trip speed past.

One hour into your voyage the plane encounters some turbulence, not entirely unwelcome as it allows for a serendipitous meeting of hands between you and your seatmate as you both grasp for your armrests. A shared laugh dissipates the fear, but as the tumult persists, you begin to worry that this isn't your average storm. Scanning the aircraft you sense similar concern on the faces of the flight attendants, who are now moving with a great deal of purpose. The wind and rain seem to intensify with every passing second and you feel more nauseated with every bump. The captain, who had previously addressed the plane with a certainty borne of experience, now speaks in a voice filled with fear. "Heads down! Brace for impact!" she shouts as you feel the plane start to list and shake.

As you regain consciousness you find yourself 100 yards from the charred remains of the plane and a quick survey of the scene reveals the worst – there are no other human survivors. Head in hands, your mind begins to race through a thousand scenarios, a convoluted mix of what might have been and "What comes next?" But you are soon interrupted by an unusual sound.

Scratch. Scraaaatch. BOOM.

Your eyes dart around your new environs until they land on the source of the racket, a mangled cage with a small sign, "Property of the Atlanta Zoo." At length, the occupant of the cage makes itself known – an Angolan Colobus monkey.

Man versus wild

Assume for the sake of our thought experiment that it will take 18 months for a search party to discover the uninhabited island where you have crashed and that you and the monkey – the lone survivors of the ill-fated flight – will be left to fend for yourselves until that time. When the rescue party arrives, whom do you think will be in better shape, you or the monkey? If you are honest with yourself, I think you will agree the monkey has better prospects than you or I when dropped in the middle of nowhere and asked to survive. When the search party arrives they may well find your sun-bleached bones, whereas the monkey seems likely to be thriving, happy to be free of the taunts of school children on field trips.

Yuval Noah Harari asks us to consider a stranger, slightly less plausible variant of this experiment in his superb TED talk, 'Bananas in heaven.'[1] Imagine that your plane was filled with 1000 humans and 1000

---

[1]   Yuval Noah Harari, 'Bananas in heaven,' TEDx (2014).

monkeys, all of which survived and were forced to live on a remote island. Would the results be the same when the rescuers landed on the shore a year and a half later? Likely not. In the second scenario, the humans have the edge for a reason that sits at the heart of our ability to build both great societies and functioning capital markets: our ability to flexibly cooperate with one another.

Sure, Harari concedes, some animals like bees and ants are able to cooperate, but do so only in a very rigid, hierarchical way. As the historian quips, bees are unlikely to plot a coup against the queen bee and have her killed in an effort to form a bee republic. Bees and ants accomplish great things but are cognitively inflexible, which limits their ascension up the food chain. Monkeys, on the other hand, are highly intelligent and have complex social structures, but they are limited by the number of social interactions they can meaningfully process. Psychologists put this number at about 150 in humans; a useful yardstick for evaluating our primate brethren. After about 100 relationships, monkeys begin to lose the ability to know their peers well enough to make accurate judgments about their behavior, character and intentions, effectively capping the size and complexity of monkey civilizations.

If bees organize by innate mandate and chimps through tight-knit social interactions, the miracle of human ascendance in the animal kingdom owes to a penchant for behaving in accordance with social narratives. To put it bluntly, we make up stories about the world and then act as if they are real. As Harari writes in the magisterial *Sapiens*, "As far as we know, only Sapiens can talk about entire kinds of entities that they have never seen, touched or smelled."[2] A monkey can say, "There is a caribou by the river," but could never communicate that, "The caribou by the river is the spiritual guardian of our city."

This ability to communicate about the unreal allows us humans to create all manner of social structures that help bring about predictable human behavior and that reliably breed trust. The State of Alabama, the Catholic church, the Constitution of the United States of America, the inalienable civil rights of man: none of these things are *real* in the strictest sense, but our shared belief in them and behaving as though they are real brings about orderly civilizations steeped in mutual trust.

[2]   Yuval Noah Harari, *Sapiens* (Harper, 2015), p. 24.

This ability to form and buy in to collective fictions is why, "…Sapiens rule the world, whereas ants eat our leftovers and chimps are locked up in zoos."[3]

If our dominance as a species is a function of our shared trust in fictions, there is one fiction in particular that reigns supreme: money. Harari pulls no punches: "Money is the most universal and most efficient system of mutual trust ever devised."[4] There is, of course, nothing inherently valuable about the pieces of paper for which we all spend our lives toiling, dreaming and fretting. Money and capital markets are shared hallucinations whose value is more psychological than physical. The human mind gave rise to financial markets and to seek to understand them without an appropriate understanding of their genesis is folly in the extreme. There is no understanding markets without understanding people.

A blessing and a curse

Whether it be the birth of a child and sleepless nights, or financial prosperity and covetous relatives, few things in life are unequivocally good. So too it goes with mankind's greatest gift, for the same narrative cohesiveness that gives rise to stock markets can lead us to poor decisions in those very same markets! Hugo Mercier and Dan Sperber, authors of *The Enigma of Reason*, argue that human reason evolved not to be "correct" in the strictest sense of the word, but rather to privilege the stability of the shared beliefs that are the cornerstone of our species' success.[5]

To more fully understand this concept, it may be useful to consider the example of belief testing in both animals and humans. A human may encounter an idea that runs contrary to a deeply held belief – for instance, that "members of my chosen political party are smart and kind" – and this may cause painful cognitive dissonance. The proof against this cherished notion may be convincing in objective terms – failed policies, incompetent leadership, scientific realities that contradict

---

3   Harari, *Sapiens*, p. 25.
4   Harari, *Sapiens*, p. 180.
5   Hugo Mercier, *The Enigma of Reason* (Harvard University Press, 2017).

the party line – but political beliefs are often quite recalcitrant to change. Since shared communal beliefs are the glue that holds humankind together, breaking those bonds is no small task, even in the face of damning contraindications. A party zealot who experiences a change of mind does so at a great social cost and will lose relationships, sever social ties and be forced to come face to face with the reality that, "I was wrong." This change of heart, as logical as it may be, is corrosive in a very real sense to what makes us human.

Now, consider a gazelle possessed of the cherished belief that, "there are no lions around here." If said gazelle becomes aware of a rustling in the brush, it will immediately run off or be eaten. Animals are capable of only literal communication and thus reason in binary, literal terms. Lion or no lion? Run and hide or stay and eat?

Humans, who are capable of much greater complexity of thought, are accordingly capable of much greater self-deception and irrationality. A gazelle that reasoned like a human would confront a rustling in the grass with a litany of reasons why that couldn't possibly be a lion and would be eaten with alacrity. Gazelles possessed with poor objective reasoning skills don't live long enough to have offspring, which is a boon for the gazelle population.

The same cannot be said of humankind, where collectivism and irrational swagger may actually lead to greater fecundity. Inasmuch as we favor in-group allegiance over almost all else, people who self-aggrandize, belittle the "other" and eschew science may attain great positions of power and respect from other people. As Mercier and Sperber write, "Habits of mind that seem weird or goofy or just plain dumb from an 'intellectualist' point of view prove shrewd when seen from a social 'interactionist' perspective."[6]

The exception to the rule

Equity markets provide an exception to the heuristic that social coherence trumps logic. You were born to fit in, but investing requires you to stand out. You are wired to protect your ego, but success in

---

[6]   Elizabeth Kolbert, 'Why facts don't change our minds,' *The New Yorker* (February 27, 2017).

markets demands that you subvert it. You are programmed to ask, "Why?", but must learn to ask, "Why not?" We owe the existence of our cities, churches, founding documents and, yes, even capital markets, to a shared allegiance to the impossible. Thus, trusting in common myths is what makes you human. But learning not to is what will make you a successful investor.

Turtles all the way down

In his 1988 book, *A Brief History of Time*, the late Stephen Hawking relates a well-known story that is emblematic of both our desire to know what the world is all about and the sometimes-spurious attributions we make in that search:

> "A well-known scientist once gave a public lecture on astronomy. He described how the earth orbits around the sun and how the sun, in turn, orbits around the center of a vast collection of stars called our galaxy. At the end of the lecture, a little old lady at the back of the room got up and said: 'What you have told us is rubbish. The world is really a flat plate supported on the back of a giant tortoise.' The scientist gave a superior smile before replying, 'What is the tortoise standing on?' 'You're very clever, young man, very clever,' said the old lady. 'But it's turtles all the way down!'"[7]

Scientists, priests and philosophers have searched for root causes from time immemorial, and although the process has been imperfect, it has brought about some impressive results when viewed on a long enough timeline. Consider the ancient practice of alchemy. We mistakenly characterize it today as the avaricious effort to transmute base metals into gold, but in reality the primary goal of the alchemist was to discover the "bottom-most turtle." As Lewis Thomas writes:

> "Alchemy began long ago as an expression of the deepest and oldest of human wishes: to discover that the world makes sense. The working assumption – that everything on earth must be made up from a single, primal sort of matter – led to centuries of hard work aimed at isolating the original stuff and rearranging it to the

[7] Stephen Hawking, *A Brief History of Time* (Bantam, 1998).

alchemists' liking. If it could be found, nothing would lie beyond human grasp."[8]

In this broadest sense then, everyone involved in finance ought to be a sort of alchemist, searching for the root causes of observed market phenomena.

This search for enduring truths about capital markets is not merely some philosophical vision quest. Quite the contrary. An understanding of what (or who, in this case) comprises markets is a necessary first step to better investing. Early ideas about the atom conceived of it as resembling a small ball bearing; a closed, hard sphere. Subsequent conceptions understood it as indivisible and even when early representations of subatomic particles began to emerge they were misguided. Electrons were initially thought to float in a cloud of positive charges that resembled the planetary model of our solar system. Basically, it was thought that the universe was made up of, well, tiny little universes. A beautiful thought that appeals to the human need for order and symmetry, but sadly useless in building descriptive and predictive models.

Much like the early study of atoms, the study of financial markets has been beset by an adherence to theories that offered more in the way of mathematical elegance than real world applicability. The traditional finance paradigm is undergird by a belief in markets with "rational" participants. This rationality has two primary features: First, rational market participants have access to information and update their beliefs immediately upon gaining access to new information. Second, rational market participants make decisions consistent with Subjective Expected Utility (SEU). The idea of Subjective Expected Utility was outlined by L. J. Savage in his 1954 book, *The Foundations of Statistics*.[9] According to Savage, we size up the personal utility of a given choice and weigh that choice by the likelihood that it will or will not happen.

It is heartening to think of the sort of noble people we would be if we adhered to the expectations of neoclassical economic theory. We would make prudent nutritional choices that nurtured our long-term health.

---

[8]   Lewis Thomas, *Late Night Thoughts on Listening to Mahler's Ninth Symphony* (Penguin, 1995).

[9]   Leonard J. Savage, *The Foundations of Statistics* (Wiley, 1954).

We would ignore the daily ups and downs of the stock market in favor of a longer-term view aligned with our personal goals and needs. And we would set aside tribalism and prejudice to elect political leaders who would work for the greatest good while speaking to us with an eye to fact and nuance. I wish that humankind were this noble, but this model of humans and markets has about as much descriptive and predictive utility as the notion of an atom as a tiny planet. Instead, we are an increasingly panicked and obese mob intent on electing leaders who magnify the worst of humanity rather than appealing to the better angels of our nature.

It is only once we viewed atoms as they are that we were able to truly harness their power. Our ability to light up a city or level it entirely are a function of having left behind more elegant models of atomic anatomy for more accurate ones. Likewise, an understanding of markets that fails to account for the humans that drive them will be of limited use. Atoms are the fundamental units of matter. Cells are the fundamental units of living organisms. Words are the fundamental units of language. People are the fundamental units of markets.

In the next section, we will undertake an in-depth look at the biology, neurology and psychology of the human animal as it intersects with investment decision-making. I imagine that you will be surprised, amused and perhaps even upset by what you learn. But I hope that you will engage deeply with the ideas, because it is only as you begin to know yourself that you will begin to grow your wealth.

What's the big idea?

- Humankind's greatest asset is an ability to build trust through shared commitment to pro-social fictions.

- Capital markets and money are perhaps the most universally cherished and highest functioning of all of these shared narratives.

- This emphasis on communal narratives means that we tend to reason in social rather than objective terms.

- People are the fundamental units of capital markets.

- Therefore, our theories about markets can only be as good as our understanding of human nature.

Chapter 2.
Investing on the Brain

"I am a brain, Watson. The rest of me is a mere appendage."

— SIR ARTHUR CONAN DOYLE,
THE ADVENTURE OF THE MAZARIN STONE

THALES OF MILETUS was the founder of the school of natural philosophy, a contemporary of Aristotle and one of the seven sages of ancient Greece. Tasked with inscribing short words of wisdom onto the Temple of Apollo at Delphi, Thales was asked what the hardest and most important task of humanity was, to which he replied, "To know thyself." He was then asked the inverse and replied that "giving advice" was the thing least profitable to humankind that came very easily.

Unfortunately for investors, Wall Street has done a great deal of the latter and very little of the former, sometimes with disastrous consequences. Fortunately for you, we are going to make that right here and now. If knowing oneself is the sine qua non of successful investing, there is no better place to start than the seat of knowing – the brain.

Old, hungry, and impatient

"My Very Educated Mother Just Served Us Nine Pizzas."

"In 1492 Columbus sailed the ocean blue."

"Thirty days hath September, April, June and November…"

Mnemonics were invented by the ancient Greeks and have been used by students of all ages ever since. Whether they take the form of an acronym (RIP Pluto!), a rhyme, or visualization, their longevity is a testament to their usefulness. As we begin our discussion of the brain as it applies to investing, I'd like you to use a mnemonic to remember three important truths about the brain by visualizing a tweed-clad septuagenarian in line at a steak buffet at 4pm. Just like the person you've imagined, your brain is old, hungry and impatient.

Age

It isn't entirely fair to say that the brain is old inasmuch as our species is not that old in evolutionary terms, but our brains are certainly old relative to the modern milieu in which we utilize them. As Jason Zweig says in *Your Money and Your Brain*:

> "*Homo sapiens* is less than 200,000 years old. And the human brain has barely grown since then; in 1997 paleoanthropologists discovered a 154,000-year-old *Homo sapiens* skull in Ethiopia. The brain it once held would have been about 1,450 cubic centimeters in volume… no smaller than the brain of the average person living today."[10]

Our brains have remained relatively stagnant over the last 150,000 years, but the complexity of the world in which they operate has exponentiated. Formal markets like our stock market are just about 400 years old. It would be a gross understatement to say that our mental hardware has not caught up to the times.

Evolutionary vestiges are apparent in the actions of modern day investors, even though the reasons for these evolutionary behaviors

---

[10]   Jason Zweig, *Your Money and Your Brain: How the New Science of Neuroeconomics Can Help Make You Rich* (Simon & Schuster, 2008), p. 62.

have long since vanished. In ancient times, our ancestors would have stored excess food supplies from the spring and summer to be relied upon in the colder fall and winter months. Oddly enough, it would appear that saving and investing behavior ticks up today in the spring and summer months too, even when controlling for the impact of seasonality, past performance, advertising, and liquidity needs. These effects have been observed in the US, Canada and even Australia, where the seasons are nearly six months out of sync with North America. Although the ancient need for food storage does not apply, modern investors inexplicably take risk in the spring and summer to be able to ride out the harsh fall and winter.[11]

One consequence of our old equipment is that the brain can end up doing double duty, with primitive structures tasked with parsing risk and reward now charged with a job foreign to their design. Emotional centers of the brain that helped guide primitive behavior like avoiding attack are now shown by brain scans to be involved in processing information about financial risks. These brain areas are found in mammals the world over and are blunt instruments designed for quick reaction, not precise thinking. Rapid, decisive action may save a squirrel from an owl, but it certainly doesn't help investors. In fact, a large body of research suggests that investors profit most when they do the least.

The fund behemoth Vanguard examined the performance of accounts that had made no changes versus those who had made tweaks. Sure enough, they found that the "no change" condition handily outperformed the tinkerers. Behavioral economist Meir Statman cites research from Sweden showing that the heaviest traders lose 4% of their account value each year to trading costs and poor timing, and that these results are consistent across the globe. Across 19 major stock exchanges, investors who made frequent changes trailed buy and hold investors by 1.5 percentage points per year.

Perhaps the best-known study on the damaging effects of our brain's action bias also provides insight into gender-linked tendencies in

[11]   Lisa Kramer, 'Does the caveman within tell you how to invest?' *Psychology Today* (August 18, 2004); and M. J. Kamstra, L. A. Kramer, D. Levi and R. Wermers, 'Seasonal Asset Allocation: Evidence from Mutual Fund Flows' (December 2013).

trading behavior. Terrance Odean and Brad Barber, two of the fathers of behavioral finance, looked at the individual accounts of a large discount broker and found something that surprised them. The men in the study traded 45% more than the women, with single men out-trading their female counterparts by an incredible 67%. Barber and Odean attributed this greater activity to overconfidence, but whatever its psychological roots, it consistently degraded returns. As a result of overactivity, the average man in the study underperformed the average woman by 1.4 percentage points per year. Worse still, single men lagged single women by 2.3% – an incredible drag when compounded over an investment lifetime. For our purposes here, the important point is that the evolutionary tendency of the brain toward action – whether caused by overconfidence or some other factor – damages investing returns.

Impatience

In an effort to understand how the brain processes patience, McClure and colleagues measured the brain activity of participants as they made a series of choices with either immediate or delayed monetary rewards. When the choices involved an immediate reward, the ventral stratum, medial orbitofrontal cortex and medial pre-frontal cortex were all used – these are parts of the brain implicated in drug addiction and impulsive behavior. The prospect of an immediate reward provided a flood of dopamine that respondents found hard to resist. Choices among delayed rewards, on the other hand, activated the pre-frontal and parietal cortex, which are parts of the brain associated with deliberation. The results of the study suggest that our ability to control our short-term impulses toward greed are limited and that we are more or less wired for immediacy. Your brain is primed for action, which is great news if you are in a war and awful news if you are an investor, fighting to save for your retirement.[12]

---

[12]   Camelia M. Kuhnen and Brian Knutson, 'The influence of affect on beliefs, preferences, and financial decisions,' *Journal of Financial and Quantitative Analysis* (June 2011).

Hunger

Adding insult to injury, your brain is not only outdated and impatient, it is also the hungriest part of your body. Like an aging iPhone model, your brain simultaneously manages to have limited functionality and even worse battery life. Although the brain accounts for just 2% to 3% of total body weight, it consumes as much as 25% of the body's energy, even when we are at rest.[13] As a result of this outsized appetite, your brain is constantly searching for ways to go into energy saver mode and not work quite so hard. And while this is a natural and even beautiful manifestation of the body's harmony, it also means that we do a lot of coasting on the ideas of others and relying on cognitive shortcuts. In lots of scenarios, this leads to us making decisions that require little mental energy and are good enough, without being perfect. A vast majority of the time these good enough shortcuts do us no harm – you can drive home from work on autopilot and barely notice – but they can be profoundly damaging when making investment decisions, as we'll see later.

*　　*　　*

Your brain is a miracle unrivaled by even the most sophisticated technology, but it is a miracle equipped for a different time and place. After millennia of fighting famine, war and pestilence, we now live in a society of greater and greater ease that is increasingly left to fight psychological battles. Obesity will kill more people this year than hunger. Suicide claims more lives annually than war, terrorism and violent crime combined. Your brain is still fighting a war won eons ago and you must steel it for a new battle that rewards patience and consistency over speed and action.

Cash rules everything around me

Some critics of behavioral finance hypothesize that irrational behavior shown in the lab when working for course credit or candy bars will disappear when real money is on the line. Put simply, as the stakes get

---

[13]   Harari, *Sapiens*, p. 9.

higher, behavior gets sharper. To put this criticism to the test, let's play a game.

There are two people in this game: a "proposer" and a "responder." During each iteration of the game, $100 is placed between the two of you and the proposer is tasked with splitting that $100 between herself and the responder in such a way that the responder accepts the offer. The proposer can split the money any way she chooses, but the rules dictate that the dyad will only get to share the loot in the event that the responder agrees to the proposed split. Assuming that you have been assigned the responder role, consider how you would reply to the following splits:

- **Scenario 1**: The proposer offers to split the money evenly, $50 apiece.

- **Scenario 2**: The proposer offers to keep $99 for herself and offers you $1.

Odds are that when you read the first scenario, you happily agreed to the deal. You likely found it fair and mutually beneficial and so said, "Yes." When you are offered a fair deal like Scenario 1 it revs up your dorsolateral prefrontal cortex, a region associated with self-awareness and complex problem solving. You evaluate the deal analytically and determine that it is a win-win.

But what about Scenario 2? If you are like me you said something to the effect of, "Oh, hell no." If you said "No," you are in good company as the *Harvard Business Review* reports that, "responders rejected about fifty percent of low offers, as they felt insulted with the low offers. The responders would rather punish the proposers than make a buck themselves."[14]

But the behavior of the responders is not the only distinction here; lowball offers are actually processed in a different part of the brain altogether! Rather than being reasoned through in the prefrontal cortex, unfair offers are processed in the anterior insula, part of the brain's emotional processing center that is implicated in feelings like fear and

[14]   Kabir Sehgal, 'What happens to your brain when you negotiate about money,' *Harvard Business Review* (October 26, 2015).

anxiety. Interestingly, this emotional part of your brain also possesses spindle cells that are more commonly found in your digestive system. As Jason Zweig quips, "When you get a 'gut feeling' that an investment has gone sour, you might not be imagining. The spindle cells in your insula may be firing in sync with your churning stomach."

Before moving on from our game, it is worth pointing out that the rational response from the responder is always to take the deal. No matter how unfair the split, the money on offer wasn't yours to begin with and you'd be leaving with more than you started with. Yet even knowing what ought to be done, it is hard to move beyond our emotional responses to money and our thoughts around fairness. Logic, it would seem, has very little to do with it.

Canonical models of economics assume that money has indirect utility, that is, it is only as good as the things we can hope to buy with it, but neuroscience tells a different story. Neural evidence suggests that money produces the same sort of dopaminergic rewards as other primary reinforcers such as beautiful faces, funny cartoons, sports cars and drugs. It would seem that we like money at a primal level, independent of what it can do for us.

Likewise, older models of consumption assume that people care about stock market returns only insomuch as they finance things that the investor cares about. But simple models like this fail to accurately describe the real world, in which investors seem to care directly for big returns, independent of what those returns produce in terms of fulfilling wants and needs. We sometimes wonder at the irrational actions of some uber-wealthy individuals who lie, cheat and steal to compound an already impossibly large fortune. But our brains appear wired to value money directly and to never be fully sated in the pursuit of more.

Another Harvard study examined the neural activity of those playing a game in which they could lose money and found a great deal of activity in the nucleus accumbens, a part of the brain implicated in motivation, reward and addiction. The closest match for this brain activity was found in the brains of drug addicts high on cocaine, whose brain scans were almost identical. In direct contradiction to those who propose that raising the stakes raises the bar, Dr. Knutson of Harvard suggests that, "We very quickly found out that nothing had an effect on people like money – not naked bodies, nor corpses. It got people riled up. Like food provides motivation for dogs, money provides it for people."[15]

Naysayers have supposed that money is so important to us that its centrality in our lives sharpens our reason and quickens our wit, but brain scans tell a different story. Money is important, sure, but it is so important that we eschew reason, ignoring what is economically best in favor of what is emotionally satisfying. In short, we kind of freak out.

Learning the wrong lesson

Imagine if you will that you and your significant other are headed out for a night on the town. You're looking for a trustworthy sitter for your young child and have asked a close friend to describe two potential childcare professionals for the evening. Your friend gives you the following descriptions and you must choose one of the two.

• **Sitter One** is described as intelligent, industrious, impulsive, critical, stubborn, and envious.

• **Sitter Two** is described as envious, stubborn, critical, impulsive, industrious and intelligent.

So, proud mama or papa, which do you choose? Being the bright person that you are, you may have deciphered that the two lists of adjectives are identical. Odds are though, you had a strong gut reaction that the first sitter is more desirable. This is due to something called the "irrational primacy effect," or the tendency to give greater weight to information that comes earlier in a list or sentence. It turns out that what's true of communication is also true of our lives generally – experiences that we associate with something when we first got to know it, or the state of something when we learned about it, affect how we see it from that point onward. The lessons we learn first are the lessons that last longest.

---

[15]   Ibid.

Primacy and recency

In a moment, I will ask you to give yourself just ten seconds to memorize the list of words below. Don't take any more than ten seconds before immediately closing the book, trying to recite the list and then returning to see how you did. Let's go:

- Enemies

- Annual

- Nervous

- Allergenic

- Century

- Hollow

- Controversial

- Blossom

- Femur

Welcome back, how did you do?

Your recall of the list probably went something like, "Enemies, Annual... um, something, something... Femur." You remembered the first and last words in the string, something psychologists call the primacy and recency effect.

This tendency to remember the first and last part of an interaction is not limited to silly parlor tricks and grocery lists – it is a very important part of how we learn and has implications for how we invest. Your early investing experiences and your recent investment experiences probably loom larger than they ought to and define your subjective experience of what markets look like.

The solution is to become a student of market history instead of falling back on your limited lived experience.

In an effort to isolate the parts of the brain implicated in making buy, sell and hold decisions, researchers placed participants in two groups with differing market conditions and then mapped their brains using electroencephalogram technology (EEG). Group One began in a market that showed steady positive growth and Group Two was placed in a more volatile market. After the participants had spent some time trading and learning the market they switched conditions, with those in the growth market entering the volatile market, and vice versa. What they observed next was fascinating and surprising: people used different parts of their brain to make future investment decisions based on their early experience with the market.

Those in Group One who had started with an orderly, predictable market organized their brain activity to create rules and search for universally applicable principles of the market. In the words of the researchers, "decision making would be supported by comparison of predicted and actual prices, and it would be driven by a rule based reasoning." Conversely, those who began in the more chaotic condition utilized entirely separate parts of the brain to cope with the volatility of their market. Since the volatility of the market did not lend itself to the formation of consistent rules, those in Group Two learned to make situational (i.e., by the seat of their pants) decisions and this improvisational style carried over even to the calmer market. They were effectively scarred by their bad experiences in the market and were never able to fully search for rules and best practices, even when they became more available.[16]

For many of life's activities it makes sense that early imprinting on the brain should inform future decisions. It is adaptive for a child born into war-torn Syria to program himself for constant vigilance from an early age, just as it is sensible for a child from Beverly Hills to learn that she is in no immediate danger. Variables of place and safety are likely to persist, but market conditions are constantly in flux and can lead us to learn the wrong lessons. An investor who begins in late 2007 may arrive at an inappropriately cruel appraisal of the market, whereas one who

---

[16]   João Vieito, Armando F. Rocha and Fábio T, Rocha, 'Brain activity of the investor's stock market financial decision,' *Journal of Behavioral Finance* (November 2014).

started in the early 1990s may characterize the market as more consistent and profitable than has historically been the case.

The lesson here is one that will be repeated throughout this book ad nauseam – mental processes that serve us very well in almost every other facet of daily living are poorly suited to the world of investing.

You will never be satisfied

Unlike most religions that are founded around a god or goddess, or several of them, the central figure of Buddhism is a man, Siddhartha Gautama, who made some shrewd observations about the human brain. Siddhartha was born into royalty and had inherited a small kingdom by the age of 29. Having acquired at a young age what many spend their whole lives striving for, he became aware of his own discontent as well as the unsettled nature of those around him. Young and old, rich and poor, dissatisfaction seemed to be a common thread.

Buddha (as he was later called) observed that when we are in lack, we long for days of greater prosperity and fulfillment. But when wealth and plenty arrive, we quickly become sated and long for an even more intense experience. The Buddha's great insight was that human suffering was less a case of providential displeasure and more an inability to control our own minds. Suffering, as he saw it, occurred when our selfish craving and desire bumped up against the inevitability of pain in the world. The Buddha may have lived around 500 BC, but he correctly anticipated one truth about the brain; when it comes to money we are never satisfied.

Part of this frustrating mirage is that anticipating a reward is deeply satisfying whereas literally receiving the reward is far less gratifying. Imagined rewards have no ceiling and don't come with any of the headaches of actually hitting it big (e.g., taxes, spoiled kids, etc...), so we take great pleasure in building castles in the sky and discussing what we would do with, say, our lottery winnings. As Jason Zweig says of this concept, "By the time you pocket the money the thrill of greed has faded into something that resembles a neurological yawn – even though you got the gains you wanted. Making money feels good, all right; it just doesn't feel as good as expecting to make money."[17] If left unchecked, our natural mental processes are a formula for dissatisfaction. We long for wealth but when we get it, the appeal of what we'd so long hoped for quickly dissipates. Psychologists refer to this Sisyphussian struggle as the "hedonic treadmill" and it is what leads us to try, and fail, to keep up with the Joneses.

We're all familiar with the term "keeping up with the Joneses," but it's doubtful that we understand just how deeply ingrained this is in our concept of success and how the neurological processes we've touched on here contribute to it. Each year, a Gallup poll asks Americans to determine "What is the smallest amount of money a family of four needs to get along in this community?" Gallup finds that the answers to this question increase in line with the average incomes of the respondents. "Enough", it seems, is a moving target that our flawed neurology won't quite let us scratch. The amount of money we need to survive is just a little bit more than we have right now.

In developed nations, the notions of "relative wealth" and "relative poverty" are very much at play. There is absolutely legitimate want in developed nations – one-in-five American children go hungry on any given day – but among the middle and upper socio-economic classes, people tend to look to others to determine whether or not they are successful rather than pointing to some static measure of wealth. In fact, studies show that the most noticeable way in which money impacts happiness is negatively! We see that the very rich enjoy a slight bump in happiness given their comparative financial superiority, but the "have nots" are made absolutely miserable as they look up at their better resourced counterparts. Given that the increase in happiness is slight and that the rich make up a small fraction of the total population, in general, the tendency of people to view money in comparative terms is the source of a great deal of woe.

Our brains push us toward comparative notions of financial wellbeing that only provide transitory joy, but understanding our limitations is a first step toward making a different choice. Indeed, the Western tendency toward outward displays of wealth and comparative measurement is not endemic to all developed countries. Switzerland is just one example of a

---

17   Zweig, *Your Money and Your Brain*, p. 35.

very wealthy country with a diametrically opposed philosophy relative to showy wealth. As opposed to the American mantra of "If you've got it, flaunt it," the Swiss take an "If you've got it, hide it" approach so as not to provoke envy in others. The Swiss model demonstrates that our views are an outcropping of a specific way of viewing wealth rather than something deterministic about human nature. We are not our worst impulses and it is up to us to determine to support each other on the way to balance and true happiness, rather than prodding each other toward jealousy and excess.

How much is enough?

Daniel Kahneman helmed a Princeton study set out to answer the age-old question, "Can money buy happiness?" Their answer? Sort of. Researchers found that making little money did not cause sadness in and of itself, but it did tend to heighten and exacerbate existing worries. For instance, among people who were divorced, 51% of those who made less than $1,000/month reported having felt sad or stressed the previous day, whereas that number fell to 24% among those earning more than $3,000/month. Having more money seems to provide those undergoing adversity with greater security and resources for dealing with their troubles. However, the researchers found that this effect (mitigating the impact of difficulty) disappears altogether at an annual income of $75,000.

For those making more than $75,000, individual differences have much more to do with happiness than does money. While the study does not make any specific inferences as to why $75,000 is the magic number, I'd like to take a stab at it. For most families making $75,000/year, they have enough to live in a safe home, attend quality schools and have appropriate leisure time. Once these basic needs are met, quality of life has less to do with buying happiness and more to do with individual attitudes. After all, someone who makes $750,000 can buy a faster car than someone who makes $75,000, but their ability to get from point A to point B is not substantially improved. It would seem that once we have our basic financial needs met, the rest is up to us.

Dopey behavior

The Ancient Greeks hypothesized two brain systems that accounted for much of human behavior – a pleasure seeking system and a pain avoidance system – and just as with the admonition to "know thyself," they were on to something. When we become aware of a potential reward in the environment, our reward system comes alive. As neurologist and trader Dr. Richard Peterson explains:

> "The reward system runs from the midbrain through the limbic system and ends in the neocortex. The neurons that carry information between the brain regions of the reward system are primarily dopaminergic… Dopamine has been called the 'pleasure' chemical of the brain, because people who are electrically stimulated in the predominantly dopamine centers of the brain report intense feelings of well-being. The dopaminergic pathways of the reward system are activated by illicit drug use, leading to street drugs being colloquially called 'dope.'"[18]

He goes on to show that activating the reward system leads to "increased risk-taking, increased impulsivity… and greater physical arousal," none of which are great for making big decisions about money. Fear understandably has the opposite effect, making us "timid, protective, fearful and risk-averse."

Intuitive enough, but what does it have to do with investing?

The fact that your brain becomes more risk seeking in bull markets and more conservative in bear markets means that you are neurologically predisposed to violate the first rule of investing, "buy low and sell high." Our flawed brain leads us to subjectively experience low levels of risk when risk is actually quite high, a concept that Howard Marks refers to as the "perversity of risk."

While we tend to think of bear markets as risky, true risk actually builds up during periods of prosperity and simply materializes during bear markets. During good times, investors bid up risk assets, becoming less discerning and more willing to pay any price necessary to take the ride. Risks compound during such periods of bullishness, but this

---

[18] Richard L. Peterson, 'The neuroscience of investing: FMRI of the reward system,' *Brain Research Bulletin* (2005).

escalation goes largely undetected because everyone is making money and the dopamine is flowing. You likely grasp this intellectually, but your brain will do everything in its power to make sure that you don't act accordingly.

Like a flower growing through the pavement, your brain is beautiful but out of place. It was formed for a place and purpose long since abandoned and your ability to create and sustain wealth is in a real sense predicated on understanding this misfit. Animals use their brains to look out on the world, but it is a unique human capability to look within. We must use the mind to understand the mind – to first, know ourselves.

What's the big idea?

- Your brain (150,000 years old) is much older than the markets (400 years old) it seeks to navigate.

- Your brain takes up just 2% to 3% of your body weight, but consumes 25% of your energy.

- Humans are wired to act; markets tend to reward inaction.

- The importance of money seems to diminish, not improve, decision-making.

- Our early experiences in capital markets imprint on our brain in ways that tend to be lasting.

- Hedonic adaptation is the process by which increases in wealth are matched pound-for-pound by increases in expectations.

- The anticipation of reward releases a flood of dopamine, which primes us to become sloppy and undisciplined; success begets failure.

Chapter 3.
Physiology

"He who conquers himself is the mightiest warrior."

— CONFUCIUS

"Ain't got no cash, ain't got no style,
Ain't got no gal to make you smile,
But don't worry, be happy,
'Cause when you worry your face will frown,
And that will bring everybody down,
So don't worry, be happy,
Don't worry, be happy now."

— BOBBY MCFERRIN

BOBBY MCFERRIN'S ODE to cheer was ubiquitous in the late '80s and, in addition to winning him Grammys for Song of the Year, Record of the Year and Best Male Pop Vocal Performance, it was a tune that launched a thousand t-shirts. If we decide to read way too much into them, the lyrics to 'Don't Worry Be Happy' reflect a common and intuitive relationship between bodily displays of affect (e.g., frowning) and the emotions that give rise to them (e.g., worry). Worry begets frowning, happiness begets smiling, we think.

But is it really that simple?

As early as 1872, a thinker no less prominent than Charles Darwin gave credence to the thought that bodily states can impact emotions just as surely as emotions can bring about bodily states. "He who gives way to violent gestures will increase his rage," Darwin wrote in *The Expression of Emotions in Man and Animals*. Darwin does not take full credit for this observation, however, ascribing it to the work of French brain anatomist Louis Pierre Gratiolet, who wrote that "Even incidental movements and positions of the body will result in associated feelings." Rather than, "Don't worry, be happy," these great men were espousing a sort of, "Worried? Smile and you'll be happy," approach.

Nineteenth century observations about the body-affect connection began to be proven out using 20th century empiricism. James Laird, a graduate student at the University of Rochester, attached non-functional electrodes to the brows, corners of the mouth and jawlines of participants and was ostensibly going to measure the activity of facial muscles under a series of changing conditions.

With the participants wired up to the phony contraption, Laird asked them assume a variety of facial postures – everything from a frown, to a smile, to a furrowed brow – and then asked them to rate a series of cartoons on their funniness on a 1 to 9 scale. Consistent with Darwin's observations 100 years previous, participants who had been made to frown rated the cartoons as significantly less funny than those who had been coaxed into smiling.

Better known still is the work of Strack, Martin and Stepper who concocted an even simpler way to get participants to smile and frown without an awareness of what was truly being measured. The researchers informed participants that they would be taking part in a study to measure "psychomotoric coordination" with an eye to helping people with disabilities learn to use a stylus to write or use the telephone. Subjects were asked to hold a felt tip pen in their mouth in one of two ways, either between the teeth, which forced a smile, or between the lips, which forced a frowning, puckered face. In results that almost identically mirrored Laird's, smiling participants rated cartoons as a 5.1 and frowning students gave an average 4.3 rating.

Since these groundbreaking studies, new applications have emerged that have corroborated the body-moves-mind hypothesis in pursuits as diverse as decreasing racism and increasing creativity. Subsequent attempts to replicate early studies have achieved mixed results, but few would argue that our understanding of the interplay between mind and body is much more a two-way than a one-way street. Understanding the impact of human physiology on investment decision-making is an underappreciated area of study that represents a unique source of advantage for the thoughtful investor.

Wired to live

Let's continue our examination of physiology and investing with a hard truth – you are not built to be happy or to make good investment choices, you are built to survive and reproduce. Asking someone built for short-term survival to become a long-term investor is a bit like trying to paint a room with a hammer. You can do it, but it's not pretty.

One consequence of being wired to live is loss aversion; an asymmetric fear of bad stuff happening to you. Loss aversion is driven by the amygdalae, two tiny almond-shaped structures that are the seat of all of your emotional responses. Evolutionarily, loss aversion makes a lot of sense and many scientists believe it is why Homo sapiens outlasted other human species on the way to the top of the food chain. As McDermott, Fowler and Smirnov (2008) point out, running out of food was fatal and so a disposition toward avoiding loss is what prompted our ancient ancestors to pack up and forage in a new spot.[19] While loss aversion is derided as being irrational in an investment context, those with a genetic predisposition against it didn't live to see a time when their even-headedness could prevail.

[19]   Rose McDermott, James H. Fowler and Oleg Smirnov, 'On the evolutionary origin of prospect theory preferences,' *The Journal of Politics* (April 2008).

Indeed, avoiding loss is so central to humanity that our bodies have actually evolved distinct neural signatures that are processed in very different parts of the brain. The nucleus accumbens of the ventral striatum is activated when we anticipate a financial gain and, unsurprisingly, this is correlated with positive arousal. Thoughts of anticipatory loss, on the contrary, are processed in the anterior insula, a region of the brain that also lights up during periods of physical pain, anxiety, and in reaction to aversive stimuli. In a very real sense, even thinking about financial loss hurts in the most physical sense possible.

It should come as no surprise that the special nature of processing loss has profound behavioral implications. Brian Knutson of Stanford has shown that investors tend to act in rational and self-interested ways... until loss gets involved. Knutson offered participants in his study one of three possible investment options: a low risk bond and two stocks of indeterminate risk and reward. The bond was simple, paying out a guaranteed $1 with each iteration of the game. The stocks, on the other hand, were more variable. One of the stocks had a large chance of paying out $10 per round and a smaller chance of losing $10. The other stock was the mirror image, with a large chance of loss and a smaller chance of gain.

Knutson observed brain activity while the investing task played out and noticed that most participants started out making rational trades and that the rational center of the brain was most active in decision-making. That is, until they suffered an unexpected loss. Once a loss had been experienced, the pain centers of the brain became aroused and future decisions tended to be less rational. Losses left investors licking their wounds and prompted an irrational preference for the certainty of bonds, which had a damaging impact on returns over the course of the game. In a strange twist, the very tendency that has led to human ascendancy is one of the primary culprits in investment underperformance.

Homeostasis

Armed with a new understanding of the bilateral relationship between mind and body, it becomes imperative for the behavioral investor to understand the very real ways in which physiological states can impact investment decision-making. Inasmuch as this construct is poorly understood and widely ignored, it represents a real source of potential outperformance for the initiated. To understand how the body impacts your financial choices you must first and foremost grasp that the primary role of the body is to maintain homeostasis.

As mentioned earlier, your body's two primary roles are to survive and reproduce. Central to your ability to do these two things is homeostasis, which is the process of maintaining physiological balance. Your homeostatic body temperature is 98.6 degrees. Get much below that and your body automatically pulls blood from the extremities. Get much above that and you cool yourself by sweating.

In order to enlist our help in this process, deviation from homeostasis tends to feel bad and induces us to grab a coat or to turn on the air conditioner (or in my case, to stop exercising). As Camerer, Loewenstein and Prelec point out, "Rather than viewing pleasure as the goal of human behavior, a more realistic account would view pleasure as a homeostatic cue – an informational signal." As a general rule, our decisions get worse as the body deviates in either direction from its homeostatic set point.[20]

Mild, positive affect, the sort you might experience on any old good-but-not-great-nothing-special-going-on day is well recognized as being positively correlated with everything from cognitive flexibility to creative problem solving. Sadness takes psychic energy and there is a freedom that comes with being upbeat in a way that is still within homeostatic bounds. But as we learned earlier, consequential financial decisions are unlikely to land in this generally-happy-but-no-big-deal decisional sweet spot. Money, it turns out, is a very big deal to us and our physiological arousal ticks up when we are making financial decisions, leading us to rapidly depart Homeostasis Station, bound for Freak Out Pass. Excessive levels of physiological arousal decrease working memory and cognition and so, just as extreme cold pulls blood

[20] C. Camerer, G. Loewenstein and D. Prelec, 'Neuroeconomics: How neuroscience can inform economics,' *Journal of Economic Literature* (March 2005), p. 27.

away from your fingers and toes, dealing with money shunts processing power away from your brain.[21]

A body that is out of homeostasis can actually alter our preferences, and in ways that we might not fully appreciate. We want to think that we make decisions based on reason, ethics and time-tested principles, but research suggests that it may have just as much to do with what we've had to eat. Judge Jerome Frank's seemingly sarcastic quip that "Justice is what the judge ate for breakfast." may contain an uneasy kernel of truth, based on the work of Shai Danziger of Ben Gurion University. Danziger examined the results of 1,112 parole board hearings from Israeli prisons over a ten-month month period.[22]

The study found that prisoners begin the day, right after the judge has enjoyed breakfast, with a 65% chance of parole, but those odds begin to plummet shortly after, with the most Draconian rulings being handed out right before lunch. After lunch, by some miracle of jurisprudence, the judges' leniency returns but then falls again until, you guessed it, snack time.

The results of Danziger's work are frankly shocking and discouraging. When peoples' lives and the welfare of the broader society are on the line, judgments ought to be made based on a dispassionate application of the law, not a hankering for a Snickers bar. Although no similar studies currently exist for investment decision-making, it seems reasonable to suppose that something as seemingly trivial as hunger could have a dramatic impact on results. Perhaps Warren Buffett's 800 calories a day of Coca-Cola are the secret to his success.

Exploring this further, another study showed that hungry people are not only desirous of food, but they also desire money and are more greedy. Related work demonstrates that individuals who are fasting tend to take riskier financial bets than those who are full. As Dana Smith reports, this tendency is not unique to humans: "This finding

---

[21]   F. G. Ashby, V. V. Valentin and U. Turken, 'The effects of positive affect and arousal on working memory and executive attention,' in S. Moore & M. Oaksford (eds.), *Emotional Cognition: From Brain to Behaviour* (John Benjamins, 2002), pp. 245–287.

[22]   E. Yong, 'Justice is served, but more so after lunch: how food-breaks sway the decisions of judges,' *Discover* (April 11, 2011).

is supported by the animal literature, in which animals are more risk-averse when sated but risk-seeking when hungry. This is presumably an evolutionarily selected trait prompting exploration and risk-seeking when in states of hunger, which could potentially lead to the acquisition of new food sources."

It would seem that homeostatic deficits in one area impact the seemingly unrelated world of financial decision-making in predictable ways. If bodily hunger can generalize to financial want, perhaps visceral control can as well. A group of researchers in the Netherlands set out to investigate, in a most unusual way.

Led by Mirjam Tuk, researchers assigned participants into two groups – the first who consumed 700ml of water and the second consumed 50ml of water. Subjects were then asked to engage in a task that would allow them to get a small reward more immediately or a larger reward upon waiting for a much longer period of time. Shockingly (to me at least!) those who drank more water and reported a very high urgency to urinate chose the delayed option with more frequency than those who'd had less water and reported less urgency to urinate! Tuk and her team propose an explanation that, while surprising, fits nicely with the spillover effects of hunger discussed above. Referring to this effect as "inhibitory spillover," the authors hypothesize that the bodily restraint needed to keep from using the bathroom had a knock on effect that increased ability to wait for a larger financial reward as well.[23] You may now put down the book – the secret to financial success is always needing to pee.

The biggest danger of physiological impediments to decision-making is that they operate surreptitiously. Ask an Israeli judge why he hands down the ruling he does and he will undoubtedly point to a leather bound tome and not his stomach. Our belief in free will and personal accountability means that we tend to ignore bodily determinants of behavior and this is much to the disadvantage of investors everywhere. But it is worth asking, are we able to rein in and control our bodily reactions to risk and uncertainty once we become aware of them? Can we better maintain homeostasis through practice?

[23] M. A. Tuk, D. Trampe and L. Warlop, 'Inhibitory Spillover,' *Psychological Science* (April 2011).

Andrew Lo examined a variety of autonomic nervous system (ANS) responses, including respiration, skin temperature, facial movements and blood volume, among traders of various experience levels. As we might expect, Lo found that more experienced traders exhibited less elevated ANS responses to market volatility than traders who were just starting out. Experienced traders were better able to maintain homeostasis, with all of the cognitive benefits that entails, but still showed "marked physiological responses." Money moves the physiological needle – period.[24]

Those hungry Israeli judges we looked at averaged 22 years of experience and their verdicts accounted for 40% of all parole decisions made in Israel over the course of the study. These were experienced professionals whose objectivity was compromised by whether they were hungry or not. Whenever I see an extreme athlete perform a dangerous stunt, say, a backflip on a motorcycle, I wonder how many broken bones it took to achieve their current level of expertise. With enough experience investors can moderate, but never be truly free of, the damaging impact of extreme physiological responses to market moves. But at what cost along the way?

Risk hurts

If I asked you to free associate for a moment on the word "stress," what are the first few words or descriptions that come to mind? You probably imagine some sort of psychic anguish: uncertainty at work, worry about the welfare of a loved one, or financial insecurities. The most commonly used colloquial definition of stress, "loss of perceived control over an event," is likewise psychological in nature. But our emphasis on stress as a mental state ignores the real bodily impact it produces and ignores some of the more practical ways in which it can be managed.

In a time when being "stressed out" seems to be such a ubiquitous part of daily life, it is amazing to consider that the idea of psychological stress was seen as hooey as recently as a century ago. The term as we currently use it today was coined by endocrinologist Hans Selye in the

[24]   A. W. Lo, 'The Adaptive Markets Hypothesis: Market Efficiency from an Evolutionary Perspective' (August 2004).

1930s and was discovered, quite by accident, as Selye was conducting research with mice.

While injecting mice with hormones, Selye began to hypothesize that the process itself – being caged, corralled, stuck with needles and scrutinized – was producing bigger changes in the mice than the hormones in the syringes. Borrowing a term from engineering, Selye proposed that a mental state of anguish was producing physical sequelae in the mice, an idea that was met with intense skepticism at the time. But what may have seen laughable in Selye's day is now understood to be deadly serious – stress hurts.

Stress is implicated in conditions as diverse as obesity, hypertension, erectile dysfunction, infertility, insomnia and cardiovascular disease. An estimated 25% of all visits to a medical doctor are stress-related conditions that end in a referral to a psychologist rather than a surgeon. Nowhere is the connection between mind and body as apparent as it is when considering stress and nothing excites our stress response quite like money.

Investors looking to manage stress en route to improved outcomes must first understand the ways in which it is a profoundly physical phenomenon. John Coates, a former trader turned neuroscientist, and investment stress researcher par excellence, said in the *New York Times*, "Most of us tend to believe that stress is largely a psychological phenomenon, a state of being upset because something nasty has happened. But if you want to understand stress you must disabuse yourself of that view. The stress response is largely physical: It is your body priming itself for impending movement."[25] A racing heart, dilating eyes, a body coursing with cortisol and adrenaline, all of this is priming you to act – now. But when the dreaded stimulus never appears or plays out over nearly 500 days (the average length of a bear market), the body has generated a physical response that is both ill-fit to the needs of the situation and presents a real health risk.

In appropriate doses and over short time frames, stress can be a lifesaver. Stress and performance have been shown to exist in what is referred to as an 'inverted U model,' shown below.

[25]   J. Coates, 'The biology of risk,' *New York Times* (June 7, 2014).

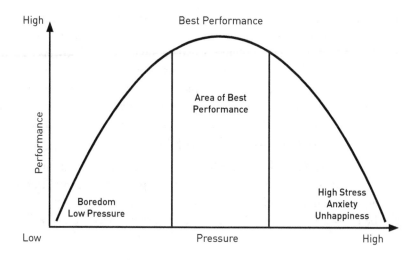

The inverted U model shows that with too little stress you never get off the couch, and with too much stress you choke. In moderation, the cortisol produced by feelings of stress is a sort of wonder drug that increases physical arousal, improves memory, promotes learning, enhances sensation seeking and increases motivation. But if stress persists over a longer period, say like that associated with most market downturns, the exact opposite occurs: behavioral flexibility decreases, immunological systems are compromised, attention wanes, depressive symptomatology emerges and learned helplessness replaces feelings of self-efficacy.

John Coates set up to study directly what previous research had only hinted at – the relationship between stress hormones and risk taking. Coates' first study was to establish a baseline effect of cortisol production during times of market volatility. His seminal research found that the cortisol levels of traders increased a whopping 68% over a period of just eight days! In a follow-up study, he pharmacologically replicated the impact of the cortisol levels on the traders and then gauged their risk taking preferences on a gambling task. The results, published in the *Proceedings of the National Academy of Sciences*, found that participants' appetite for risk fell by an incredible 44% as a result of the elevated levels of cortisol.[26]

[26]   N. Kandasamy, B. Hardy, L. Page, M. Schaffner, J. Graggaber, A. S.

Formerly thought of as primarily a mental construct, Coates' findings turned traditional notions of risk tolerance on their head, and painted a more dynamic picture of the interplay between mind and body. As he opines in *The Biology of Risk*, "Most models in economics and finance assume that risk preferences are a stable trait, much like your height. But this assumption, as our studies suggest, is misleading. Humans are designed with shifting risk preferences. They are an integral part of our response to stress, or challenge." [*]

Once again, we observe that decisions and ideas that feel internally volitional can be greatly manipulated by physical externalities. Advantageous financial risk taking is not some intellectual puzzle that can be reasoned through and taken advantage of by sheer force of will.

The intransigence of fear

From 1900 to 2013, the US stock market experienced 123 "corrections" (a 10% or greater drawdown) – an average of more than one per year! The more dramatic losses that are the hallmark of a bear market occur only slightly less frequently, averaging one every 3.5 years. Although the media talks about 10% to 20% market losses as though they are the end of the world, they arrive as regularly as spring flowers and have not negated the tendency of markets to dramatically compound wealth over long periods of time. It is incredible to consider that over that 100 plus years, one could expect both double-digit annualized returns with attendant double-digit percentage losses. But to be able to realize these great gains amid great pain, investors must check their fear of loss at the door, a task that your imperfect biology will make extremely difficult. As much as we may wish it were otherwise, our bodies seem uniquely skilled at holding on to fear and letting it loose at just the inopportune time.

In a paradigmatic experiment that bears this out, LeDoux (1996) fear conditioned rats by repeatedly pairing an electric shock with an auditory stimulus. In a move that would make Pavlov grin, the rat eventually need only hear the tone to begin to worry. But once the animal had been

---

Powlson, P.C. Fletcher, M. Gurnell and J. Coates 'Cortisol shifts financial risk preferences,' *Proceedings of the National Academy of Sciences of the United States of America* (March 4, 2014).

sufficiently conditioned to fear, researchers then began to extinguish the fear by providing the stimulus (the tone) with no accompanying shock. Eventually, the fear response abates and the rat goes about its rat business upon hearing the tone. We might now assume that the fear has dissipated entirely and that the rat has overcome its original fear, but the reality is far more bizarre.

The researchers (who really must hate rats) next severed the neural connections between the cortex and amygdala and presented the tone again, at which time the rat promptly freaked out. The fear was not gone at all! Rather, the fear was being suppressed by the cortex but remained, hidden in the amygdala, for such a time as the painful stimulus might reappear. LeDoux's findings suggest that the body, ever intent on preservation, actually hangs on to bad experiences and brings them right back to the surface when similar bad news re-emerges.

Four Steps to Managing Stress

Michele McDonald developed the R.A.I.N. model, a simple but powerful system for managing an episode of acute stress. Try this the next time you are stressed:

1. **Recognition** – Deliberately observe and name what is occurring in your body and mind. For instance, "I feel my heart and mind racing."

2. **Acceptance** – Acknowledge and accept the presence of whatever you observed above. You don't have to love it, but fighting will make it worse.

3. **Investigation** – Ask yourself what stories you are telling yourself and examine what thoughts are present.

4. **Non-identification** – Now that you have recognized, accepted and investigated your stress, you must realize that you are more than your emotions. You can feel something without being defined by it.

What's the big idea?

- Physical states can impact emotion just as surely as the reverse is true.

- Loss aversion kept our ancestors alive. It keeps you from being a successful investor.

- The body longs for homeostasis. Thinking about money disrupts homeostasis.

- Stress is as much a physical as it is a psychic phenomenon.

- Taking financial risk causes real bodily pain.

- Fear is impossible to extinguish since the body stores it for a rainy day.

- Bad news in the stock market is more regular than your birthday.

PART TWO.
INVESTOR PSYCHOLOGY

"If you don't know who you are, Wall Street is an expensive place to find out."

— ADAM SMITH, *THE MONEY GAME*

A S A CHILD I loved reading Rudyard Kipling's *Just So Stories*, a collection of tales originally crafted as bedtime stories for his daughter who demanded that they be told "just so" (using the same words she was accustomed to). Each of the stories provides a magical take on evolutionary biology and describes how various animals acquired their most distinctive features.

In 'How the Whale Got His Throat' we learn that whales can only eat plankton as a result of one having swallowed a mariner who subsequently tied a raft inside its throat to prevent others from meeting his fate. In 'How the Camel Got His Hump' we learn that the dromedary's hump is a result of being lazy and being cursed by a genie with a hump that allows for greater work between periods of rest. In each case, the animal endures some hardship but is ultimately rewarded with a distinctive feature that is evolutionarily adaptive. Just like the stories themselves, the animals are created "just so."

It is satisfying to think of a world where nature conspires to work in our favor, but it is sadly not reflective of our reality when it comes to financial decision-making. As you now know from the previous chapters, your body and brain were created to do a great many things with remarkable efficiency, but investing happens not to be one of them. In fact if a demigod, evil genie, or vengeful mariner set out to design the worst investor possible, they would have designed you. When it comes to investing, you were not created just so.

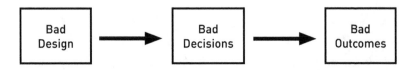

The flaws in your design quite naturally lead to quirks in your behavior and creating a system that accounts for these quirks is a foundational element of any sound investment philosophy. Just as good defense wins championships but the quarterback gets the girl, risk management drives performance but big returns get all of the press. And so before we answer the question, "How can I become a skilled investor?" we must first answer the less-sexy-but-more-important question, "How can I not suck at investing?" Said more gently, we must learn to manage risk.

If you accept this as a fact and pick up a textbook on risk management, you are likely to read about two primary types of investment risk – systematic and unsystematic.

Systematic risk, also known as "market risk," is the chance that you will lose money as a result of moves in the broad market as opposed to factors relating to any business in particular. Unsystematic risk, also referred to as "business risk," is the chance that an investment in an individual security will depreciate in value due to factors pertaining to that business. What your textbook will likely omit altogether is a third type of risk – behavioral risk – and this is the most important risk of all.

Codifying a universe of behavioral risk is a prerequisite to successfully managing it. After all, how can you fight a monster that you can't see? In many cases, our universe of behavioral risk is generated from studies of investor misbehavior. As Daniel Kahneman says in *The Undoing Project*, "How do you understand memory? You don't study memory. You study forgetting." *Misbehaving*, Richard Thaler's incredible origin story of the field of behavioral economics, recounts the simple but effective way that he set the discipline on its current course. Incredulous about what he was learning about efficient markets, Thaler set out to brainstorm all of the real-life ways in which the people he knew differed from the "Econs" (i.e., fictional individuals who optimize utility and always make rational financial decisions) he was learning about in his theory courses. Using nothing more than a simple thought experiment, Thaler created a list of behavioral anomalies that spawned numerous research projects and vastly deepened our understanding of how mere mortals make financial decisions.

While the discovery and documentation of these behavioral anomalies was an important first step, they lack utility to investors inasmuch as there is no broader organizing framework. We now have long lists of the ways in which we are imperfect, but little in the way of practical next steps. As research has shown, bad news without a concrete solution set can actually exacerbate the problem!

Inspired by the simple elegance of Thaler's approach, I put on my catastrophic thinking cap and set out to brainstorm every possible way someone's behavior could negatively impact investment decision-making. I found over 117 different biases and heuristics that could lead an aspiring investor from making optimal decisions! Ouch. To make this universe more useful to investors, I looked for common psychological underpinnings among the various modes of error and grouped them accordingly. I began this process without preconceptions of how the information would shake out. At the end, four consistent types of behavioral risk emerged:

1. Ego

2. Conservatism

3. Attention

4. Emotion

All behavioral risk has one or more of these four risk factors at its core. This classification is unique to this book and provides an important starting point for the creation of behaviorally informed investment management processes.

We'll now move on to examine each of these pillars of investor behavior in turn in the chapters that follow.

Did you know?

Research by Lo, Repin and Steenbarger suggests that there is no "best" trader personality type. Despite the popular portrayal of successful investors as brash, extroverted, risk-seekers, success in financial markets is more about mastering the four facets of behavioral risk and less about fitting a certain investor mold.

Chapter 4.
Ego

"Don't be so humble, you're not that great."

— GOLDA MEIR

"**Y**OUR CHILD'S INTELLIGENCE is in the average range." As soon as I spoke the words I could feel my body tensing for a rebuttal. As a graduate student in psychology I was commonly called upon to assess the IQ of grade school children and quickly found that "average" was the word no parent wanted to hear. Giftedness is its own reward and a learning disability mobilizes parents in search of intervention, but average? Average? No one wanted to be average. Ever since the 1969 publication of *The Psychology of Self-Esteem*,[27] wherein Nathaniel Branden posited that self-esteem was the single most important facet of personal well being, the self-esteem movement has been one of far-reaching influence. The US has been a nation in search of a well-fed

---

[27]   Nathaniel Branden, *The Psychology of Self-Esteem: A Revolutionary Approach to Self-Understanding that Launched a New Era in Modern Psychology* (Jossey-Bass, 2001).

ego. In the 1970s and 1980s anything seen as detrimental to feelings of self-worth was done away with. Gold stars proliferated while red pens gathered dust. First place trophies gave way to awards for participation. In this new milieu, everyone was a winner; everyone was special.

As this well-intentioned movement garnered support, scholarly research followed. In the 30-year run up to the 21st century, over 15,000 articles were written on the impact of self-esteem on, well, pretty much everything imaginable. However, the results of these myriad studies were often confusing or inconclusive. In an attempt to make sense of the general trajectory of the literature on self-esteem, the Association for Psychological Science asked Dr. Roy Baumeister, an admitted proponent of the theory, to meta-analyze the extant data on the subject. What followed was what Dr. Baumeister would go on to refer to as "the biggest disappointment of my career."

Of the 15,000 studies taken into consideration, a paltry .013% of them (that is, 200) met the rigorous standards for inclusion in the meta-analysis. To begin with, it became apparent that many of the theories about self-esteem that had impacted policy were simply junk science. What's more, the studies that did pass muster didn't have much good to say about the construct's predictive power. Self-esteem did not predict academic or career achievement, nor did it predict drug usage or violent behavior. The biggest finding to emerge from the self-esteem movement was that praise did not predict self-esteem, accomplishment did. Telling someone that they are special is insufficient if they have not worked to earn it. We have an accurate internal sense of when we have earned praise and when we have not. If we feel as though we are being patted on the back undeservingly, it does not move the self-esteem needle one inch.[28]

Unasked in this frenzy of self-congratulation is, "Do we even need this?" Because if feelings of positive self-worth are important (and they don't seem to be) there is still nothing to suggest that they are lacking in most people. In fact, most people likely have too much rather than too little belief in self. You learned earlier that we make "good enough" decisions because we have big, hungry brains whose energy consumption our body is looking to curtail. In many cases, the cost

[28]   Daniel Crosby, *You're Not That Great* (Word Association Publishers, 2012).

of boosting our decision-making precision outweighs the benefits and so we streamline those choices in a very particular way: we engage in "egosyntonic satisficing."

In a world full of ridiculous phrases, this has to be among the most ridiculous, but inasmuch as using it will impress people at cocktail parties, let me explain. Something that is *egosyntonic* is consistent with the goals of the ideal self-image; it's an idea that allows us to believe the best of ourselves. *Satisficing* is the process of selecting a "good enough" option on the basis of its availability rather than superiority. Thus, egosyntonic satisficing is the process of making easy decisions that support a belief in a self that is good, kind and generally above average. So much of human behavior – political, religious, financial – can be explained by the fact that we want to think the best of ourselves and don't want to work very hard to do it.

There is lots of evidence for this. When worldwide mathematical proficiency is considered, American high school students are squarely middle of the pack. However, when these same students are asked about how confident they are in their abilities, they lead the world. James Montier reports that over 95% of people think they have a better than average sense of humor. Peters and Waterman, in a book titled *In Search of Excellence*, found that 100% of men surveyed felt that they were better than average interpersonally and that 94% of men felt as though they were athletically better than average.

We are more in love with ourselves than is warranted, a fact that has dangerous implications for investment decision-making. In an effort to keep this love fest going and preserve precious cognitive processing power, we engage in a three step process: we look for supporting evidence, we congratulate ourselves for believing as we do, and we react violently against attacks to our worldview.

Words to live by

"If one were to attempt to identify a single problematic aspect of human reasoning that deserves attention above all others, the confirmation bias would have to be among the candidates for consideration. Many have written about this bias, and it appears to be sufficiently strong and pervasive that one is led to wonder whether the bias, by itself, might account for a significant fraction of the disputes, altercations, and misunderstandings that occur among individuals, groups, and nations."

— RAYMOND S. NICKERSON

"Be careful. People like to be told what they already know. Remember that. They get uncomfortable when you tell them new things. New things... well, new things aren't what they expect. They like to know that, say, a dog will bite a man. That is what dogs do. They don't want to know that man bites a dog, because the world is not supposed to happen like that. In short, what people think they want is news, but what they really crave is olds... Not news but olds, telling people that what they think they already know is true."

— TERRY PRATCHETT, THROUGH THE
CHARACTER LORD VETINARI, IN *THE TRUTH*
(A DISCWORLD NOVEL)

Looking for truth in all the wrong places

"The human understanding when it has once adopted an opinion (either as being the received opinion or as being agreeable to itself) draws all things else to support and agree with it."

— FRANCIS BACON

It is human nature to try to confirm our existing beliefs rather than disconfirm them. To think, "I'm probably right" rather than, "Why might I be wrong?"

This tendency to seek out information that agrees with our existing preconceptions is a big part of how we maintain our ego and is known in psychological literature as confirmation bias. Although we have only lately named and studied confirmation bias with scientific rigor, it has been observed throughout history. The Greek historian Thucydides (460 BC – circa 395 BC) wrote, "for it is a habit of mankind to entrust to careless hope what they long for, and to use sovereign reason to thrust aside what they do not fancy." *The Divine Comedy* features St. Thomas Aquinas cautioning Dante upon meeting in Paradise that, "opinion – hasty – often can incline to the wrong side, and then affection for one's own opinion binds, confines the mind." In his essay, *What is Art?* famed novelist Leo Tolstoy speaks to this human tendency, saying:

> "I know that most men – not only those considered clever, but even those who are very clever, and capable of understanding most difficult scientific, mathematical, or philosophic problems – can very seldom discern even the simplest and most obvious truth if it be such as to oblige them to admit the falsity of conclusions they have formed, perhaps with much difficulty – conclusions of which they are proud, which they have taught to others, and on which they have built their lives."

Dick Cheney famously personified this tendency when he demanded that only Fox News be playing when he entered the room. The Vice President, highly criticized by his Democratic counterparts and liberal news outlets like MSNBC, wanted to surround himself with less critical viewpoints. And while it's easy to pick on Vice President Cheney (he did shoot his friend in the face, after all), we are all guilty of surrounding ourselves with like-minded others and comfortable half-truths. A 2009 study out of Ohio State found that people spend 36% more time reading an essay if it aligns with their opinions. In the 2016 US Presidential election, a majority of those who voted for either of Donald Trump and Hillary Clinton did not have a single friend who was voting for their non-preferred candidate.

Regrettably for honest seekers of truth, it is becoming easier and easier to avoid information that doesn't square with a cherished personal narrative. The proliferation of news sites and highly specialized pundits means that we increasingly live in a world in which accepted truths chase an audience rather than an audience searching for truth. Don't like what you're hearing? Change the channel to the polarized tastemaker that fits your existing worldview.

In general, we flock to those with whom we share a cultural, religious, political or ideological identity. In so doing, we surround ourselves with a chorus of *yes people* who reinforce the validity of our opinions. Given the emotional wrangling involved with confronting conflicting ideas, immersing ourselves in an ideologically homogenous pool is infinitely easier than the alternative. If everyone with whom we associate looks, acts and thinks like we do, we are able to "successfully" skirt a number of tough internal struggles.

Give yourself a hand

Our preservation of ego is not limited to searching for truth in all of the wrong places. It also extends to conducting intense internal promotional campaigns that serve to strengthen existing beliefs, referred to as "choice supportive bias" in the literature. To illustrate this concept, let's try an exercise.

Let's pretend for a moment that you have agreed to be a part of a study I'm conducting. I bring you into a room and present you with six works of art. I then ask to you to rank the six paintings from 1 to 6, with 1 being your most preferred and 6 being your least preferred. I further explain that you'll be able to leave today with a painting of your choosing.

Now that you've completed the ranking assignment, I tell you that you can choose any one of the six paintings to take home. Naturally, you choose Number 1 seeing as how it was your most preferred and I retire to the back of the room to retrieve it. I return shortly with a worried expression and apologetically tell you that the paintings you ranked 1, 2, 5 and 6 are all picked over, leaving the ones you ranked 3 and 4 remaining. You can still have your pick of either 3 or 4 and you decide on 3 given that it was your slight preference.

Now imagine that I give you two weeks off and invite you back into my office to rank the same six paintings in order of your preference. What do you hypothesize will have happened? Would your preferences remain the same, or would they have shifted? What might account for them changing or staying the same?

Most people who participate in this experiment (commonly referred to as the "Free Choice Paradigm") change their preferences upon their return. Typically we see the painting that was chosen, previously ranked Number 3, will now be ranked more highly. Conversely, the painting that was not chosen, previously ranked Number 4, will now be rated less well. What accounts for such a dramatic change over such a short period of time? After all, both of the paintings represented a sort of middling preference, neither greatly prized or greatly disliked at the initial ranking. How have they now migrated closer to the respective extremes? The answer lies in our need to maintain ego and to think of ourselves as competent, capable decision makers who make choices based on rational criteria.

Dr. Dan Gilbert, Harvard professor and happiness researcher extraordinaire describes the thought process of participants thusly: "The one I got is really better than I thought. That other one I didn't get sucks."[29] The takeaway is this – once we have made a decision, we immediately start to look for all of the reasons why we were right. We may tell ourselves that we prefer the shading or the texture, or the way the painting frames a previously blank space in the living room. But whatever the specific reasons we construct, the general principal remains: we are not looking for truth, we are looking for comfort. We

[29]   Dan Gilbert, 'The surprising science of happiness' TED Talk (February 2004).

simultaneously play the other side of the fence and begin to mount an offensive against the road not taken. We are at least as tenacious at tearing down the unchosen option as we are at building up our commitment. Just ask anyone who has ever been broken up with by a partner that they "didn't like anyway."

Incredibly, the choice supportive bias is such a powerful tendency that it seems to exist somewhere so deep within us that it is even present in those unable to form short-term memories. Dan Gilbert and his team examined the impact of the Free Choice Paradigm on a group of subjects with anterograde amnesia; in other words, a group of hospitalized individuals unable to form new memories. Like their neurotypical (that is, without brain damage) peers, the amnesiac patients were asked to rank the paintings from 1 to 6 and were given the option to keep either painting 3 or 4. Upon choosing a painting, the researchers promised to mail the chosen painting in a few days and left the room.[30]

Returning just 30 minutes later, the members of Dr. Gilbert's team reintroduced themselves to the amnesiacs who, unable to form new memories, had no recollection of having met with them before or having performed the exercise. To ensure that the amnesic patients were truly unable to form memories, the researchers then asked them to point to the painting that they had chosen before, a task at which the patients performed less well than chance guessing! The patients were then put through the whole ranking exercise again, with astonishing results. Just as with the neurotypical control group, the amnesic patients "talked up" the choice they made and dismissed the painting not chosen, even though they had no memory of having made a choice at all! Our need to view ourselves as competent and maintain ego lives somewhere so deep within us that not even cognitive impairment can touch it.

The science of belief

The 2004 Presidential campaign pitted the incumbent President George W. Bush against the Democratic challenger John Kerry. It also provided an opportunity for brain researchers to study the science of what makes belief so "sticky." Researchers began by gathering participants who

[30]   Ibid.

professed to have a well-defined preference for one candidate over the other. Participants were given seemingly contradictory statements either from President Bush, Senator Kerry, or a third politically neutral public figure. They were also given further information that made the seeming contradiction appear more plausible. They were then asked to determine whether or not the individuals in question had in fact made statements that were inconsistent.

During the evaluation and thought process, research participants were monitored inside a magnetic resonance imaging (MRI) machine that allowed the scientists to observe their brain activity. As subjects evaluated seemingly contradictory statements made by their less-preferred candidate, the emotional centers of their brain remained inactive. This allowed them to make cold, rational judgments about these statements. However, as the subjects evaluated the statements of their preferred candidate, the emotional centers of their brain became highly aroused. When the results were tallied, there were clear differences in the evaluations.

Subjects were very likely to endorse their less preferred candidate as having said something contradictory, but were highly unlikely to say the candidate of their choice had made such a rhetorical error. Simply put, when their guy said something incorrect, their emotions drowned it out, but when "the other guy" said something implausible, they rationally pointed out the fallacious thinking. In simple terms, we rationally evaluate things that do not intersect with our worldview and emotionally evaluate those that do, as part of our ongoing effort to maintain a belief in our own "rightness."

As with all of the behavioral quirks that we have discussed, there is method to the madness of self-congratulations around belief. The theory is that this is a form of regret aversion designed to minimize unhappiness, promote wellbeing and save cognitive processing power for more important tasks. I mean, can you imagine how tired and depressed you'd be if you went around second-guessing yourself all of the time? Interestingly, we show no choice supportive bias when assigned an option through chance or random selection. It is only when our personal choices and pet beliefs come under scrutiny that we rally the ego to our defense.

Backfire

"My characterization of a loser is someone who, after making a mistake, doesn't introspect, doesn't exploit it, feels embarrassed and defensive rather than enriched with a new piece of information, and tries to explain why he made the mistake rather than moving on."

— NASSIM TALEB

"Paper or plastic?"

It's a question you've been asked a thousand times but one you've likely never thought too deeply about. But since I'm asking now, which do you think is better for the environment? Which do you choose when presented with alternatives at the grocery store? If you're like me, you likely choose paper, assuming that you're doing Mother Earth a favor in the process. If that's what you think, consider these facts from the You Are Not So Smart (YANSS) podcast:

- Making a paper bag takes three times the amount of water as making a plastic bag.

- Only 24% of people reuse paper bags versus 67% reuse of plastic bags.

- Paper production creates 70% more air pollution than plastic production.

- It takes 91% more energy to recycle a pound of paper than a pound of plastic.

Pretty shocking, right? In light of this new information, will you do things differently the next time you go to the grocery store? If you had previously opted for paper, you might well reconsider that now. Given that you had a low level of emotional investment in the paper versus plastic discussion it is easy to update your beliefs in light of the new information you've just received. Next, let's try something a little, OK a lot, more emotionally laden – gun control.

"The laws around gun control should be more restrictive."

Whether you agree or disagree with the statement above, odds are that you feel more passionately about it than you did the paper versus plastic conversation. You may have even noticed some changes in your respiration, posture, or thoughts as you readied to engage in a more meaningful conversation and prepared to defend your deeply held beliefs. Consider the following points about gun control, also from the YANSS podcast, in light of this new awareness of how it has impacted your body:

- 98% of guns used in the commission of a crime are stolen.

- Over 100,000 people successfully defend themselves with a gun each year.

- 9 times out of 10 gun owners defend themselves without firing a shot.

- More people drown each year than have been accidentally shot since 1980.

- Kitchen knives kill ten times as many people each year as assault weapons.

To be clear, I could come up with a list of facts just as compelling in favor of tighter gun control, but that's not the point here. The point is to observe your reaction to hearing information that does or does not conform to your deeply held beliefs.

If you were previously in the paper bag camp and received information that called that opinion into question, you would likely revise your beliefs with no particular angst. But if you are in favor of tighter gun control and heard someone quoting statistics like the ones above, your reaction would likely be much different. Far from seamlessly assimilating new ideas into existing belief frameworks, research shows that we actually tend to get more firm in our cherished beliefs when those beliefs become challenged.

Lee Ross and Craig Anderson completed a series of experiments using a structure called a "debriefing paradigm" to test the recalcitrance of belief to new information.[31] Participants in these studies read fake evidence for

---

[31]   Lee Ross and Craig Anderson, 'Shortcomings in the attribution process: On the origins and maintenance of erroneous social assessments,' in Daniel

an idea, after which time the change in their attitudes was measured, before the fakery was eventually exposed in detail. Their attitudes were then measured again to search for lingering effects of the now debunked idea. Even though they had been told in some detail that the original evidence was entirely fictional, a residue of bad belief tended to persist even after a full debriefing. A similar study at Stanford assigned students to read suicide notes and determine from the note whether or not the person in question had subsequently taken their own life. Some students were told they were immensely gifted at sorting completed suicides from those who had not gone through with it, while others were told they were not good at all at making the prediction. The only problem – the whole task was a ruse.

The students who had been told that they were nearly always right were no more gifted than anyone else at the task. In part two of the study, the deception was revealed and the participants were informed that the true aim of the study was to gauge their reactions to thinking that they were right or wrong. They were then asked to rate how they had actually done on the task in light of this new information and something strange happened. The students who had received fake news of their giftedness persisted in their belief that they were far more talented than average and those who had received bad scores in round one remained committed to their idea of having done poorly. True or false, once an idea takes root it can be very hard to dislodge.

This tendency for beliefs to get even stronger in the face of contradictory evidence, known as the backfire effect, is even more pronounced when the information presented is ambiguous or unclear. A Stanford study presented participants with strong feelings about the death penalty with a sheet that set forth evidence both for and against capital punishment. Of those surveyed, 23% said that their views had become more extreme after reading the document and all of those whose views had changed had moved in the direction of their pre-existing bias.

Taber and Lodge conducted a similar study in which those with strong opinions about gun control and affirmative action were asked to read arguments on both sides of those two issues. Those with the strongest

Kahneman, Paul Slovic and Amos Tversky (eds.), *Judgment Under Uncertainty: Heuristics and Biases* (Cambridge University Press, 1982), pp. 129–152.

previous feelings and well-identified political preferences showed even greater polarization in the direction of their extant beliefs. When presented with beliefs that challenged their own, the radical became even more radical.

In cults, the process whereby the most militant members remain in the group is known as the "evaporative cooling of beliefs." When a deeply held belief of the cult (say, that the world will end on a certain date) fails to materialize, the more moderate members realize their mistake and exit the group. The most radical among them, however, double down on the existing story and look for reasons to sustain the thinking such as, "Maybe we weren't righteous enough to bring about the prophecy." The cult subsequently becomes even more radicalized and the process repeats until you see tragedies the likes of Jonestown or Heaven's Gate.

When you step on the scale and like what you see, what do you do? In all likelihood, you jump right back off and go about your day, secure in the knowledge that you are reaching your weight loss goals. But what about when you step on the scale and don't like the number staring back at you? At those times you likely step off and step back on, being careful not to lean too much or put undue pressure on the bearer of bad news. Get a clean bill of health and you skip out of the doctor's office, get a scary diagnosis and you double and triple check in disbelief. We are programmed to accept self-affirming truths at face value and to be deeply skeptical of anything that offends us.

Deeply aware of the negative implications of ego, some investment shops appoint a dedicated "Devil's advocate" to challenge the thinking of the portfolio manager. But research on people critical of vaccinations shows that when these people are presented with facts that disagree with their unscientific views, they actually become more entrenched in their wrongheaded position. The behavioral investor realizes that course-correcting bad ideas is nearly impossible and that designing a system inoculated against untruth is the far better route.

The most ignored phrase in investing

"Those who do not know the torment of the unknown cannot have the joy of discovery."

— CLAUDE BERNARD

Sir John Templeton famously opined that the most expensive words in investing were, "This time is different." After all, this sort of new era thinking is to blame for everything from the excesses of the Jazz Age (that led to the Great Depression) to the astronomical valuations of the dot.com bubble. When trusted metrics like profitability and sales growth give way to "mindshare" and "eyeballs on the page," disaster is not far off. But if "this time is different" is the most expensive phrase in investing, I would like to nominate "I don't know" as the most overlooked phrase in investing, with "I was wrong" as a close second. As is so often the case, the usefulness of these beliefs in an investment context is directly proportional to their behavioral difficulty. Acceptance of uncertainty and a belief in personal fallibility are remunerative precisely because they come so hard to humankind.

It is strange to consider that many of the most effective tactics in investing have "I don't know" at their core. Passive investing is the embodiment of "I don't know" investing; if you're not sure what's good and what's not, just buy the market. In large part due to this attitude of humility, passive vehicles have spanked active funds over just about any timeframe you'd care to consider. Just look at the results of the SPIVA Scorecard, a comparison of how active managers have done relative to their passive counterparts. Over five and ten-year periods, respectively, 88.65% and 82.07% of large capitalization money mangers were beaten by passive approaches to investing (and that's before their fees!). The results for small capitalization stocks, often considered to be less efficiently priced and therefore more favorable to active management, are just as damning: 87.75% of small cap managers were bested by passive approaches.

Diversification is likewise rooted in an ethos of, "you can't be sure of anything so buy everything" and is proof that conceding to uncertainty does not have to mean compromising returns. In fact, broad diversification and rebalancing have been shown to add half a percentage point of performance per year, a number that can seem small until you realize how it is compounded over an investment lifetime.

For evidence of the efficacy of diversification and rebalancing take, for example, the case of European, Pacific and US Stocks cited in *A Wealth of Common Sense*. From 1970 to 2014, the annualized returns were as follows:

- European Stocks: 10.5%

- Pacific Stocks: 9.5%

- US Stocks: 10.4%

Similar returns, but let's examine what happens when all three markets are combined, equally weighted and rebalanced each year-end to maintain consistent portfolio composition. In what can only be described as a diversification miracle, the average return of the portfolio over this time is 10.8% annualized – greater than any of its individual parts! Not bad for not having a clue.

Despite the efficacy of "I don't know" investing, it still remains an underutilized approach. The reasons for this lie in our deep-seated needs for felt personal competence and are hard to extinguish, even in the face of compelling evidence.

I don't know

"The quest for certainty is the biggest obstacle to becoming risk savvy."

— GERD GIGERENZER

Aerophobia (also known as aviophobia) is the fear of flying in airplanes or helicopters and impacts an estimated 25% of air travelers in some form or another. The fear of flying is no respecter of persons and negatively impacts such notables as gangster rapper KRS-One, football coach John Madden, tattooed drummer Travis Barker (of Blink-182), and the despotic duo of Joseph Stalin and Kim Jong-il. An appetite for committing crimes against humanity, it would seem, is no guarantee of a stomach for flying. But despite our widespread fear of flying, it remains one of the safest, if not the safest, means of travel available. Statistics from 2014 from the National Travel Safety Board found that zero people were killed on commercial airliners in one calendar year,[32] compared with 38,300 fatalities and 4.4 million injuries in automobile accidents over that same period. Assuming you fly once a year, you would surpass your risk of injury by car by driving a mere 12 miles! Considering that most Americans drive more like 12,000 miles per year, the numbers are laughably discrepant.

But the safety of air travel has not always been as exceptional as it now is and those improvements owe largely to a commitment to "I don't know" and "I was wrong." The airline industry has embraced simple but powerful best safety practices such as religious reliance on pre-flight checklists and System Think, a program that brings pilots, mechanics, air traffic controllers, regulators and the airlines themselves together to discuss past errors and consider a safer future for the passengers they serve.

Shockingly, this commitment is not shared by one place you'd definitely expect it to be readily adopted – hospitals. As Gerd Gigerenzer says of hospitals in *Risk Savvy*, "National systems of reporting and learning from serious errors, as in aviation, rarely exist."[33] Which is the biggest reason why the Institute of Medicine estimates that somewhere between 44,000 and 98,000 patients are killed each year by preventable medical errors. That's right, hospitals may kill twice as many people as car accidents and medical errors are the third leading cause of death in the US, behind only heart disease and cancer! In capital markets, we pay a steep price for our hubris. In hospitals, that debt is paid in human life.

One perverse quirk about our search for certainty is that the more random an event is, the more certain we become. Jason Zweig shares that participants in one ambiguous study reported 68% certainty in their ability to determine whether a drawing had been created by an Asian or European child. Likewise, college students reported 66% certainty that

---

[32] 2014 NTSB US Civil Aviation Acccident Statistics.
[33] Gerd Gigerenzer, *Risk Savvy: How to Make Good Decisions* (Penguin, 2015).

they could name which US states had the highest graduation rates. In both cases, the actual results were at or below chance levels.

A related concept, perhaps my favorite in all of psychology, is what is known as the Dunning-Kruger effect. To put their findings indelicately, David Dunning and Justin Kruger of Cornell University found that dumb people are too dumb to know how dumb they are.[34] Their inquiry into the subject was inspired by the case of McArthur Wheeler, a bank robber who attempted to disguise his identity by covering his face in lemon juice. Aware that lemon juice was used as invisible ink, McArthur reasoned that it would likewise make his face invisible. By studying this idiot and others like him, Dunning and Kruger found reliably that incompetent people fail to recognize their own lack of skill and have difficulty gauging the skill level of others.

To recap, doctors and investment advisors have specialized knowledge and are highly esteemed, which contributes to the difficulty they have relying on something as banal as a checklist or uttering something as self-effacing as, "I have no idea." On the other end of the spectrum, those with limited knowledge tend to overstate their competence by their very lack of competence. And to put a cherry on top of the whole mess, the more random a situation is, the more certain we tend to be of the outcome. Smart or stupid, young or old, expert or novice, we have a really difficult time with uncertainty and admissions of wrongdoing.

Exceptional mediocrity

Willard Van Orman Quine was a logician, philosopher and professor at Harvard University. He is one of the most influential philosophers of the 20th century and is celebrated for an unusual mutation to his office computer – he removed the question mark key, stating, "I deal in certainties." While Professor Quine's extraction is comical and grandiose, it is a fine metaphor for how most of us go about our lives. We see ourselves as the center of the universe, overstating the likelihood of positive occurrences and delegating the dangerous. This tendency

---

[34] Justin Kruger and David Dunning, 'Unskilled and unaware of it: How difficulties in recognizing one's own incompetence lead to inflated self-assessments,' *Journal of Personality and Social Psychology* 77:6 (1999), pp. 1121–34.

gets us out of bed, gives us the courage to talk to the attractive person at the bar and encourages us to start restaurants and businesses, neither of which is rational in a purely probabilistic sense.

But in a refrain that is by now becoming familiar to you, the adaptions that serve us so well elsewhere in life are ill fit to the needs of the investor. Becoming a behavioral investor means examining the world in ways entirely foreign to us, with ourselves as an insignificant part of a much larger tapestry, with no special gifts, knowledge or luck. It means owning that we are, on average, average.

But the paradox in owning our personal mediocrity is that it makes us, in the strictest sense of the word, exceptional. It is not about believing in yourself – in fact, it's quite the opposite. It's about realizing that the less you need to be special, the more special you'll become. As investor and author James P. O'Shaughnessy says in *What Works on Wall Street,* "The key to successful investing is to recognize that we are just as susceptible to crippling behavioral biases as the next person." Exceptional investment outcomes are attainable by all of us, if we just stop trying so hard.

What's the big idea?

- "Believe in yourself" is really bad advice for investors.

- You tend to search out information that proves what you already believe.

- You nearly break your arm patting yourself on the back for the decisions you make.

- We react violently to challenges to cherished beliefs and may double down.

- "I don't know" is a profitable if seldom uttered sentiment.

- Paradoxically, the more ambiguous a situation, the more certain we become.

- If you feel passionately about an investment idea, you probably haven't thought hard enough about it.

Chapter 5.
Conservatism

"It's only after we've lost everything that we're free to do anything."
— CHUCK PALAHNUIK, *FIGHT CLUB*

SOME YEARS AGO, a German town was presented with an almost unheard of opportunity – the chance to totally reinvent itself. The town sat atop valuable mineral reserves that the West German government desperately needed. Vast swaths of the town would have to be razed to access the lignite being mined, but in return, the government offered to rebuild the town just down the road to whatever specifications the townspeople desired.

Part of the reason the government felt so comfortable destroying the town was that it was nothing to speak of. It had developed haphazardly over the generations, winding in a serpentine path that made travel difficult, and was not particularly functional or beautiful. When asked to create a new town plan that would be entirely bankrolled by the government the townspeople set forth a plan that looked – you guessed it – just like the ugly little hamlet that was to be destroyed.

Given the chance to be anything they wanted to be, they engaged in the very natural human tendency to be what they had always been. This broad tendency to privilege sameness over change accounts for a host of human behaviors and is our second pillar of investor behavior, *conservatism*.

The devil that you know

This year, roughly 10,000 people will die in drunk driving accidents. One-in-three people will be involved in an alcohol-related crash in their lifetime. A majority (55%) of all family violence occurs in the homes of alcoholics.

While we are all familiar with the dangers of alcohol abuse at a high level, statistics like these still stagger the mind. Given the damage done by drinking to excess it seems natural that those negatively impacted by alcoholism in their youth would take pains to avoid it in adulthood. Why is it then that fully 50% of children of alcoholics go on to marry alcoholics themselves?

There are a number of psychological variables at play that account for this tendency to prefer the "devil that we know." One reason is that there is comfort in sameness. People want to know what they are getting into – even if it is boring, bad or unfulfilling. Pain researchers have found that expected pain is much less disruptive than unexpected pain, even if the painful stimulus delivered is of exactly the same intensity. As Kurt Cobain crooned, "I miss the comfort in being sad."

Conservatism is also buttressed by our natural tendencies to avoid regret, to esteem things we have as more valuable than those we don't, and to fear loss more than we seek gain. Whatever the specific psychological underpinnings, the pitfall of our natural conservatism is universal; it keeps us stuck. In an investment context this can look like everything from holding losers too long, to failing to rebalance, to under allocating to risk assets, all the way to a more general paralysis.

Change requires much of us that is psychologically difficult – cognitive effort, adaptation, the potential for regret and loss – but it is also fundamental to becoming a behavioral investor. In life and markets, change is the only constant.

Thinking is hard

How many decisions would you guess that you make in a given day? Take a second, mentally walk through your day and hazard a guess. Most people I ask this question land somewhere around 100, which is way off – try 35,000.[35]

That's right, you make 35,000 decisions per day.

Canonical models of decision-making deal with two types of decisions – *certain* (i.e., with a known set of alternatives with given outcomes) and *uncertain* (just the opposite). In theory, decisions made under conditions of certainty involve ranking the known alternatives and choosing the most preferred option, simple enough. Uncertain decisions operate from a similar theory, with the only kink being that subjective probabilities are assigned to the different outcome likelihoods. Thus, decision makers weigh the desirability of a given option by the chance that it will or won't occur.

These are nice ideas and make some sense until you consider the sheer volume of decisions we make each day. When you consider that you make 12,775,000 decisions each year, thinking that each determination is made by weighing its probabilistic utility starts to strain credulity. Making that many decisions sounds exhausting and, indeed, the research supports that it is. This leads us to disproportionately stick with the familiar.

In their 'Status Quo Bias in Decision Making' paper, Samuelson and Zeckhauser found that classical models of decision-making vastly under predict the degree to which we stick with what we are already doing. When considering decisions as diverse as voting, making business decisions, choosing health insurance and managing retirement accounts, the two researchers found that we overwhelmingly default to the status quo.

---

[35] Joel Hoomans, '35,000 decisions: The great choices of strategic leaders,' *Roberts Wesleyan College Leading Edge Journal* (March 20, 2015).

They illustrate the strength of this tendency using the metaphor of an incumbent politician taking on a challenger. In their words, "An extrapolation of our experimental results indicates that the incumbent office holder would claim an election victory by a margin of 59% to 41%. Conversely, a candidate who would command as few as 39% of the voters in the neutral setting could still earn a narrow election victory as an incumbent."[36] Think that voters dispassionately weigh the pros and cons of politicians when making a choice? Think again. More often than not they pull the lever for the person that's already seated.

Wansink and Sobal of Cornell found that we are similarly impacted by conservatism in the way that we the well over 200 food decisions that we confront each day.[37] In their first study, the professors examined how aware participants were of having actually made a decision around food. The 139 participants in their study underestimated the number of food decisions they made by an average of 221! It is a testament to the degree to which we are on autopilot that we can make decisions so wholly beneath our awareness. Their second study looked at those who overate by virtue of having been given an "environmental default" (a large bowl). When asked why they overate, almost no one attributed it to defaulting to the status quo. Twenty-one percent of participants denied having overeaten altogether. Seventy-five percent attributed it to hunger and a scant 4% copped to the fact that, yeah, I just filled up the bowl because it was there.

There is a reason that the arthouse films and documentaries in your Netflix queue never get watched – your brain is exhausted. After a long day at work you want Michael Bay, not Lars von Trier. You are confronted with a staggering number of decisions to make each day

Drawing on this very idea, Edwards (1968) found that our tired brains mean that we don't update our beliefs rationally and that, "The more useful the evidence, the greater the shortfall between actual updating and rational updating."[38] Pause for a moment and consider

[36] Samuelson and Zeckhauser, 'Status quo bias in decision making,' *Journal of Risk and Uncertainty* (1988), p. 9.
[37] Brian Wansink and Jeffery Sobal, 'Mindless eating,' *Environment and Behavior* (January 1, 2007).
[38] W. Edwards, 'Conservatism in human information processing,' in B.

how incredible that statement is. Important information is almost of necessity hard to digest. Our mental fatigue ensures that we leave relevant new information to the side and rely instead on well-trodden mental paths of dubious quality.

As was previously mentioned, your brain is the most metabolically inefficient part of your body and one way that you conserve energy is by going with defaults. You don't calculate how much cereal you need to fuel your morning, you just fill up the bowl. You don't create a spreadsheet comparing the pros and cons of your workplace retirement options, you just go with the one you've had for the past five years. You don't rebalance your portfolio, you let it ride.

Conservatism is a fact of life that exists in no small part because your decision-making abilities are stretched to their limit. It's not good or bad, it just is. And as we will discuss in subsequent chapters, there are very real ways to make this construct work in your favor.

Inaction means never having to say you're sorry

Imagine that you are at home alone with a young child asleep in her crib. You have an urgent errand to run that is time sensitive but should be fairly quick, say 15 minutes. Would you wake the child and take her with you on the errand or leave her asleep, knowing that she is contained in the crib even if she awakes? Most people (myself included) automatically say that they would wake up the child and take her along on the trip and for a very specific reason. Regret avoidance. If, in the course of you running your errand, the house caught fire or was robbed with the child inside, your guilt would be unbearable. All of this of course ignores the probability that harm will come to the child in one or another instance. Home fires are extremely rare and the likelihood that a sleeping child in a crib will be harmed in 15 minutes is infinitesimal. Auto accidents, on the other hand, are very common and the risk that the child will be harmed as your companion in running errands is very real. The imagined regret of not protecting a child you left alone is more salient and vivid than the statistics surrounding auto fatalities.

Kleinmutz (ed.) *Formal Representation of Human Judgement* (Wiley, 1968).

Stories ignite the mind while probability puts us to sleep, and so we bring her along.

We engage in such fallacious thinking, say Kahneman and Tversky, because "individuals feel stronger regret for bad outcomes that are the consequence of new actions taken than for similar bad consequences resulting from inaction."[39] Action begets feelings of culpability and taking responsibility for uncertain outcomes is a hard pill to swallow. If Investor A makes dramatic changes to her portfolio before the market drops 20%, all else being equal she will feel worse than Investor B who might suffer a similar loss but had not made recent changes to her holdings. Investor A will feel more responsible and that responsibility hurts. This concept of inaction as a form of regret avoidance was driven home to me in an unforgettable way by my first ever therapy client, a woman I'll refer to here as Brooke.

Although I have spent my entire career applying behavioral principles to the world of finance, my PhD is in clinical psychology. As one of the components for completion of my doctoral program, I was required to provide thousands of hours of counseling to clients in crisis, a skill set that has proven invaluable in speaking to panicked investors. My first client, Brooke, entered my office holding six envelopes that she immediately placed on the desk before me, saying, "I have a problem." Brooke was attractive, well dressed, articulate and, I understood from her file, an exceptional student. I frankly couldn't imagine what could be troubling someone so poised.

As the session went on, Brooke began to expound upon her problem and I did my best not to look like the scared rookie that I was. Brooke was an aspiring scientist and had applied to a number of prestigious PhD programs, all of which had responded to her via post – these were the six letters presented to me at the outset. She had dreamed of being a scientist since she was a young child, had spent her time at high school in solemn preparation for acceptance to a good college and had been a diligent student throughout her university years. Everything she had ever done had been preparing for this moment!

---

[39] D. Kahneman and A. Tversky, 'Choices, values and frames,' *American Psychologist* 39 (1984), pp. 341–350.

The letters had arrived and she had… done nothing. Having poured so much time and intention into preparing for this moment, she was now paralyzed by the prospect of actually discovering whether or not she had been accepted. With the deadlines for enrollment looming, she had to face her fears, open the envelopes and take action, but she was paralyzed. She could not bear the thought of being rejected at something she had worked so hard to bring about.

Throughout the session, I was a mess. Brooke's presenting concerns had not been covered in any of my textbooks and I was nonplussed that someone so seemingly together could act so erratically. I distinctly remember fumbling over words, actually dropping my files at one point and just generally being useless. I had been taught not to give direct advice, but rather to ask the sort of pointed questions that would help the client arrive at her own solutions. Easier said than done in the moment.

Frustrated with my own inability to lead her in a good direction, I finally blurted out, "It seems to me that by being afraid to take a risk, you're bringing about the inevitability of the very thing you're afraid of." It wasn't pretty, but it worked. Brooke and I both realized that day that our best efforts at managing uncertainty can sometimes bring about certain disappointment – a reality as true in investing as it is in life. Brooke irrationally feared that by taking action she would feel regret. Ironically, through her inaction, she nearly brought about the inevitability of the very thing she feared.

Like Brooke, many investors take the ostrich route to investing, burying their head in the sand and hoping that nothing bad will happen. While the impulse toward complacency is understandable, the sting of the poor financial results it produces is in no way lessened.

Synthesizing happiness

Another means by which we act too conservatively is rooted in our tendency to value what we have or what we have done over that which we don't have or haven't done. Consider the free choice paradigm experiment from before where participants were asked to select a painting for which they had no particular preference, but simultaneously generated a preference for the painting simply by virtue of their ownership of it. Daniel Gilbert refers to this process as "synthesizing happiness" and it has a great deal of positive real-world application. Having an irrational preference for and unrealistically high opinion of, say, your spouse, has positive implications for a stable society. But if we can give true love a pass for being blind, we should not be so accommodating with our investment decisions. Good marriages are built on forgiveness and tolerance for imperfection. Good investing is based on clear-eyed decision-making and buying and selling wholly on merit.

This tendency to love the one you're with is known as the endowment effect. Its existence has been established in hundreds of experiments but has never been as described as beautifully as in Ayn Rand's novel, *The Fountainhead*. Within, Wynand describes the effect in easily relatable terms, "I am the most offensively possessive man on earth. I do something to things. Let me pick up an ashtray from a dime-store counter, pay for it and put it in my pocket – and it becomes a special kind of ashtray, unlike any on earth, because it's mine." Like so many of the concepts discussed in this book, the endowment effect exhibits deep evolutionary salience. It has now been observed in three different primate species and has been shown to be more intense when life-sustaining needs (e.g., food) are involved versus simple wants (e.g., toys).

The most famous study on the endowment effect was conducted at Cornell University and involved chocolate bars and coffee mugs. The two items, each with identical market values, were given to students who had previously reported liking them in roughly equivalent terms. About half of the students preferred the coffee mug and about half wanted the chocolate bar. The two items were then handed out at random and students were subsequently allowed to trade for the item they had professed to initially prefer. Given that the items were doled out randomly, you would assume that about half of the students involved would have received their non-preferred item and would swap accordingly. The observed effect was that only 10% of the participants in the study made the trade. They may have initially preferred one item over the other but as soon as it became theirs it became valuable to them.

The implications for investing are clear; we tend to overvalue what we own and undervalue unowned alternatives. Even professional traders exhibit a tendency not to sell investments they already hold, even though in many cases they admit that they would not buy the holding in question today if asked to start afresh.

Our tendency to overvalue physical objects under our care makes sense when considered in a certain light, but it also extends to the ways that we evaluate decisions on which we have spent time and money. In a cruel twist, the more time and attention we give a decision, the more warped our sense of what is right may become. This sunk cost fallacy, as it is known, means that the larger the past resource invested in a decision, the greater the inclination to continue the commitment in subsequent decisions. The member of a gym he has never once visited may not cancel his monthly membership fee because to do so would mean that the whole thing had been a waste. A Farmville addict may spend hours a day, ignoring real life responsibilities, to tend to digital crops, because to cease doing so would mean that the hundreds of hours previously invested would be for naught.

This phenomenon would be little more than a blurb in a Psych 100 textbook if its impact were limited to digital crops and couch potatoes, but history is full of examples in which decisions made with an eye to sunk costs had a dramatic impact. Samuelson and Zeckhauser share the following in 'Status Quo Bias in Decision Making':

- The Teton Dam, which eventually burst and killed 11 people and 13,000 cattle, was known to be faulty during its construction. These imperfections were ignored by the government who insisted on pushing forward in order to complete the task.

- With the help of millions in taxpayer funds, Lockheed continued to build the never-profitable L-1011 aircraft in an attempt to justify past research and development efforts.

- The huge investment of American life and treasure is seen as the motivating force behind the Vietnam War going on far longer than it should have.

- The billion dollars spent on the Manhattan Project is viewed as contributing to Truman's decision to use atomic weapons against

Japan in World War II. Had the bombs not been used to end the war, the resources devoted to the project would likely have been viewed as wasted.

While certainly not as consequential as the examples mentioned above, investment managers commonly fall prey to the sunk cost fallacy when making buy and sell decisions. Consider the seemingly reasonable impulse to want your investment manager to do in-person site visits with potential investment targets.

For starters, you begin with a sort of optimism bias about the whole affair because no investor ever vetted a deal he didn't believe to be worthwhile. Once the sunk costs begin to accrue, analysts and fund managers have a built-in bias for the result of the meeting to be positive. After all, if the management being scrutinized is disappointing, the trip and all of the time invested were for naught. Do you know how expensive it is to fuel a private jet?

A second problem is getting straight answers from the people being vetted, who will obviously be putting their best foot forward and are also subject to subconscious biases about their own viability. In examining the Duke CFO optimism survey data, Graham and Harvey found that almost 90% of tech CFOs thought their stock was undervalued near the peak of the tech bubble. Everyone thinks their baby – and their business – is more beautiful than all of the others, no matter how statistically impossible that is. As a result of this overconfidence, you can be sure that management is misleading you even if they are not aware that they are! Finally, we have a worse-than-chance ability to tell if someone is being honest with us.

In-person due diligence of management, for all its common-sense appeal, is really little more than an expensive boondoggle that gives fund managers false confidence while increasing sunk costs that obscure decision-making.

Hopeful new research out of the University of Maryland suggests that experience may lessen the impact of the endowment effect. John List observed that experienced sports memorabilia traders were much less prone to conservatism than their more callow counterparts. Whereas newbies tended to overvalue their holdings and be slow to buy and sell, more experienced traders sized up deals on an individual basis and made dispassionate decisions less prone to the endowment effect. If it is human nature to want to cling tightly to what we own, even in the face of better options, it is encouraging to think that we can be broken of this habit with sufficient experience.

I can't, I can't, I can't stand losing

There are many paths to conservatism – avoidance of regret, privileging of what we own, the consideration of sunk costs – but all have an aversion to loss at their core. Regret aversion is fundamentally about avoiding the loss of perceived competence. The endowment effect is an evolutionary land grab designed to keep us from being taken advantage of. And the sunk cost fallacy is rooted in a fear of wasting time and resources. All paths to conservatism, it would seem, run through some form of loss aversion.

It is perhaps the most widely disseminated finding of behavioral finance that our risk and reward preferences are asymmetrical and that we care far more about avoiding loss than we do about achieving gain. What is less understood is the brain science behind this phenomenon As reported in *Scientific American*, Dr. Russell Poldrack and his colleagues found that, "...the brain regions that process value and reward may be silenced more when we evaluate a potential loss than they are activated when we assess a similar sized gain." Loss aversion is as much a physiological construct as it is a psychological one. Poldrack found enhanced activity in the reward circuitry of the brain as gains were made, but even stronger responses to potential losses – something the researchers dubbed "neural loss aversion."[40] The fear of loss and the attendant behavioral paralysis that can accompany that fear have biological roots that run deep, but they must be shaken if we are to achieve our true potential as people and investors.

Think about the most meaningful thing you have ever done. I would wager that it took a measure of risk, uncertainty and hard work to achieve. In this, as with all risk, comes a valuable lesson: to strive for certainty is to doom oneself to mediocrity. Nothing is less safe than playing it safe and nothing guarantees loss like trying to avoid it. Consider the person who remains unattached to avoid risking heartache and finds loneliness in the process. Or the would-be entrepreneur who never makes the leap of faith and wastes a career working at jobs they hate. Or the investor paralyzed by a fear of volatility that arrives at retirement with resources inadequate to meet their needs. Indeed, the irony of obsessive loss aversion is that our worst fears become realized in our attempts to manage them.

The sweet taste of familiarity

Like any good child of the '80s, I have a keen recollection of the Soda Wars. Tired of being the red-headed-stepchild of soft drinks, Pepsi ran a series of commercials that pitted Coke and Pepsi head to head in a blind taste test. Much to the delight of Pepsi (and much to the surprise of most of the blind taste testers), the results of these blind taste tests favored their product more often than not. Pepsi touted the results of this "scientific" study in a legendary ad campaign that was everywhere from the mid-1970s well into the '80s. It stands to reason of course that if a slight majority of people prefer one soft drink over another, the preferred beverage should also enjoy a sales advantage over the less preferred beverage. And yet, as of the writing of this book, Coke enjoys a 17% share of the US soda market, roughly double that of Pepsi. Likewise, Diet Coke weighs in at a 9.6% market share compared to just 4.9% for Diet Pepsi.

There are a number of reasons that might account for this difference (e.g., Pepsi is sweeter and outperforms in sip tests but can be cloying

40   Russell A. Poldrack, 'What is loss aversion?' *Scientific American*.

over the course of a whole can), but a huge part of the chasm between preference and purchasing seems attributable to conservatism. Coke beat Pepsi to market by 12 years and what the Coca-Cola Company achieved in terms of brand building is nothing short of miraculous. By employing lifestyle advertising before there was a name for such a thing, Coke has woven itself into the fabric of American life in a way that is unprecedented. It is hard to imagine a brand that feels like more of a known quantity than Coca-Cola. As a result, Coke was relatively unimpacted by the Pepsi challenge, despite their relatively poor showing. Pepsi banked on soda drinkers making a change based on updating rational preferences, but Coke won by realizing that nothing tastes quite as good as familiarity.[41]

What's the big idea?

- Thinking is metabolically taxing – we have to parse tens of thousands of decisions per day.

- The best information is also the hardest to assimilate because it is often expressed mathematically or via complex ideas.

- Holding outcomes equal, action is more likely to lead to regret than inaction.

- We synthesize happiness (but fail to learn from mistakes) by building up the choices we make and denigrating the road not taken.

- We immediately ascribe higher value to things we own.

- An emphasis on sunk costs can lead us to work for completeness over quality.

[41]   Gus Lubin, 'Here's the real difference between Coke and Pepsi,' *Business Insider* (December 19, 2012).

Chapter 6.
Attention

QUICK! NAME ALL the words you can that begin with the letter "K." Yes, I'm serious. Take a moment and make the most complete list you can.

How many were you able to come up with? Now, make a second list with all of the words you can think of with K as the third letter. How many could you name this time?

No doubt you found it easier to generate a list of words that begin with K. But, did you know that there are three times as many words in which K is the third letter as there are words that start with K? If that's the case, why is it so much easier to create a list of words that start with K?

It turns out that our mind's retrieval process is far from perfect and that a number of cognitive quirks play into our ability to recall information.

Psychologists call this fallibility in your memory retrieval mechanism the availability heuristic, which simply means that we predict the likelihood of an event based on how easily we can call it to mind rather than how probable it is.

Kahneman and Tversky first observed this effect in their 1973 paper where they noted that an information signal is salient (i.e., memorable) if it has characteristics that differ from the background or a past state. Thus, we have a good memory for both the exceedingly commonplace (by virtue of repetition) and the exceptionally strange. Behavioral economist Robert Shiller suggested that the ubiquity of the internet made it easier for investors to bid up the prices of internet stocks to unprecedented levels during the dot.com bubble. Evidence of the usefulness of the WWW was everywhere, making it easy to create internal narratives about how the internet could be paradigm changing. Likewise, we see the effects of black swan events like the Great Recession linger in the public consciousness for years after the fact, unusual and impactful as they are.

Unfortunately for us, the imperfections of the availability heuristic are hard at work as we attempt to gauge the riskiness of different ways of living and investing.

The power of story

The basic premise of the *attention* pillar is that we make probability-insensitive judgments because of our reliance on information that is vivid over information that is factually accurate. Our propensity to rely on salience over math was powerfully illustrated by researchers at the University of Massachusetts using the humble jellybean. Let's have you play along, using language just slightly different from that of the original experiment.

Imagine that you are tasked with drawing a jellybean, blindfolded, from one of two bowls. If you draw a white jellybean you will get nothing (well, besides one delicious white jellybean), but if you draw a red jellybean you will get $100. The first bowl has nine white jellybeans and one red, and bowl two has 91 white jellybeans and nine red. From which of the bowls would you draw for the chance to win the $100?

A quick step back from the problem shows that bowl one has a 10% probability of success while bowl two has a mere 9% chance of winning – bowl one is the rational choice. But if you're like most people, bowl one doesn't *feel* like the best choice. Bowl two feels more likely to pay off, even if you stop and consider the math.

What accounts for this nagging feeling? Why is it that two-thirds of participants chose bowl two even after being directly informed of the probabilities? As one participant said, "I picked the (bowl) with the more red jellybeans, because it looked like there were more ways to get a winner, even though I knew there were also more whites, and that the percents (sic) were against me."[42] People think in stories, not percentages, and the second bowl offers nine different storylines that end in success, whereas bowl one offers just a single story with a happy ending.

There's a reason why teachers from Jesus to Aesop have used parables as the medium for their message: stories stick. We may know this intuitively, but Uri Hasson of Princeton took our understanding of the power of story a step further by examining the brains of people both telling and listening to stories. Hasson found that when a woman shared an emotional story with a group of strangers, "... their brains synchronized. When she had activity in her insula, an emotional brain region, the listeners did too. When her frontal cortex lit up, so did theirs. By simply telling a story, the woman could plant ideas, thoughts and emotions into the listeners' brains." Listening to and telling a story creates not only a shared narrative but also a common physical response. It is as if the storyteller is opening her mind and directly placing the thoughts in their pure form in the heads of those gathered to listen.

Storytelling bypasses many of the critical filters we apply to other forms of information gathering, which is what makes a movie so immersive to watch but can also give misinformation a superhighway to our mind. For this reason, stories are the enemy of the behavioral investor.

To look more closely at the power of story, consider how much you would pay for a single, sequined glove, in a dated 1980s fashion. Not much, I'd wager. Now, how much would you pay if I told you that the

42   Zweig, *Your Money and Your Brain*, p. 22.

glove had been worn by Michael Jackson? The story completely changed the means by which you valued the item. This is not so dangerous with 1980s pop paraphernalia, but very dangerous when buying stocks.

Nowhere is the power of narrative more fully realized than in IPO (initial public offering) investing. IPOs are novel, often focused in new and growing sectors, and companies tend to go public at times of great bullishness. Almost every investor I know has gone through the mental storyboarding of how much money they would have if they had only bought (Apple, Tesla, Amazon, whatever) on the first day that it went public. The power of narrative, emotion and fear of missing out combine to make IPOs extremely appealing to both professional and retail investors.

How has all of this excitement over IPOs served the investing public? Cogliati, Paleari and Vismara show in 'IPO Pricing: Growth Rates Implied in Offer Pricing' that the average IPO in the US has gone on to underperform the market benchmark by 21% per year in the first three years following its release. Despite this massive underperformance, there is no good reason to suppose that the demand for IPOs will wane in popularity in the years to come. After all, there will always be stories.

If it bleeds it leads

If stories in general have a powerful hold on our minds, then one type of narrative is particularly powerful – scary stories. Like all stories, scary tales bypass some of our critical filters but also have enormous staying power for evolutionary reasons. Dangerous, scary memories are sticky precisely because they help us survive. Good news won't kill you and so is quickly expelled from the memory. Learning the lessons taught by traumatic events, on the other hand, has an important evolutionary function with no margin for error. The reality of this was brought home to me when, as a newlywed, I was given the not-so-unpleasant task of teaching at a college on the North Shore of Oahu. Although our lodging was humble, my wife and I were thrilled to be together in paradise and eager to immerse ourselves in all the local culture and natural beauty it had to offer. That is, until I watched Shark Week.

For the uninitiated, Shark Week is the Discovery Channel's seven-day documentary programming binge featuring all things finned and scary. A typical program begins by detailing sharks' predatory powers, refined over eons of evolution, as they are brought to bear on the lives of some unlucky surfers. As the show nears its end, the narrator typically makes the requisite plea for appreciating these noble beasts, a message that has inevitably been overridden by the previous 60 minutes of fearmongering.

For one week straight, I sat transfixed by the accounts of one-legged surfers undeterred by their ill fortune ("Gotta get back on the board, dude") and waders who had narrowly escaped with their lives. Heretofore an excellent swimmer and ocean lover, I resolved at the end of that week that I would not set foot in Hawaiian waters. And indeed I did not. So traumatized was I by the availability of bad news that I found myself unable to muster the courage to snorkel, dive or do any of the other activities I had so looked forward to just a week before.

In reality, the chance of a shark attacking me was virtually nonexistent. The odds of me getting away with murder (about 1 in 2), being made a Saint (about 1 in 20 million) and having my pajamas catch fire (about 1 in 30 million), were all exponentially greater than me being bitten by a shark (about 1 in 300 million). My perception of risk was warped wildly by my choice to watch programs that played on human fear for ratings and my actions played out accordingly. My story is silly and low stakes, but our tendency to cling disproportionately to scary information has damaging implications for our health and our wealth.

No event has impacted the modern American psyche like the terror attacks of September 11, 2001. The 9/11 attacks cost the lives of thousands of innocent civilians and also set in motion procedural, political and military decisions that have had an ongoing impact on how we do everything from vote to board an airplane. As you might expect, Americans began to fly less in the wake of the 9/11 attacks. After all, the narrative of the ultimate scary plane story was still very fresh in the shared national psyche. Just as surely as the 24-hour news machine played and replayed the video of the planes hitting the towers, a parallel mental loop was playing in the heads of many US citizens. Sure, nothing like this had ever happened before, making it a low probability event. But that is small comfort for a nation in the grip of a visceral pain that makes the danger seem very real. As a result, more and more Americans began to drive, with disastrous consequences. German risk specialist Gerd Gigerenzer estimates that 1,595 more lives were lost to the tendency to drive rather than fly in the year following 9/11, a number equal to half the lives lost in the Twin Towers.

The larger point here is that risk management cannot be decoupled from considerations of scope and probability. It is only once we are able to view risk with clear eyes that we are effectively able to manage it.

Of stories and stocks

The flipside to the "If I'd just bought Apple when it IPO'd" narrative is that buying individual stocks is, in isolation, a truly risky endeavor. According to JP Morgan, 40% of stocks have suffered "catastrophic losses" since 1980, meaning that they fell by 70% or more! But what happens when we pool those risky individual names into a diversified portfolio? Jeremy Siegel found in *Stocks for the Long Run* that in every rolling 30-year period from the late 1800s to 1992, stocks outperformed both bonds and cash. In rolling ten-year periods, stocks beat cash over 80% of the time and there was never a rolling 20-year period in which stocks lost money. Bonds and cash, considered safe by most measures of risk, actually failed to keep up with inflation most of that time.

As Siegel says of this twisted logic, "You have never lost money in stocks over any 20-year period, but you have wiped out half your portfolio in bonds [after inflation]. So which is the riskier asset?" Over the past 30-year rolling periods stocks have returned 7.4% after inflation on average whereas bonds have barely kept up, clocking a real return of just 1.4%. I'm not sure what you'd call an asset class that outperforms by an average of 500% a year and does so with great consistency, but I wouldn't call it risky.

Another danger is to become mired in the day-to-day gyrations of the market instead of focused on the long term. Once again, stocks do seem very scary if you're looking at them every day. Greg Davies shows that if you check your account daily, you'll experience a loss just over 41% of the time. Pretty scary when we consider that human nature makes losses feel about twice as bad as gains feel good! Look once every five years and you would have only experienced a loss about 12% of the time and those peeking every 12 years would never have seen a loss.[43] Twelve years may seem like a long time, but it's worth remembering that the investment lifetime for most individuals is likely in the range of around 40 to 60 years.

Equity investing activates our "story brain" in the direction of both greed and fear because there are salient examples throughout history of both great wealth creation and wealth destruction. But risk, real risk, is the probability of permanent loss, not the bumps and bruises along the way. To manage risk in any meaningful sense means stepping outside of the stories we tell ourselves and considering information in as emotionless a manner as possible. If properly diversified and considered against an appropriate timeline, a portfolio with equities as its primary driver provides a great deal of reward with very little risk in the most meaningful sense of the word. Now that's a story worth telling.

When less is more

It is often assumed that there is a positive, linear relationship between information and market efficiency. It stands to reason, at least to a point, that the more publicly available information we have about a security, the greater our ability to accurately price that security. But is it possible that too much information can be as bad for efficiency as too little? As reported in *Scientific American*, the amount of data that we produce doubles each year. To put it more concretely, in 2016, humankind produced as much data as in the entire history of the species through 2015. The publication's best estimate for the future of data is that in the next decade there will be 150 billion networked measuring sensors, 20 for every man, woman and child on earth. At this point, the amount of data that we produce will double every 12 hours.

We are a culture in love with data and tend to take a *more is better* approach when it comes to measuring and reporting on every part

[43] Greg B. Davies, *Behavioral Investment Management: An Efficient Alternative to Modern Portfolio Theory* (McGraw-Hill, 2012), p. 53.

of our world. But the glut of information flooding our lives has real consequences, many of them negative. Consider the following studies:

Lenton and Francesconi analyzed 3,700 human dating decisions across 84 speed dating events. The authors found that the more the daters varied along various dimensions (height, job, education), the fewer proposals got made. The daters were overwhelmed by the variety and so did nothing.

Dimoka studied the brains of volunteers engaged in complicated, combinatorial auctions. As early information began to roll in, so did brain activity in the dorsolateral prefrontal cortex, a part of the brain implicated in decision-making and impulse control. But as the researchers gave the participants more and more information, the brain activity suddenly fell off, as if snapping a circuit breaker. "With too much information," says Dimoka, "people's decisions make less and less sense."

Ever had a hankering for sweets only to arrive in the candy aisle and become totally overwhelmed by your options? Research shows that lots of choices lead to both paralysis and dissatisfaction with your eventual choice. Several experiments suggest that when those presented with an extensive array of options make fewer purchases and are less happy with the purchases they make than those operating from a more limited decisional universe.

Another consequence of financial information overload is that it leads to drawing spurious correlations between variables. As Nate Silver reports, the government produces data on 45,000 economic variables each year![44] Pair this reality with the fact that there are relatively few dramatic economic events (e.g., there have been 11 recessions since the end of World War II) and you get what Silver refers to as putting data into a blender and calling the result haute cuisine.

And then consider the strange case of the correlation between moves in the S&P 500 and Bangladeshi butter production. Yes, you read that right – Bangladeshi butter production. This relationship, which accounts for 95% of covariance, is of course spurious even though the

[44] Nate Silver, *The Signal and the Noise: Why So Many Predictions Fail – but Some Don't* (Penguin, 2015), p. 185.

fit is nearly perfect. The relationship was discovered and set forth by researchers anxious to prove the old axiom that correlation does not equal causation and to show that by analysing a glut of information you are bound to find relationships, even if no causal relationship exists.

In a world of big data, we all too often fail to see the forest of "is this a good business?" for looking at the trees of esoteric data points. No matter what exotic economic measures professors and pundits may dream up in the future, there will always be some that show some fleeting correlation with stock returns, but fail to pass the sniff test of "Should it matter when determining whether or not to become partial owner of a business?" The coming wave of big data seems just as likely to yield a ton of false positives as it is any great new insights about the way markets behave.

Too much of a good thing

Daniel Kahneman and Amos Tversky's 'Linda the Bank Teller' study provides yet another powerful example of how more information is not always better. The two researchers set out to prove something that they had observed empirically – that emotional signals can overwhelm probability. We now refer to this as *base rate fallacy*. The two men posed the question:

Linda is 31-years-old, single, outspoken and very bright. She majored in philosophy. As a student, she was deeply concerned with issues of discrimination and social justice, and also participated in anti-nuclear demonstrations.

Which is more probable?

1. Linda is a bank teller.

2. Linda is a bank teller and is active in the feminist movement.

If you consider the question rationally and probabilistically, you understand that the number of feminist bank tellers is a subset of the larger population of bank tellers. But most people answered that (2) is more likely, falling victim to a host of noise among the true signal of probability. Our minds are populated with preconceptions about the type of people that are involved in the feminist movement and Linda checks many of those boxes.

Just as more information about Linda made us less capable of judging what really mattered, so much of what passes as investment advice is marketing or clickbait with a thin educational veneer. A part of any sensible approach to security selection is determining what matters most and a focus on those variables to the exclusion of the cacophony all around. If everything matters, nothing does.

Andrew Haldane, Executive Director of Monetary Analysis and Statistics at the Bank of England, makes a compelling academic argument for simplicity in his speech, 'The Dog and the Frisbee'. Haldane begins his comments by relating the example of catching a Frisbee, a process that "requires the catcher to weigh a complex array of physical and atmospheric factors, among them wind speed and Frisbee rotation." His question: how is such a complicated process attainable by most humans and even more admirably performed by dogs? The answer lies in the use of a simple rule of thumb – run at a speed that keeps the moving disc roughly at eye level. Haldane argues that the more complex a problem, the more simple the solution must be to avoid what statisticians call overfitting.

Haldane gives a number of examples of overfitting, beginning with complicated sports betting algorithms that examine historical measures of performance. He finds that such complex approaches are beaten by a recognition heuristic – simply picking the name of the player or the team that you have heard of. He goes on to relate that, "experimental evidence has found the same to be true across a range of other activities. Among physicians diagnosing heart attacks, simple decision trees beat a complex model. Among detectives locating serial criminals, simple locational rules trump complex psychological profiling… and among shopkeepers understanding repeat purchase data out-predicts complex models." Complex problems yield noisy results that can only be understood using big-picture, simplifying frameworks.

Haldane contrasts rules for governing known risks versus operating in a situation fraught with uncertainty, like investing in the stock market. He says:

> "Under risk, policy should respond to every raindrop; it is fine-tuned. Under uncertainty, that logic is reversed. Complex

environments often instead call for simple decision rules. That is because these rules are more robust to ignorance. Under uncertainty, policy may only respond to every thunderstorm; it is coarse-tuned."

It is precisely because the variables impacting the market are so varied and complex that it requires a simple set of rules for mastery. Just as a human trying to calculate velocity, rotation, wind speed and trajectory would drop the Frisbee, an investor mired in every piece of market minutiae is doomed to both a prodigious headache and poor performance.

The upside of noise

In science and engineering, the signal-to-noise ratio (or SNR) is a metric that compares the level (typically in decibels) of a desired measure against that of extemporaneous background noise. The parallels to investing are obvious; signal is information that is additive whereas noise can be thought of as a red herring that distracts from the task of divining fair value. For all of the flack that noise and "noise traders" get, financial markets could not exist without them. Consider a market with no noise whatsoever, an efficient market with only signal interpreted unambiguously by perfectly rational market participants. In such a market, next to nothing would ever happen. After all, if people only paid fair prices for widely understood assets, why would you ever buy or sell?

As Fischer Black notes, "Noise makes financial markets possible, but it also makes them imperfect." No noise, no action. The more noise there is, the more liquidity the market enjoys because assets change hands frequently. The obvious Catch 22, however, is that you now have a noisy market in which the assets that are now liquid are imperfectly priced. More confusing still is that noise can become signal if it is widely intuited to be so. In markets as elsewhere, perception in a very real sense becomes reality.

It's also worth mentioning that just because noise traders are necessary for the market to function, it doesn't mean that you should sign up for the job of keeping markets inefficient. Being a noise trader is like being a boat owner – it's best left to the other guy. In order to profit from the noisy markets in which we find ourselves, we must have an understanding of why people trade on noise in the first place. Fischer Black provides two ideas: 1. It gives them a sense of belonging and 2. They don't realize that it's noise.

Behavioral investors, as the sworn enemies of noise traders, must do just the opposite: 1. Revel in principled contrarianism and 2. Cultivate an understanding of the empirical and psychological markers of signal.

Become an informed consumer of investment media

- **Evaluate the source** – does this individual have the appropriate credentials to speak to this matter or were they chosen for superfluous reasons such as appearance, charisma or bombast?

- **Question the melodrama** – while volatility can be the enemy of good investing, chaos and uncertainty are a boon to media outlets hungry for clicks and views.

- **Examine the tone** – does the report use loaded language or make ad hominem attacks? These are more indicative of an agenda than an actual story.

- **Consider motive** – news outlets are not charitable organizations and are just as profit-driven as any other business. How might the tenor of this report benefit their needs over yours as a decision-maker?

- **Check the facts** – are the things being presented consistent with best academic practices and the opinions of other experts in the field? Are facts or opinions being expressed and in what research are they grounded?

"Don't be a nerd"

Following a particularly volatile few weeks in the market, I was called on by a major financial news network to share my opinion on what was happening and what it meant for investors. While I'm always grateful for a good PR opportunity, my previous appearances on TV had been a bit hard to acclimate to. Appearing on cable news means that you are speaking into a camera in some far flung location without any idea of what's going on with the person interviewing you. Worse still is that your earpiece not only picks up the words of the show host, but also includes a line for the producer who is often barking orders, counting down time and otherwise calling the shots. Having dueling voices in your head produces a sort of manufactured schizophrenia that I still find a bit difficult to navigate.

On this particular day, I had shared some of my high level remarks with the producer who had asked me, in no uncertain terms, to be more bombastic and dogmatic in my opinions. I demurred in mumbled tones, hoping that I would not be asked to compromise my integrity on the altar of media sensationalism. The producer began to count down "We're on in 5, 4…" I did my preemptory cough and throat clearing, "3, 2…" I offered my best TV smile, "1… we're live. Don't be a nerd, we're selling news here." I was shocked in a way that I'm sure registered on my face as it was picked up on camera.

I engage with the media under no pretense that they are always acting in the best interests of the investor, but even with my jaded worldview it was shocking to hear such a cynical admission of, "we're selling news here." Financial news is designed for clicks and eyeballs, not dollars and cents. Any ideas I had to the contrary were put to rest that day. When news is designed to arouse and not to inform, we get results like the latest Franklin Templeton Global Investor Sentiment Survey. Survey participants were asked how the S&P 500 had performed in 2009, 2010 and 2011, years in which the benchmark saw double-digit gains in the first two years in question and a small uptick in 2011. Despite the exceptional performance of the market over the period in question, large numbers of investors responded that it had been down sharply. We have evolved to hang on to information that is scary and unusual, especially when presented in narrative form, as the media does so well.

We live in a time when information is more available than ever, but the availability of information says nothing of its usefulness.

As news outlets become more and more partisan and specialized, the value of information can become so diminished that it can actually become harmful. Those who ought to be selling signal have by and large become purveyors of noise. What's more, the coming glut of information means that we will be compelled to rely more and more heavily on heuristics. After all, what are heuristics but evolutionary shortcuts designed to help us make decisions in the face of an overwhelming volume of information?

But signal masquerading as noise benefits the behavioral investor who is awake to the accompanying perils. Rudyard Kipling begins his coming-of-age classic, 'If', with the following stanza:

> If you can keep your head when all about you
> Are losing theirs and blaming it on you,
> If you can trust yourself when all men doubt you,
> But make allowance for their doubting too;
> If you can wait and not be tired by waiting,
> Or being lied about, don't deal in lies,
> Or being hated, don't give way to hating,
> And yet don't look too good, nor talk too wise

Keeping your head in an information age designed to help you lose it is the never-ending task of the behavioral investor. Cultivating principled contrarianism, an understanding of behavior and a familiarity with enduring empirical principles of finance may not come naturally, but they are the keys to weeding out disinformation en route to mastery of self and wealth.

What's the big idea?

- We tend to confuse ease of recall with probability.

- People think in stories, not percentages.

- We overestimate the likelihood of high-impact-low-probability scary events.

- Risk measures that fail to account for behavior are useless.

- Both too little and too much information makes markets inefficient.

- Complex dynamic systems paradoxically require simple solutions to avoid overfitting.

- Noise is what makes markets possible. It is also what makes them almost impossible to beat.

Chapter 7.
Emotion

"The world is a tragedy to those who feel, but a comedy to those who think."

— HORACE WALPOLE

Emotion: friend or foe?

IT MUST BE stated from the outset that there is some disagreement within the behavioral finance community about whether emotion is a help or hindrance when making investment decisions. One camp thinks emotions provide valuable information that deepen context, while another feels they obscure rational thinking. Both are right to a point and we'll now consider some of the relevant research in an attempt to see where emotion does and does not fit in the context of becoming a behavioral investor.

It is correctly argued by those in the pro camp that, in a very real sense, emotion is a prerequisite to being able to make decisions at all. Denise Shull points out in *Market Mind Games* that those with damage to the emotional centers of their brain often have difficulty making even simple decisions like what to wear to work or what to eat for breakfast.[45] Even quotidian, low stakes decisions have an emotional undercurrent that is noticeable only in its absence. Further, Zajonc (1980) argues persuasively that automatic, emotional reactions have an orienting effect that provides directional support for subsequent information processing and judgment.[46] They might not tell the whole story, but they point us in a good direction, get us most of the way there and then allow finer grained reasoning to sort out the rest.

As Loewenstein and Schkade point out, there are plenty of instances that come to mind when emotion serves this orienting function nicely. They write, "Undoubtedly, the great majority of predictions of feelings are reasonably accurate. People know they will feel bad if they lose their job, get rejected by a lover, or fail an examination, that they will be stressed on the first few days of a new job, and that they will experience a post-jog 'high.'" The importance of quick and dirty directional shortcuts for a brain overwhelmed by its processing demands cannot be overstated and emotion does the job nicely.

In addition to being cognitively expedient, there are profound evolutionary benefits to emotion. Paul Slovic and company go so far as to say that it is our emotional processing, "that enabled human beings to survive during their long period of evolution. Long before there was probability theory, risk assessment, and decision analysis, there were intuition, instinct, and gut feeling to tell people whether an animal was safe to approach or the water was safe to drink."[47] It is only after life became more complex, suggest Slovic et al., that we began to diminish the importance of emotion relative to more analytical means of making decisions. Andrew Lo of MIT seconds this notion, saying, "From an evolutionary perspective, emotion is a powerful adaptation that dramatically improves the efficiency with which animals learn from

[45]   D. Shull, *Market Mind Games* (McGraw-Hill, 2011).

[46]   R. B. Zajonc, 'Feeling and Thinking,' *American Psychologist* (1980).

[47]   P. Slovic, E. Peters, M. L. Finucane and D. G. MacGregor, 'Affect, risk, and decision making,' *Health Psychology* (2005).

their environment and their past."[48] The evolutionary evidence seems clear: no emotion, no humans.

But evidence of former evolutionary utility is not necessarily proof of modern-day necessity. Just ask your appendix. As surely as emotion assists in some facets of decision-making, it seems to hinder others. The previously mentioned orienting effect of emotion can be, well, downright disorienting. Emotion may correctly tell us that being broken up with will be painful, but may mistakenly lead us to believe that a bigger house or a higher salary are the keys to happiness. The literature has shown that both of these later are demonstrably untrue.

Isen found that low levels of positive affect can improve creative decision-making, but positive mood has also been shown to impair other aspects of cognition such as memory, deductive reasoning and planning.[49] Some studies have shown that positive emotion can impact the recall of positive information, whereas others have found that being happy inhibits processing and can cause cognitive processing impairments. Happiness has been shown to improve performance on some tasks (e.g., Duncker's Candle Task), but has hurt measures of executive function on others (e.g., Stroop Test, Tower of London Test).

Confused yet?

While positive emotion seems to improve some sub-facets of decision-making and harm others, one finding is less controversial: happiness leads to greater reliance on heuristics, or cognitive shortcuts. Bodenhausen, Kramer and Susser (1994) found that positive mood increases reliance on stereotypes to judge other people.[50] Forgas and Fiedler (1996) likewise argue that positive affect leads to greater discrimination against those in the outgroup.[51] The takeaway here seems

[48] A. W. Lo and D. V. Repin, 'The psychophysiology of real-time financial risk processing,' *Journal of Cognitive Neuroscience* 14:3 (2002), pp. 323–339.

[49] A. M. Isen, 'Positive affect and decision making,' in M. Lewis & J. M. Haviland (eds), *Handbook of Emotions* (Guilford Press, 1993), pp. 261–277.

[50] G. V. Bodenhausen, G. P. Kramer and K. Süsser, 'Happiness and stereotypic thinking in social judgment,' *Journal of Personality and Social Psychology* 66:4 (1994), pp. 621–632.

[51] J. P. Forgas and K. Fiedler, 'Us and them: Mood effects on intergroup discrimination,' *Journal of Personality and Social Psychology* 70 (1996), pp. 28–40.

to be that the human mind is a happiness preservation machine and facilitates that by remaining superficial when things are going well. Nothing kills your buzz like having to think in nuance or, in the case of an investor, read an in-depth analysis of company financials.

Considered from the highest level, emotion is a mixed bag, but when examined in terms particular to the context of investment decision-making, we are able to make more specific recommendations about the uses and misuses of emotion. Emotion leads to greater reliance on heuristics, which has a number of related sequelae: ignoring rules, deemphasizing probability, truncating timelines, homogenizing behavior and shifting risk perception. As always, context is king. Many of the aforementioned impacts are positive in life or death situations in which time is limited. But we no longer live in a jungle and the concrete jungles that house financial markets play by an altogether different set of rules.

A poor, wayfaring stranger

Imagine that you are seated in your favorite theater, eagerly awaiting the start of a new release, *Star Wars Episode 19: Return of the Return of the Jedi*. If you were to pause and observe the other people gathered in the theater, you might observe a host of different behaviors. One married couple might be discussing the best schooling options for their young children. The proprietor of a comic book store might be wolfing down popcorn as he intently scours reviews of the new flick, being sure to avoid spoilers. Children might be poking and bothering their siblings. A young couple on their first date might be awkwardly trying to get to know one another. In short, there would be a great heterogeneity of behavior in spite of your common locale and shared interest in a galaxy far, far away.

Next, picture someone standing up in the very same theater and yelling "FIRE!" at the top of their lungs. Now what would happen to the behavior of the gathered cinephiles? In a frantic rush, the former heterogeneity of behavior would give way to a singular purpose – make it to the door. Low levels of emotion give rise to a high dispersion of ideas and behaviors, but strong emotion has a decided homogenizing effect that can harm the investor with even the best intentions. Emotion makes you a stranger to your rules.

In *Predictably Irrational*, Dan Ariely reports on some – um, stimulating – work done by himself and a group of colleagues that demonstrates how emotion can override obedience to rules. Ariely and company asked a group of students 19 questions about their sexual preferences, including their propensity to engage in "odd" sexual behaviors, cheat on a partner, practice safe sex and engage respectfully with their partner.

They first asked these questions of the students in a "cold" state in which they were emotionally and sexually unaroused. As you might have guessed, the tendency among the students in the cold state was to advocate for safe, consensual sex that respected the wishes of the partner and occurred within the context of an existing relationship.

Next, Ariely and team introduced emotion into the exercise in the form of pornographic images aimed at sexually and emotionally arousing the participants. When sexually aroused, the answers of the participants to the 19 questions changed dramatically. They were 136% more likely to cheat on a partner, 72% more likely to engage in odd sexual activities and 25% more likely to have unprotected sex. Ariely sums it up thusly, "Prevention, protection, conservatism, and morality disappeared completely from the radar screen. They were simply unable to predict the degree to which passion would change them."

The lurid nature of the experiment may lead us to believe that its impact is limited to sexual arousal, but that would be a mistake. As Ariely says in a footnote, "…we can also assume that other emotional states (anger, hunger, excitement, jealousy, and so on) work in similar ways, making us strangers to ourselves."[52]

The students in the study knew all of the rules – you always wear a condom and you never cheat on your partner – they just didn't care about the rules in the heat of the moment. So too are you aware of many of the rules of smart investing – they just seem obsolete in a moment of fear or greed.

[52]   Dan Ariely, *Predictably Irrational* (HarperCollins, 2009).

Psychologist and trading coach Brett Steenbarger says it well, referring to a group of traders he studied: "…the net effect of emotion on trading appears to be a disruption of rule governance… Under emotional conditions… their attention became self-focused to the point where they were no longer attentive to their rules. Often, it wasn't so much a case that under emotional conditions they doubted their rules; rather, they simply forgot them."[53] No matter how smart, an emotional investor is a stranger to himself and his rules.

The Minnesota Multiphasic Personality Inventory (MMPI) is a widely used assessment of mental disorders that provides interesting insights into the American national psyche. Between 1938 and 2007, the levels of psychopathology in the US, as measured by the MMPI, have risen greatly. Specific areas on the rise include:

- Moodiness

- Restlessness

- Dissatisfaction

- Instability

- Narcissism

- Self-centeredness

- Anxiety

- Unrealistically positive self-appraisal

- Impulse control

For all the societal progress made over that time, it would appear that emotional wellbeing remains more elusive. Arbitraging emotionality seems to be an enduring form of investing advantage – one that may actually be increasing.

[53] B. N. Steenbarger, *The Psychology of Trading: Tools and Techniques for Minding the Markets* (Wiley, 2007), p. 54.

Emotion impacts our assessment of probability

One of the things that makes adhering to probabilities so difficult (and profitable) for an investor is that emotion has a pronounced impact on how we assess probability. Predictably, positive emotion leads us to overstate the likelihood of positive occurrences and negative emotion does just the opposite. This coloring of probability leads us to misapprehend risk.

Anger has been shown to make people less threatened by risk, while sadness makes them more threatened. Our personal affinity for a behavior also makes it seem more or less risky. Boating and skiing, both relatively dangerous, are largely overlooked as sources of bodily harm because they are so enjoyable. Good investing, tedious as it can be, is inappropriately labeled as risky when it is really just boring. All too often, when assessing risk we ask ourselves, "Is this fun?" and not, "Is this dangerous?"

Happy people are much more likely to think that they will win the lottery but, news flash, this doesn't improve their odds. Even if the overarching tendency to associate emotion with risk seems intuitive, the intensity with which we distort probability may still surprise you. Rottenstreich and Hsee (2001) showed that if the outcome of a bet is emotionally rich, its attractiveness or unattractiveness is insensitive to changes from probability as great as from .99 (nearly certain) to .01 (highly unlikely).[54] Loewenstein et al. (2001) found that participants' self-assessed likelihood of winning the lottery was the same whether the probability was 1 in 10 million or 1 in 10,000.[55] They further noted that emotion gives uncertain outcomes an all-or-none quality that focuses on "possibility" rather than "probability."

We are all much more like Jim Carrey's character in *Dumb and Dumber* than we might like to admit. When told by the object of his affection that he has a 1 in 1,000,000 chance of ending up with her, he smiles with relief and says, "So you're telling me there's a chance." All too

---

[54] Y. Rottenstreich and C. K. Hsee, 'Money, kisses, and electric shocks: On the affective psychology of risk,' *Psychological Science* (2001).

[55] G. F. Loewenstein, E. U. Weber, C. K. Hsee and N. Welch, 'Risk as feelings,' *Psychological Bulletin* 127:2 (2001), pp. 267–286.

often we confuse the intensity of our longing with the probability of our winning.

Rainy days and Mondays

Hirshleifer and Shumway examined the impact of cloud cover, which directly impacts mood, on the daily returns of 26 different stock exchanges. In 18 of the 26 markets, cloud cover was associated with low daily stock returns. In New York City, a hypothetical portfolio that invested only on days projected to be cloudless returned 24.8%, versus 8.6% on cloudy days. Looks like it's time to call up your local meteorologist and start a hedge fund!

Time travel

"Time flies when you're having fun" is a cliché that masks a larger truth: emotion dramatically impacts our perception of time. Specifically, intense emotion truncates our timelines and makes the here-and-now seem like all that is or will ever be. Investors, for whom time is the great wealth compounder, are profoundly hurt by this tendency of emotion to ground them in the short term.

Lynch and Bonnie's (1994) longitudinal study of smoking behavior is proof that strong emotion in the moment can lead to a lifetime of harmful decisions. High school students in their study were asked if they would still be smoking five years hence. Among occasional smokers, 15% predicted that they would be smoking in five years, compared to 32% of those who smoked one pack a day. Five years later, 43% of the occasional smokers were still puffing away while a full 70% of the heavy smokers had maintained their bad habit. A thousand emotional cravings had been strung together until they created a lifetime of bad decisions. Correspondingly, investors who mire themselves in the day-to-day minutiae of the markets and experience all of the accompanying emotions are likely to make a thousand tiny decisions that end in a penniless retirement.

Functional sociopaths

If intense emotion has such a negative impact on investment outcomes, it is interesting to consider the results of minimizing or abolishing emotion altogether. Sokol-Hessner et al. (2012) found that lowering emotion by reducing stakes and taking broader perspectives led to decreases in physiological arousal and improved decisional outcomes. Research from the University of Miami suggests that individuals learn better from financial news when it is general in nature than when it pertains to specific holdings in their portfolio. Participants are able to remain dispassionate about the general financial news but emotion warps the learning process when the news has a dollars and cents impact on their lives. Finally, the *Scientific American* cites evidence that bilingual folks make better decisions when thinking in a foreign language because it requires them to be less reflexive and emotional.

The evidence is starting to mount that emotion, adaptive as it may be elsewhere, is an impediment to sound investing. To examine this more directly, Lo, Repin and Steenbarger looked at the behavior of 80 volunteers in an online trading course and measured the impact of emotional reactivity on normalized profits and losses. They found that those who exhibited the most emotion – both positive and negative – "exhibited significantly worse trading performance, implying a negative correlation between successful trading behavior and emotional reactivity." The researchers went on to say, "…our results are consistent with the current neuroscientific evidence that automatic emotional responses such as fear and greed often trump more controlled or 'higher level' responses. To the extent that emotional reactions 'short circuit' more complex decision-making faculties… it should come as no surprise that the result is poorer trading performance."[56]

If inhibiting emotion is good, is it possible that doing away with it altogether is even better? This is the line of thought pursued in a Stanford University study titled, 'Investment Behavior and the Negative Side of Emotion'. Within, the researchers pitted 15 individuals with brain damage to their emotional processing centers

---

[56] Andrew W. Lo, Dmitry V. Repin and Brett N. Steenbarger, 'Fear and Greed in Financial Markets: A Clinical Study of Day-Traders,' MIT Sloan Working Paper No. 4534–05 (March 2005).

against 15 "neurotypical" peers in a gambling task. The study found that the brain damaged participants handily outperformed their no-damage counterparts through a combination of being willing to take bigger bets and being able to bounce back quickly after setbacks. The neurotypical participants played more safely throughout but became particularly risk averse after periods of poor performance (which in markets tend to coincide with attractive periods of investment). The brain-damaged participants, not feeling the need to lick their wounds or salve a damaged ego, maintained a consistent style throughout and emerged victorious.

The moral of the story: get a lobotomy and get rich. OK, maybe not, but the truth remains that emotion appears to be the enemy of great investing. In a joking-but-not-really moment, neurologist Antoine Bechara ventured that investors ought to be like "functional psychopaths" to excel at making money. Effectively, they ought to drive out emotion at every turn.

Too much of a good thing

Being the first in line at a traffic light is both an honor and a sacred privilege. With this power comes great responsibility, in particular remaining alert enough to be quick off the line and to allow as many people as possible to make the turn or the light. Not everyone views this as the same high calling as I do, however, and from time to time people will be slow to turn or miss the light entirely because they are texting or otherwise engaged. At times like these, I give my car horn a quick tap to alert the person in front of me to their dishonorable behavior.

One weekend in the recent past, I was behind such a distracted driver and gave my customary honk. In an instant, the person ahead of me gave me an angry look and shot me their middle finger before making the turn. As luck would have it, I pulled up next to them at the next light and the offending party rolled down his window to apologize. "I should have been paying attention," he offered, "I hate it when people do that to me." His initial, emotional response was anger toward me for honking. It was only after further consideration that he gained some empathy into how he had treated others and his "thinking slow" response allowed him to take some responsibility. As much as I would like to believe that those who shirk traffic light responsibilities are a unique brand of evil, this man was much like all of us – he let his emotions register before his thinking eventually took over.

LeDoux (1996) and his colleagues have done some interesting work that speaks to what I observed at the traffic light: the primacy of affect over reason. Based on their studies of rats, they discovered a direct neural connection from the sensory thalamus (where basic signal processing is performed) to the amygdala, or emotional center of the brain. This direct connection, that does not meander through the neocortex, means that signals are processed emotionally before they can ever be reasoned through. Rats are quite literally able to be afraid before they can even know why, a system that provides them with a quick but crude assessment of their behavioral options. This builds on previous work from Zajonc (1980, 1984, 1998) demonstrating that humans too can identify a gut-level like or dislike of an object before they can even say what it is. Further, our emotional response to a stimulus is shown to linger in memory far beyond any of the particulars of that stimulus. For instance, you may retain a strong visceral dislike of a movie for which you remember no details.

The extent to which rational and emotional approaches to decision-making interface is largely a discussion of intensity. When emotion is measured, it appears to play an advisory role that informs without overwhelming. This can be useful and may carry information that can benefit the decision-maker. But emotion is tuned for volume, not subtlety, and at greater levels of intensity, emotion almost precludes decision-making altogether. As George Loewenstein writes, "No one 'decides' to fall asleep at the wheel, but many people do."

Research by Anthony Greenwald (1992) has shown that anything the human brain has affectively tagged is primed for easy recall, whereas rational facts have no such retrieval mechanism. A study of 1400 ad campaigns with emotional appeals was pitted versus those with strictly rational appeals. Twice as many of the campaigns with emotional appeals were recalled as were those with more rational appeals. The researchers attribute this effect to the fact that emotion is effortlessly processed and stickier in our brains. As Rita Carter (1999) writes,

"Where thought conflicts with emotion, the latter is designed by the neural circuitry in our brains to win." Trying to fight emotion with logic is bringing a knife to a gun fight.

Reserve emotion for when it is useful

Most animals have evolved adaptive stress responses that protect them in times of peril. A threatened cobra raises its hood, a puffer fish puffs itself out and a turtle retreats into its shell. The human animal, conversely, seems destined to do just the wrong thing under pressure. We sweat profusely when we need to look our best. Our mouths go dry as we wait offstage to give a big speech. Our ability to forecast, anticipate and worry may separate us from the rest of the animal kingdom, but it can also separate us from a great deal of money. The best parts of life are times of elevated emotion: a marriage, the birth of a child, watching a friend graduate from college. Even life's saddest moments have an enduring ability to teach and shape behavior by virtue of their singular memorability. But as surely as emotion enriches as the soul, it depletes the wallet, and it is best kept for the times and seasons for which it is most useful.

What's the big idea?

- Our love of money makes us less, not more, reliant on emotion when making financial decisions.

- Emotion provides crude but important shortcuts that preserve mental capacity.

- Strong emotion leads to greater reliance on heuristics.

- Emotions are good for making life and death, time-sensitive choices, but are less useful in other contexts.

- Emotion makes us a stranger to rules we would otherwise profess to follow.

- Powerful feelings have a homogenizing impact on behavior.

- We tend to conflate our desire for an outcome with its likelihood.

- We are prone to viewing enjoyable activities as less risky (and vice versa).

- Intense emotion truncates timelines and leads us to ignore our future selves in favor of our immediate selves.

PART THREE.
BECOMING A
BEHAVIORAL INVESTOR

"We create our fate every day... most of the ills we suffer from are directly traceable to our own behavior."

— HENRY MILLER

JAPANESE DIRECTOR AKIRA Kurosawa is perhaps best known for his masterpiece *Seven Samurai*, but it was a different film, *Rashomon*, that was actually his breakthrough work. *Rashomon*, winner of the 1952 Academy Award for Best Foreign Language Film, depicts the trial of a notorious criminal who stands accused of murdering a samurai and raping his wife. The incident is recounted by four different witnesses – the accused, the deceased (through a spiritual medium), a priest and a woodcutter – all of whom present conflicting but earnest stories. The film is an examination of the subjective nature of truth and plays up the ways in which experience, motivation and personality impact our judgments. The moral of the story being that the various testimonials said more about the people speaking than the actual events under scrutiny.

One of the first to study the subjectivity of truth in a controlled academic setting was Sir Frederick Bartlett, head of the psychology department at Cambridge University. Bartlett operationalized this concept by asking participants in his study to read a Native American folk tale and recall it at several later dates. Bartlett found that when subjects were asked to recount the story, they tended to alter it to reflect their own priorities and cultural milieu. They omitted parts of the story they found unpleasant or foreign and swapped out Native American cultural particularities in favor of their own norms. As Mo Costandi points out, Bartlett pioneered the idea that memory was as much reconstructive as it is reproductive.[57]

Left to our own devices, we create portfolios in our own image. Americans buy American stocks. Steel workers are overweight manufacturing, while financiers double down on bank stocks. The timid fail to allocate to equities and the overconfident hold large positions in single stocks. Like an old married couple, our holdings start to look just like us, and there is great danger in that similarity.

The interpersonal differences born of our biological, psychological and neurological differences are what make the world a fascinating place, but Wall Street is no place to give voice to that uniqueness. The job of an individual is to craft a story that only she can write and to see the world through a lens unlike any other. The job of an investor, on the other hand, is to view the market today the way that others will tomorrow. Becoming an individual requires expression of self, but becoming a behavioral investor requires subjugation of self. Bending your will against its most primal bio-psycho-social longings is one the hardest and potentially most rewarding things you will ever do. In Part Three, we will examine specific ways to do just that.

Sigmund Freud began his study of the human psyche by outlining how it was broken (hint: your Mom) and the discipline of psychoanalysis continued down that path for over a century. It was roughly 150 years before the study of clinical psychology was offset at all by the research into what we now call positive psychology – the study of what makes us happy, strong and exceptional.

For a clinical psychologist, a diagnosis is a necessary but far from sufficient part of a treatment plan. No shrink worth his $200 an hour would label you pathological and show you the door, yet that is largely what behavioral finance has given the investing public: a long list of biases with very few solutions. But that all ends today, as we will take the four pillars of behavioral risk management identified in Part

---

[57]   Mo Costandi, 'Reconstructive memory: Confabulating the past, simulating the future,' *Neurophilosophy* (January 9, 2007).

Two and speak to the particulars of what they mean in the context of managing money. By way of quick reminder, they are:

1. **Ego** – tendency toward overconfidence and behaving in ways that maintain feelings of personal competency over clear-eyed decision-making.

2. **Conservatism** – asymmetrical preference for gain relative to loss and for the status quo relative to change.

3. **Attention** – disposition to evaluate information in relative terms and let salience trump probability when making decisions.

4. **Emotion** – perceptions of risk and safety that are colored by both our transitory emotional state and personal level of emotional stability.

Having read Parts One and Two, you now understand the "Why does this happen?" of misbehavior, but still lack clarity around the "So, what do I do about it?"

Let us begin that journey by examining the means by which we can construct ego-resistant by portfolios by asking, "Do we really have anything to be cocky about?"

Chapter 8.
The Behavioral Investor Overcomes Ego

"One of the painful things about our time is that those who feel certainty are stupid, and those with any imagination and understanding are filled with doubt and indecision."

— BERTRAND RUSSELL

"Part of me suspects that I'm a loser, and the other part of me thinks I'm God Almighty."

— JOHN LENNON

THE SINKING OF the Titanic, the nuclear meltdown at Chernobyl, the tragedy of Space Shuttle Challenger, the Deepwater Horizon spill, and the founding of your favorite restaurant may not seem to have much in common, but all of these events are rooted in a deep sense of overconfidence. It must be plainly stated that overconfidence isn't all bad, at least in certain contexts. We more or less demand ego from our politicians and it is also required of restaurateurs and entrepreneurs, both of whom start new enterprises in the face of overwhelmingly negative probabilities.[58] So, what determines if overconfidence is the "get you out of bed to chase your dreams" kind or the "catastrophic disaster" kind? To begin to answer this, we will examine the evolutionary roots of ego and the different contexts in which it can help and hinder us.

Dr. Tali Sharot, professor of cognitive psychology at University College London suggests that over-optimism impacts about 80% of us. Citing a humorous example, she reports that 75% of people thought good things were in store for their families but just 30% thought families in general were headed for good times.[59] In *Thinking Fast and Slow*, Daniel Kahneman also gives a nod to the ubiquity of overconfidence, calling it "the most significant of the cognitive biases" and suggesting in an interview that it is the one he'd choose to eliminate if he could do so with the wave of a magic wand.[60] Kahneman has also suggested that overconfidence is the bias that emboldens all other biases, justifying sloppy and ill-considered behavior. Understanding that human nature does not evolve arbitrarily, it seems evident that overconfidence must serve us well in some places and at some times and indeed that is the case.

To begin to unpack the evolutionarily adaptive elements of overconfidence, we must first understand that it is itself a multifaceted construct. In specific, there are three types of overconfidence:[61]

1. **Overprecision** – excessive certainty in the precision of private beliefs.

2. **Overplacement** – elevated belief in personal skill relative to others.

---

[58] An Ohio State study found that 80% of restaurants fail in the first three years: Lorri Mealey, '10 reasons restaurants fail,' *The Balance Small Business* (October 10, 2016).

[59] T. Sharot, 'The optimism bias' (May 2012).

[60] D. Shariatmadari, 'Daniel Kahneman: 'What would I eliminate if I had a magic wand? Overconfidence',' *Guardian* (July 18, 2015).

[61] D. Moore and S. A. Swift, 'The three faces of overconfidence in organizations,' in David De Cremer, Rolf van Dick and J. K. Murnighan (eds.) *Social Psychology and Organizations* (Routledge, 2012).

3. **Overestimation** – unrealistic optimism about the level of control and odds of success.

Overprecision

Take overprecision, for example. If I asked you to name how many books there are in the Bible and instructed you to provide a range that you were certain encompassed the actual number, what range would you provide? Go on, give it a shot.

You might give a range of something like 25 to 50 books (there are actually 66 books in the King James Bible, 80 if you count the Apocrypha). But stop and think about the question for a moment. I asked for a range that would almost certainly provide the correct number, so why didn't you guess "1 to 10 million"? An answer like 1 to 10 million has the distinction of being technically correct but practically useless. Under conditions of uncertainty, we humans do our best to be useful, even if that precision is found lacking with regularity.

Likewise, if a stock analyst is asked for her forecast on the share price of Apple one year hence she is likely to provide an overly precise number like $173.42. This is well intended, to be sure, and is rooted in the understandable tendency to privilege faux-precision over vague accuracy. Sadly, it can also be unintentionally misleading and cause others who act on these predictions to believe in a world that is more predictable than it actually is.

As a direct result of overprecision, contrarian investor David Dreman found that most (59%) Wall Street "consensus" forecasts miss their targets by gaps so large as to make the results unusable – either under- or overshooting the actual number by more than 15%.[62] Further analysis by Dreman found that from 1973 to 1993, the nearly 80,000 estimates he looked at had a mere 1 in 170 chance of being within 5% of the actual number.[63]

James Montier sheds some light on the difficulty of forecasting in his *Little Book of Behavioral Investing*. In 2000, the average target price of

[62]   J. Zweig, in Benjamin Graham, *The Intelligent Investor* (HarperBusiness, 2006), p. 374.
[63]   C. H. Browne, *The Little Book of Value Investing* (Wiley, 2006).

stocks was 37% above market price and they ended up 16%. In 2008 the average forecast was a 28% increase and the market fell 40%. Between 2000 and 2008, analysts failed to even get the direction right in four out of the nine years.

Finally, Michael Sandretto of Harvard and Sudhir Milkrishnamurthi of MIT looked at the one-year forecasts of the 1000 companies covered most widely by analysts. They found that the analysts were consistently inconsistent, missing the mark by an annual rate of 31.3% on average.[64] The only accurate equity forecast is, "I have no idea and neither does anyone else," but estimates like that don't provide lobster lunches and fail to meet our need for a belief in a knowable future.

Overplacement

Overplacement is what most people think of when they think of overconfidence; we judge our own performance as being superior to others. In a 2006 study entitled 'Behaving Badly,' researcher James Montier found that 74% of the 300 professional fund managers surveyed believed that they had delivered above-average job performance. Of the remaining 26% surveyed, the majority viewed themselves as average. Incredibly, almost 100% of the survey group believed that their job performance was average or better. Clearly, only 50% of the sample can be above average, suggesting the irrationally high level of overconfidence these fund managers exhibited.

In their, 'The Evolution of Overconfidence,' Johnson and Fowler suggest that overconfidence may increase resolve, ambition, persistence and competition for scarce resources.[65] They present a model that suggests that overconfidence is a natural and even desirable evolutionary outcome that maximizes individual fitness and group stability when the resources at stake in a conflict are greater than the cost of competition.

[64] B. Malkiel, *A Random Walk Down Wall Street* (W. W. Norton & Company, 2016).
[65] D. D. P. Johnson and J. H. Fowler, 'The evolution of overconfidence,' *Nature* (2011).

Overestimation

Overestimation is evident in a Cook College study in which people were asked to rate the likelihood that a number of positive events (e.g., win the lottery, marry for life) and negative events (e.g., die of cancer, get divorced) would impact their lives. What they found was hardly surprising – participants overestimated the likelihood of positive events by 15% and underestimated the probability of negative events by 20%. Likewise, Heather Lench and Peter Ditto performed a study where participants were shown six positive and six negative life events as well as their accompanying probability in the general population. Respondents endorsed 4.75 of the 6 positive life events as probably impacting them.

In her TED talk, Dr. Tali Sharot speaks to some of the ways in which overestimation can impact our reasoning. She relates that overconfidence makes it hard for us to learn from new information and suggests that we are prone to revise our beliefs only when it suits us. She shares that patients who assume that they have a 50% chance of cancer and are informed that their odds are lower, say 30%, revise their opinion to around 35% when asked for a second estimate. However, when the new information is not in their favor, say a 10% estimated chance of cancer with a 30% actual incidence, their second guess is only slightly revised upward to 11%. Overestimation means that we tend to see our lives as subject to a different set of rules and probabilities than the rest of the world and not even factual information can do much to alter that view.

* * *

Overconfidence is largely presented in a comical, "Aren't we so silly and cocky?" manner that belies its complexity and the real social, financial and evolutionary advantages that can accrue to the egotistical in many domains. Overconfidence has been shown to confer advantages in sports, politics and even health. Overconfident people show more resiliency in the face of setbacks, tackle more ambitious projects and are even deemed more mentally healthy than their lower confidence counterparts.[66]

[66] M. Muthukrishna, S. J. Heine, W. Toyakawa, T. Hamamura, T. Kameda

But while overconfidence may confer some specific advantages, our particular interest in the construct is more niche; and when it comes to business in general and investing in specific, there appears to be very little to recommend it. A Bain study found that 80% of CEOs believe that they are delivering a "superior experience" to customers, while only 8% of customers agree.[67] The Employee Benefit Research Institute (EBRI) found that 60% of those surveyed felt they'd be able to save enough for a comfortable retirement but that only 41% of those surveyed had ever tried to calculate how much money they'd actually need for a comfortable retirement.[68]

Statman, Thorley and Vorkink found that investors absolutely "confuse brains with a bull market," attributing their own success to skill and not the fact that a rising tide had lifted all boats.[69] As a result, trading volumes were found to rise dramatically following good times and fall precipitously in bad times, effectively buying high and selling low. The authors of 'Positive Illusions and Forecasting Errors in Mutual Fund Investment Decisions' discovered that most participants had consistently overestimated both the future and past performance of their investments.[70] One-third of those who believed that they had outperformed the market had actually lagged by at least 5% and another quarter of people lagged by 15% or greater. Even more damning research is found by Glaser and Weber who discovered that, "Investors are unable to give a correct estimate of their own past portfolio performance. The correlation coefficient between return estimates and realized returns was not distinguishable from zero."[71]

---

and J. Henrich, 'Overconfidence is universal? Depends what you mean' (2015).

[67] J. Allen, F. F. Reichheld, B. Hamilton and R. Markey, 'Closing the delivery gap,' Bain & Company (2005).

[68] M. W. Riepe, 'Is overconfidence affecting your investing outcomes?' Charles Schwab (February 12, 2018).

[69] M. Statman, S. Thorley and K. Vorkink, 'Investor overconfidence and trading volume,' AFA 2004 San Diego Meetings (2003).

[70] D. A. Moore, T. R. Kurtzberg, C. R. Fox and M. H. Bazerman, 'Positive illusions and forecasting errors in mutual fund investment decisions,' *Organizational Behavior and Human Decision Processes* 79:2 (August 1999), pp. 95–114.

[71] M. Glaser and M. Weber, 'Why inexperienced investors do not learn:

The finding that investors would misstate their returns is not entirely surprising, but the size and scope of the problem is. Only 30% of those surveyed considered themselves to be "average" investors and the average overestimation of returns was 11.5% per year! More shocking still, portfolio performance was negatively tied to the difference between estimates and actual returns; the lower the returns, the worse investors were at remembering their realized returns. Overconfidence simply made it impossible for them to accurately recall and report how they had done.

An elevated sense of self may get you a spouse or a Senate seat, but the same ego that elevates the politician can destroy an investor. Rational behavior, truly considered, is less about conforming to some universal standard of clear thinking and more about tailoring your approach to the context in consideration. When it comes to investment decision-making, the most rational among us will check the ego at the door.

Tools for combatting ego

If you're now convinced of the need for greater humility in your investment approach, a natural next question is, "Where do I start?" The journey toward admitting ignorance and culpability is winding and difficult, but has both financial and relational rewards.

Here are some things you can do.

Spread the wealth

My favorite part of any public speaking event is connecting with the attendees who approach the stage once I have finished. These interactions (which are as close as you get to the comments section of a web article in real life) typically take one of three forms – compliment, criticism, or consulting. I can almost invariably discern which is coming from the look on the face of the approaching party. On one memorable occasion, I was approached by an unusually long series of individuals who, as expected, thanked me for my work, told me I was an idiot, and asked me for free advice.

They do not know their past portfolio performance,' *Finance Research Letters* 4:4 (2007).

While the person who told me I was an idiot was arguably the most interesting (and accurate?), I'd like to focus on the person who asked for my advice on one stock in particular, Apple. The gentleman, after a brief thanks for the presentation, asked for my opinion of Apple stock as it made up a large portion of his $2 million portfolio. Now, I held the stock in my separate account strategies at the time and it was the highest rated stock in my investable universe at that very moment; I could not have been more bullish on Apple.

But rather than providing my take on what I saw to be Apple's considerable upside, I keyed in on another part of his question. "How large is your position?" I asked. "Half of my wealth," he replied sheepishly. My reply was reflexive, "You're being an idiot and you know it. No matter what I think of it, you're grossly misallocated." Since that time, Apple shares have gone from $74 to $142, but I still hope that the man heeded my advice that day to diversify his position. One of the most important rules of behavioral investing is that results matter less than the process; you can be right and still be a moron.

Diversification has become such a broadly accepted good in asset management that it seems many have forgotten the underlying reasons for doing it. Considered from a behavioral lens, diversification is humility made flesh, the embodiment of managing ego risk. Diversification is a concrete nod to the luck and uncertainty inherent in money management and an admission that the future is unknowable.

As evidenced by the JP Morgan research in the following table, single stock ownership can indeed be harrowing, with nearly half of all stocks suffering catastrophic losses in their lifetime.

But diversification is a lot like medicine (or candy, or children) in the sense that some is good but more is not always better. In fact, diversification can be achieved with fewer holdings than most understand and over-diversification can be an impediment.

Catastrophic losses of single stocks

Sector	Total % of companies experiencing catastrophic loss, 1980–2014
All sectors	40%
Consumer Discretionary	43%
Consumer Staples	26%
Energy	47%
Materials	34%
Industrials	35%
Health Care	42%
Financials	25%
Information Technology	57%
Telecommunication Services	51%
Utilities	13%

Source: Isaac Presley, 'How Concentrated is Too Concentrated? A Mistake That Costs You the Whole War', blog.cordantwealth.com

It does not take hundreds of stocks to create a truly diversified equity portfolio. One of the earliest studies to refute this misconception was conducted by John Evans and Stephen Archer of the University of Washington. Evans and Archer found that the benefits of diversification dropped off precipitously when more than 20 stocks were added to a portfolio. Reilly and Brown second this idea in their book, *Investment Analysis and Portfolio Management* when they note, "...about 90% of the maximum benefit of diversification was derived from portfolios of 12 to 18 stocks." Further, billionaire investor Joel Greenblatt says in his book *You Can Be a Stock Market Genius* that nonmarket (i.e., diversifiable) risk is reduced by 46% by owning just two stocks, 72% with four stocks, 81% with eight stocks and 93% with as few as 16 stocks. Greenblatt's work shows just how quickly most of the benefits of diversification can be achieved and also how quickly they begin to erode after about the 20 stock point.

Finally, Morningstar examined the volatility of high-conviction (i.e., less than 40 stocks) versus those with more than 200 holdings and found that, "…concentrated funds aren't more volatile than more diversified funds on average, and some are surprisingly steady despite their small number of holdings." It is no coincidence that there is almost universal consensus among the world's greatest investors about the appropriate number of holdings to balance diversification and performance, as you can see below.

Famous investors and their ideas about diversification

- **Benjamin Graham** – 10 to 30 holdings of "large, prominent, conservatively financed companies".

- **John Maynard Keynes** – 12 or 13 companies "which one thinks one knows something about and in the management of which one thoroughly believes".

- **Warren Buffett** – five to ten holdings, "if you are a know-something investor, able to understand business economics and to find sensibly-priced companies that possess important long-term competitive advantages".

- **Seth Klarman** – 10 to 15, because you are "better off knowing a lot about a few investments than knowing only a little about each of a great many holdings".

Diversification, truly understood, is not some game whereby we accumulate large numbers of holdings for their own sake, but rather an attempt to insulate ourselves against catastrophic loss. Considered in this light, it becomes just as important that we know something about what we own as it is to own the appropriate quantity.

Much of the work of the behavioral investor is to cut through the extreme notions of various schools of thought and to find a sensible middle path. The idea that owning just a few stocks is sufficient flies in the face of everything that we know about luck, uncertainty and human fallibility and is therefore foolish. But on the flipside, the idea that one must buy the entire market to be diversified is just as ridiculous. The idea that nothing can be known about a security and that none of the information available – prices, trends, financial and quality metrics, the behavior of insiders – gives any insight into how risky an investment is, is so pessimistic as to be absurd. It is egoistic in the extreme to assume that you can predict the future, but nihilistic in the extreme to assume that nothing can be known.

A sensible middle ground guards against catastrophic loss by diversifying a portfolio adequately to minimize idiosyncratic risk while holding few enough securities that they can be properly vetted. As Buffett wrote in a 1993 shareholder letter, "We believe that a policy of portfolio concentration may well decrease risk if it raises, as it should, both the intensity with which an investor thinks about a business and the comfort-level he must feel with its economic characteristics before buying into it. In stating this opinion, we define risk, using dictionary terms, as 'the possibility of loss or injury.'"

Seth Klarman further speaks to the relationship between conviction and risk management in the aptly named *Margin of Safety*: "My view is that an investor is better off knowing a lot about a few investments than knowing only a little about each of a great many holdings. One's very best ideas are likely to generate higher returns for a given level of risk than one's hundredth or thousandth best idea." Protection against ruinous wealth destruction is partially a numbers game but is equally a product of deep understanding.

A desire for conformity is part of the human condition, even (and perhaps, especially) for those who deny this most vehemently. *Exactitudes*, a contraction of the words "exact" and "attitudes", is a book that showcases the ways in which even self-professed non-conformists adhere to a rigid set of social norms. The brainchild of photographer Arie Versluis and stylist Elly Yttenbroek, the book chronicles sets of 12 individuals who belong to cultural subgroups like punks, soccer hooligans, "pin up girls" and backpackers. The irony of these photos of ostensible deviants is the total lack of deviation among their dress and postures. The studded leather chain, Mohawk and ripped jeans of a gutter punk are no less a uniform than the blue blazer and loafers of a preppy. We are all snowflakes, just like everyone else.

Similarly, something like 100% of active managers you speak to would mention contrarianism as a foundational value, even as three quarters of them imitate a benchmark for a disgustingly high fee. Passive management is sensible. True active management is sensible. High fee, low conviction asset management, which currently accounts for most of what passes as active, is a cancer to investors that should be conspicuously avoided. Diversification is a concept that has more nuance than is commonly realized and for its potential to be truly realized it must be numerically robust, fundamentally vetted and express a unique viewpoint.

Those who can, teach

A quick question for you, gentle reader, "Do you know how a toilet works?" On a scale from 1 to 10, how familiar would you say you are with the workings of a toilet? Go ahead and answer. All done? Great! Now, explain to me in detail the mechanics of a toilet, I'll wait. Done? OK, now let me ask again – on a scale of 1 to 10, how well do you understand the workings of a toilet?

Research by Steven Sloman of Brown and Philip Fernbach at the University of Colorado shows that having to teach a concept has a humbling effect that brings our beliefs more in line with our actual understanding. The pair have used this technique to moderate beliefs about everything from single payer healthcare to, well, toilets and have found that, "As a rule, strong feelings about issues do not emerge from deep understanding."

This exercise is commonly referred to as the Feynman Technique and is named for the theoretical physicist of the same name. Richard Feynman, known for his work in quantum mechanics, set forth a simple, three-part formula for gaining greater knowledge:

1. Figure out what you don't know.

2. Educate yourself.

3. Teach it to a child or novice.

Feynman's technique, elegant in its simplicity, speaks both to the human tendency to overestimate our own capabilities and to conflate complexity with understanding. The act of writing, teaching or explaining a concept to an absolute beginner has a humbling effect that provides a more accurate measure of our understanding. The next time you feel as though you *must* buy or sell a security, or that you are certain of where the financial markets are headed, take a moment to explain, in detail, the factual reasons why this is so. You're likely to find that your enthusiasm has gotten the best of your brain and nothing brings them back into sync like having to teach.

Take the outside view

When making a decision we tend to rely on what social scientists call the *inside view*. The inside view is our perception of a decision as informed by our own biases, anecdotal experience and a convenience sample of whatever data pops to mind first. Conversely, taking the *outside view* means a more dispassionate appraisal that depends more on probability and facts than convenience and personal experience. In *Think Twice*, Michael Mauboussin sets forth four steps to taking an outside view of a problem. They are:

1. **Select a reference class** – compare your problem to other problems like it.

2. **Assess the distribution of outcomes** – examine rates of success and failure.

3. **Estimate probabilities** – based on the external evidence, estimate timelines, failure rates and obstacles to success.

4. **Fine tune your prediction** – let bumps in the road and changing circumstances alter your estimate accordingly.

By relying on external data, you are likely to arrive at a much more realistic picture than by leaning on your personal experience. If it takes most people two years to complete a task, you are unlikely to finish yours in six months. The outside view is an effective way of combating ego risk by reminding you that you're pretty much just like everyone else.

Man of steel

You've likely heard of a straw man argument in which a weakened caricature of an opposing opinion is presented, only to be dismantled. A less discussed but more effective critical thinking technique is to create a steel man, which represents the very best thinking and most rigorous empirical proof of an opinion with which you disagree. Rather than using the straw man as a rhetorical punching bag to feed your ego, build a steel man that will sharpen your thinking, cause to you to look in dark corners and consider new vantages.

Love the questions

In *Letters to a Young Poet*, Rainer Maria Rilke writes to his protégé:

> "I want to beg you, as much as I can, dear sir, to be patient toward all that is unsolved in your heart and to try to *love the questions themselves* like locked rooms and like books that are written in a very foreign tongue. Do not now seek the answers, which cannot be given you because you would not be able to live them. And the point is, to live everything. *Live* the questions now. Perhaps you will then gradually, without noticing it, live along some distant day into the answer."

Western culture is in love with certainty and bravado, but the uncertainty of markets necessitates that we pursue a dynamic approach that is rooted in a fascination with the process rather than looking for silver bullets. The paradoxical truth is that only by learning to love the questions will we ever find the answers.

Take your time

For years, scientists have puzzled at the evolutionary reason for depression. Species tend not to adapt in ways that are self-harming and yet depression on its face does very little good and a whole lot of harm to the organisms it touches. But more recent research shows that deep sadness may have a strong evolutionary purpose that is rooted in the depressive tendency to ruminate on problems. By playing and replaying a negative event over and over in our minds, we often arrive at solutions that can be called upon at a future date. What hurts in the moment may be profoundly beneficial down the road.

We would do well to follow the admonition of John Dewey in *How We Think*: "To be genuinely thoughtful, we must be willing to sustain and protract that state of doubt which is the stimulus to thorough enquiry, so as not to accept an idea or make a positive assertion of a belief, until justifying reasons have been found."

Listen to the master

David Dunning of Dunning-Kruger fame gives four tips for managing overconfidence:[72]

1. **Always be learning** – It is a strange quirk of human behavior that the more you learn, the less certain you tend to become. Dunning suggests a lifelong commitment to learning as a paradoxical means by which to attain humility.

2. **Beware beginnings** – Pursuant to the first recommendation, Dunning cautions that a "little knowledge is a dangerous thing" and that early immersion in an idea or project can give a thin veneer of knowledge that feels more meaningful than it is.

3. **Slow down** – Fast thinking is biased thinking. Moving at speed requires us to rely on heuristics that have worked in the past rather than thoroughly examining a problem from top to bottom. While this is a fine way to make low stakes, quotidian choices, it's no way to invest time or money in matters that are truly important.

4. **Know when to be confident** – Dunning appropriately acknowledges that confidence has its place, especially when it comes to persuading others about our ideas. He suggests that we should be cautious in the appraisal and preparation of a proposal and confident in its eventual delivery.

Follow the crowd

The *herd* tends to get a bad reputation in behavioral finance circles, but under certain circumstances there is indeed wisdom in the opinions of many different stakeholders. Pooled judgments have shown great

[72]   J. Stillman, '4 tricks to avoid overconfidence,' Inc. (December 1, 2014).

predictive power in areas as diverse as Hollywood blockbusters, sporting outcomes and election results. Averaged economic indicators are also greatly improved over the judgment of the typical estimate.[73] What's more, this effect is seen relatively quickly, with as few as 8 to 12 estimates providing results nearly as robust as much larger samples.[74]

All of this, of course, assumes different sources of error, a nerdy way of saying that the people involved should have different ideas and assumptions. The danger here is that given the human tendency toward confirmation bias, we are prone to surround ourselves with people that are like us in many respects, thereby minimizing the potential benefit of this crowd wisdom.

The practical fallout of this research for investors has at least two logical applications. First, we must always be able to articulate an edge when we expect prices to deviate sharply from their current state. After all, the price of a security at any given time reflects the consensus estimate of millions and millions of market participants. If we are bold enough to suggest that millions of people will soon be proven wrong, we'd better have a very strong reason for thinking so. Second, investment teams should make every effort possible to be as psychologically diverse as possible. All too often, investment committees are comprised of participants with nearly identical educational, socioeconomic, racial, and gender makeup, which is likely to result in cognitive homogeneity as well.

Guess again

You now know that there is some wisdom in the crowd and that estimates with diverse sources of error tend to be better than those originating from a single source. But what's a savvy behavioral decision maker to do when she finds herself all alone? Fear not, because through the process of *dialectical bootstrapping*, you can divide your mind in a way that tends to reduce decisional error.

[73] S. M. Herzog and R. Hertwig 'The wisdom of many in one mind,' *Psychological Science* 20:2 (2009).

[74] R. M. Hogarth, 'A note on aggregating opinions,' *Organizational Behavior and Human Performance* 211 (February 1978), pp. 40–46.

The dialectical part of this tongue-twisting concept arises from the work of the philosopher Georg Hegel, who proposed a three-part method for discussing ideas that would lead to truth. First, there is the thesis or original idea, which then comes into contact with the antithesis, or some contrary opinion. After some discussion, Hegel thought rhetorical combatants ought then to arrive at a synthesis, a sort of logical middle ground between the two competing ideas.

In security analysis as in Hegel's philosophy, you likely have an opinion about a security that stems from a certain set of assumptions. Perhaps you are bullish on Acme Corporation's stock given your belief in their competitive moat, the strength of the broader economy, or any host of other considerations. This is your thesis and most financial analysts stop here. But what if you turned some of these assumptions on their head, performing a sort of pre-mortem as discussed previously? What if an upstart competitor threatens the Acme brand? What if an imbecilic President threatens a trade war that jeopardizes the economy? By considering these alternate scenarios you arrive at an antithesis with a new accompanying price target. By averaging the price targets that are a result of your original and revised assumptions, you would arrive at a synthesis – a midpoint between the best and worst case scenarios.

In an empirical examination of this idea, Herzog and Hertwig found that dialectical bootstrapping was a powerful tool for making better decisions. Although not quite as powerful as aggregating different peoples' opinions, the process of synthesizing multiple estimates based on different assumptions reduced error estimates in 75% of their sample.[75] You may not always have access to the wisdom of a crowd, but with the use of this simple process, a single mind can simulate the wisdom of many.

*   *   *

In summary, ego risk is made manifest in behaviors that privilege our need for felt personal competency at the expense of clear-eyed decision-making. Specific examples might include good old-fashioned

---

[75]   Herzog and Hertwig 'The wisdom of many in one mind.'

overconfidence, a tendency to become defensive when pet ideas are challenged (backfire effect), or a belief that one's mere involvement in a project makes it more likely to succeed (the awesomely named IKEA effect).

Ego risk leaves specific evidence of its presence in a trading log that might include overly concentrated positions, churning and the use of excessive leverage. Whatever the specific manifestation, the source is always the same – an ego that privileges its own care and feeding over making good decisions. It is a natural and unavoidable human tendency to want to feel different or better than average, but the enduring lesson of overconfidence for the behavioral investor is that it must be kept in its place. In love and life – hope for the best; when investing – play the odds.

Crafting ego resistant portfolios

- **Fact**: We should check the ego, as investing has elements of both luck and skill. **So what?** Adherence to rules trumps personal genius.

- **Fact**: Forecasts have a coin-flip likelihood of being correct. **So what?** Projections about the future, if they must be proffered at all, should be based on an assumption around base rates on long-term averages, not stories.

- **Fact**: Investors dramatically misremember their returns in their own favor. **So what?** Keep a log of trading decisions and monitor hit rate, performance and external variables that might negatively impact financial decision-making. Also, ignore braggarts at cocktail parties.

- **Fact**: Diversification is the lived embodiment of humility and its primary good is the preservation of capital. **So what?** Remember that protecting against catastrophic decline is part owning enough different things and part knowing what you own.

- **Fact**: Everyone thinks that they are a contrarian. **So what?** True contrarianism is painful and should cause considerable self-doubt. If your brand of swimming upstream doesn't hurt, it's unlikely to work.

Chapter 9.
The Behavioral Investor Conquers Conservatism

"Everyone thinks of changing the world, but no one thinks of changing himself."

— LEO TOLSTOY

"A ship is safe in harbor, but that's not what ships are for."

— WILLIAM G. T. SHEDD

I T'S A QUIET Saturday morning and you are sitting on your couch, enjoying the morning's first cup of coffee and an engrossing read by your favorite novelist. Quite unexpectedly, you hear a knock at the door and rise to see who has so thoughtlessly interrupted your weekend reverie. Standing at the door is an officious-looking man with a receding hairline, aviator sunglasses and a black suit. Flashing a badge ever so briefly, he introduces himself as Mr. Smith and informs you that he has some news that may be hard to hear.

"There has been a terrible mistake," he begins, your early morning buzz now quickly turning into anxiety. "Your brain has been plugged by error into an experience creation machine created by neurophysiologists. Everything you have ever experienced in your life is a vivid simulation, a waking dream." Pausing to let the enormity of this revelation sink in, Mr. Smith now offers you a choice: he can unplug the simulation, allowing you to engage in "real life", albeit a life you know nothing of, or you can remain hooked to your simulation. Mr. Smith is not a patient man and emphasizes that you must make a decision immediately. Which path do you choose?

This scenario is a variant of a question posed by Felipe De Brigard, a researcher at Duke University, and his results might surprise you. Intuition tells us that contact with reality is an important consideration and that most of us will want to live in "the real world" rather than drift along in some simulation cooked up in the mind of a neuroscientist. But among respondents to this study, 59% opted to stay hooked up to the machine compared to just 41% who opted for the "red pill" option. Our impulse to engage with reality may be strong, but it's not quite as strong as our pull for the familiar.

Our tendency toward conservatism is also on display in arguably the most famous business case study of all time; Coca-Cola's introduction of New Coke in the 1980s. New Coke is discussed in B-schools as a once-in-a-generation business miscalculation, but the logic of Coke executives would have been sound if they were dealing with rational *Homo Economicus* and not fickle *Homo Sapiens*.

Coke would never undertake a change of that magnitude without extensive focus group testing and indeed their numerous taste tests had found that blind taste testers preferred the sweeter flavor of New Coke by a significant margin. However, once introduced, Coca-Cola Classic continued to outsell New Coke by a factor of three-to-one! As articulated nicely in Samuelson and Zeckhauser's article in the *Journal of Risk and Uncertainty*, even though there was a clear preference for the new beverage, the old favorite continued its sales dominance. People may have preferred the taste of New Coke, but that preference was overwhelmed by their comfort with the familiar.[76]

[76] W. Samuelson and Richard Zeckhauser 'Status quo bias in decision

The sources of conservatism

If our penchant for the status quo were just limited to silly *Matrix* scenarios or cola preferences, it might not be worth our time, but the impact of our preference for conservatism has profound implication on the quality of both our lives and investment decisions.

Military personnel often reenlist simply because they are unaware of what other options might be at their disposal.[77] Sales professionals, who work so hard to position their product or service above that of the competition, are actually up against a far more formidable foe: inertia. According the Sales Benchmark Index, 60% of qualified leads culminate in a "no action," meaning that the potential customer just didn't make a choice. Retirement savers, tasked with the all-important mission of preparing a financial future, tend to just opt for whatever the company's default choice is, a tendency deftly turned to investor advantage by Richard Thaler and colleagues.[78] Yes, conservatism is everywhere. Psychological and neurological processes help account for its ubiquity.

A study conducted at University College London examined neural pathways involved in status quo bias and found that the more difficult the decision we face, the more likely we are not to act. Participants in the study, which was published in the *Proceedings of the National Academy of Sciences*, were involved in a tennis "line judgment game" while their brains were scanned using functional magnetic resonance imaging (fMRI). Participants were shown a tennis ball landing near the line and had to determine whether it was in or out.

In each case, they were given a default option and had to continue to hold down a button to assent to the default option and release the button to vote for a change. The results showed a consistent bias toward the default and noted that this bias became increasing pronounced as the judgment calls become more pronounced. This tendency led to

making,' *Journal of Risk and Uncertainty* 1:1 (March 1988), pp. 7–59.

[77] R. Henderson, 'How powerful is status quo bias?' *Psychology Today* (September 29, 2016).

[78] Simon Rooze's review of R. Thaler and C. Sunnstein's *Nudge* (Penguin, 2009) in *Amsterdam Law Forum* 1:4 (2009).

errors that became increasingly pronounced as the difficulty of the task increased. Meanwhile, the fMRI scans demonstrated that the sub-thalamic nucleus (STN) became activated in scenarios where the default was rejected. Researchers also noticed an uptick in activity in the pre-frontal cortex, a region known for dealing with difficult mental problems. This early research suggests that the STN may be among the foremost parts of the brain involved with making difficult decisions and moving away from the status quo, an act that is effortful and cognitively expensive.[79]

A second study found that erroneous rejections of an existing state have a more profound neural impact than erroneous status quo acceptances. Put simply, if you're going to make a mistake, your brain would rather you make a mistake by doing nothing. This asymmetry is consistent with the psychological notion of regret aversion, which finds that people are more upset with themselves when taking an action and suffering a loss than when staying put and suffering that same loss. Maintaining the status quo is not seen as a choice, however wrongheaded that is, and thus we tend to go easier on ourselves when complacency culminates in a bad outcome.[80]

Much of what we observe as a behavioral bent toward conservatism may actually be down to how the brain processes information. In a calm state, it takes around eight to ten seconds for the brain to process new information and that response time is lengthened considerably by the presence of stress. Having slowed the process to a crawl, stress may actually lead us to fixate on a single solution – likely the default or existing solution – and be unable to consider other options. Evolutionary psychologists think that this near paralysis may actually give some animals a survival advantage inasmuch as predators are unlikely to see prey that is stationary. But, just as the impulse for a

---

[79]   S. M. Fleming, C. L. Thomas and R. J. Dolan, 'Overcoming status quo bias in the human brain,' *Proceedings of the National Academy of Sciences of the United States of America* 107:13 (February 2010), pp. 6005–6009.
[80]   A. Nicolle, S. M. Fleming, D. R. Bach, J. Driver and R. J. Dolan, 'A regret-induced status quo bias,' *Journal of Neuroscience* 31:9 (March 2011), pp. 3320–3327.

deer to freeze is better in a forest than a freeway, your tendency to seize up belongs on the African plains and not on Wall Street.

The human propensity toward conservatism, driven by some of the neurological processes discussed before, appears behaviorally as the interaction of a constellation of non-rational cognitive processes including the endowment effect, mere exposure effect, home bias, regret avoidance and loss aversion. Remember from our earlier discussion that the human brain and body are always looking to operate in the most parsimonious manner possible. Relying on what has worked in the past or what has always been done is a very cognitively efficient way to do just that. It's no wonder that as decisions become more complicated or the tradeoffs become more tiring to consider, the tendency to stay put becomes more pronounced.

Richard Thaler has suggested that this tendency is rooted in the endowment effect or our proneness to value something simply because it is ours. Whether that something is a method of viewing the world, a political ideology or even a physical item, we tend to love it just because we own it. While this tendency has obvious salutary effects on our feelings of self-worth, it makes it much harder to dispassionately evaluate the true worth of something familiar versus a new way of being. Daniel Kahneman attributes our inert behavior to our aversion to loss, arguing that the status quo becomes our reference point and that deviations from it – even some positive deviations – are seen as a loss. Given that potential losses are feared more than twice as much as potential gains are prized, old ways of acting tend to calcify.

Tools for combatting conservatism

You are now armed with the realization that you have a tendency to lean on the safe and familiar when making decisions and that this tendency can have dangerous consequences. How, practically, can we overcome this natural tendency toward conservatism?

Give yourself the world

Home bias, the tendency toward viewing domestic equities as more safe and knowable than their international counterparts, means that people all over the world are underinvested in countries outside of their own. As a rule of thumb, your percentage ownership of the equities of a given country should align roughly with the size of that market on the international stage. According to Morgan Stanley, the combined market capitalization of all US stocks accounts for just under one-half of the world's total market value. However, US investors have an average allocation to US stocks of an incredible 90%![81] This geographical favoritism even extends to regions of the United States, with Northeasterners tending to be overweight financials, Midwesterners tending to be heavy on agriculture and energy.

And if this tendency to buy what you know is dangerous in the economic superpower that is the United States, consider how damaging it can be in countries that account for a smaller part of the world's market value. For instance, the average British investor keeps nearly 80% of their equity investments in British companies, in spite of the fact that Great Britain represents less than 10% of global market value.

Incredibly, home bias seems to impact professional investors just as dramatically as novices. Researchers at the University of Manchester and Lancaster University surveyed fund managers in the United States, Great Britain, Continental Europe and Japan and asked them about their expectations about US stocks. Completed between 1995 and 1999, the 12-month forecasts of US managers were far more bullish than among fund managers in other parts of the world. Similarly, when US managers were asked about stocks in the other parts of the world, their expectations for growth were much lower than those of the managers in those countries.[82]

Mark Twain famously quipped that, "Travel is fatal to prejudice, bigotry, and narrow-mindedness, and many of our people need it sorely on these accounts. Broad, wholesome, charitable views of men and things cannot be acquired by vegetating in one little corner of the Earth all one's lifetime." Twain was of course speaking of literally visiting new places, but investors would be wise to heed his view as it pertains to investing.

---

[81] 'Overcoming home bias in equity investing,' Janus Henderson Investors (September 2017).

[82] M. Hulbert, 'A plan to overcome investors' home bias,' *New York Times* (January 23, 2000).

There is a pervasive narrow mindedness around investing in places unfamiliar. We would all be wise to recognize that industriousness and ingenuity are not the purview of any one place and invest accordingly.

Choose tomorrow over today

The evolutionary roots of our system of self-preservation make sense. It was not all that long ago (in terms of evolutionary time) that our forebears were called upon daily to make life and death decisions. For people living on the savannahs of Africa, choosing to zig when you should have zagged could spell the end. Historically, decision-making has been very wrapped up in preserving physical safety and ensuring that physical needs were met. In this life-and-death scenario, minimizing risk at the expense of self-actualization is only logical. However, in the intervening millennia, things have changed and our thought patterns have not kept pace.

In the developed world, most people have the base of Maslow's pyramid met – they have adequate food, water, sleep and safety. Having now met these basic needs, they are left to wrangle with more metaphysical concerns such as belonging and self-actualization. What we are left with is a brain and a decision-making modality that is ill-suited for our modern milieu. We are programmed to choose safety, even at the expense of joy, in an environment where safety abounds and joy is hard to find. Unless we learn to train our brains to evaluate risk and reward on a more even keel, we will remain trapped in a life of risk-aversion that keeps us from taking the very risks that might make us happy.

Imagine that you are presented with just two different investment options – Asset A and Asset B – and that you must choose the least risky of these two options. Over the last hundred plus years, Asset A has outperformed Asset B in 80% of rolling ten-year periods and has been on top in 100% of rolling 30-year periods, a timeframe consistent with saving for retirement. Asset A has beaten inflation 100% of the time in rolling 20-year periods, whereas Asset B has only beaten inflation 31% of the time. The inflation-adjusted annualized return of Asset A is 7%, whereas Asset B clocks in at 1%.

Which of the two assets would you say is riskier – Asset A or Asset B?

With the two assets de-identified like this, almost everyone would choose Asset A as the less risky of the two. After all, failing to outperform inflation, as Asset B did a majority of the time, is just a fancy way of saying "losing money." Asset A is stocks, generally considered to be far more risky than Asset B, bonds.

How is it then that our perception of risk is so grossly decoupled from the actual performance of these two asset classes? In markets as in life, people tend to evaluate risk in terms of short-term harm rather than long-term reward. Stocks undoubtedly offer the potential for short-term harm, despite the fact that they have been enormously predictable and rewarding over time. By privileging today over tomorrow and certain mediocrity over possible greatness, fearful investors provide behavioral investors with an equity risk premium that is improbably large. This premium can be earned by doing the opposite: by privileging tomorrow over today.

Buy what you (don't) know

If I asked you to name the single most famous painting of all time, which would you choose? Odds are that many readers would have landed on DaVinci's *Mona Lisa*, arguably the most iconic piece of art in the world. But did you know that what we now consider his masterwork was not too long ago considered a rather mediocre representation of his work? The story of how the Mona Lisa became the avatar of artistic excellence is one of criminal activity and intrigue that relies heavily on human psychology.

In 1911, a handyman at the Louvre removed the painting from its place in the museum and took it home. The utter lack of security measures surrounding the Mona Lisa is a testament to its unextraordinary reputation at the time. It was over 24 hours until anyone even noticed that the painting was missing! But as newspapers started to report on the robbery, awareness of the painting increased as the mystery surrounding the heist became a full-blown media sensation. After it was recovered two years later, the Mona Lisa became the most popular painting in the museum, as interested patrons clamored to see what all of the fuss had been about. Only after the heist and in light of its newfound popularity did the Mona Lisa earn the reverence and esteem of the art world. We imagine that the Mona Lisa is popular because it is so special, but in reality, it is seen as special precisely because it first became popular.[83] The psychological term for this phenomenon is *mere exposure effect*, a process by which we develop a preference for something simply because we are familiar with it.

Peter Lynch famously encouraged investors to "buy what you know"; to look at the products and services you use every day to source the next great stock pick. With all respect due to a truly incredible investor, this is profoundly dumb advice. Our conservative nature already means that we see less risk in the familiar and so are likely already overweight what we know. Our proclivity to conflate the known with the advisable is so pronounced that we actually perceive stocks with pronounceable tickers (e.g., MOO) to be less risky than those with hard to pronounce tickers (e.g., NTT). So, rather than trying to scour your local mall for the next big investment idea, put in place a plan that diversifies across geographies and asset classes, both familiar and foreign.

Don't know what you own

The trolley problem is a formulation used in many philosophy and ethics courses. A slight modification of the general form of the problem is as follows:

There is a runaway trolley barreling down the railway tracks. Ahead, on the tracks, there are five people tied up and unable to move. The trolley is headed straight for them. You are standing some distance off in the train yard, next to a lever. If you pull this lever, the trolley will switch to a different set of tracks. However, you notice that there is one person, a friend of yours, tied up on the side track. You have two options:

1. Do nothing, and the trolley kills the five people on the main track.

2. Pull the lever, diverting the trolley onto the side track where it will kill your friend.

Which of those admittedly unpleasant options would you choose? From a utilitarian standpoint, saving the most lives by pulling the lever is the most desirable outcome. All else equal, I think that many of us would

---

[83] D. Sassoon, *Becoming Mona Lisa* (Harvest Books, 2003).

agree that saving five lives is preferable to one. However, I imagine that many of you choose not to pull the lever, despite the fact that it would have a dramatically more positive outcome in the most practical sense. There are two reasons why you likely chose as you did, both of which have their roots in conservatism.

First, choosing to pull a lever to change the status quo feels like making a decision. Make no mistake, it's a decision either way, but action feels more volitional than inaction. Second, your friend benefits from a familiarity bias that you don't enjoy with the other five people. You know your friend and that knowing fundamentally alters your perception of right and wrong. A similar (though admittedly less dramatic!) version of this is at play whenever you research, purchase and follow a stock. Through the endowment effect, your familiarity with and ownership of the security means that you elevate its perceived above it's actual worth.

The surest way around this? You shouldn't know what you own. This suggestion strikes most people as dramatic, but it is rooted in common sense. In fact, some fund managers have already embraced this idea. A *USA Today* article on behaviorally minded investment manager C. Thomas Howard reads:

> "Thomas Howard may have one of the oddest investment approaches ever. The 66-year-old former business school prof buys and sells stocks without even knowing the names of the companies. He's got no idea how much he has paid for the stocks. And he doesn't bother to keep track of whether the stock is winning or losing. But, hey, in 12 years, through the wild ups and downs of Wall Street, this close-your-eyes approach has managed to average roughly 25 percent annual returns on his flagship Athena Pure fund, making it one of the better investment products out there."[84]

Inasmuch as ownership distorts perceptions of value and leads to poor buy and sell decisions, knowledge of ownership should be kept from the fund manager. Only then can he make rules-based, dispassionate decisions about what to buy and sell that are free from the shackles of the endowment effect.

[84] S. Butler, 'To get rich, stifle emotion-driven investment picks,' *USA Today* (January 25, 2015).

Embrace the messiness of risk

"An exit door procedure at 30,000 feet? Mmmhmm, the illusion of safety."

Tyler Durden's *Fight Club* rant about the duplicity of airline safety protocols could just as easily be applied to the futile dance of financial advisors giving clients risk tolerance questionnaires. Risk tolerance questionnaires (RTQs) give the illusion of safety and insight, and fly in the face of research that suggests that risk-taking behavior is domain specific, context driven and dynamic. Some academics try to skirt this point through a bit of esoteric sleight of hand that distinguishes risk tolerance from risk perception.

Risk tolerance is defined as your static, long-term attitudes about risk, whereas *risk perception* is the dynamic, contextual piece more likely to fluctuate during periods of market upheaval. Risk tolerance, academics are quick to point out, is unchanging and they have the studies to prove it. Essentially, they say, you can have the right idea at heart about risk-reward tradeoffs (risk tolerance) even as you are engaging in the wrong behavior due to your risk perception in the heat of the moment. This Ivory Tower factoid is of very little practical use to investors who enter and exit the market at all the wrong times or the beleaguered investment advisors who take panicked phone calls from their clients. In the end, risk-taking behavior is all that matters and the fact remains that it is changeable and context-dependent.

Some RTQs attempt to arrive at investor risk preferences by asking about non-financial risk taking behavior. And while this invariably has the effect of spicing up what can otherwise be a fairly staid affair, your propensity to go bungee jumping has nothing to do with your ability to hold on to stocks during a bear market. As Nicholson, Fenton-O'Creevy, Soane and Willman point out, "no single psychological questionnaire predicts risk-taking behavior across multiple domains, or explains why someone highly risk-averse in financial decision-making contexts would pursue extremely dangerous sports."[85]

---

[85] N. Nicholson, E. Soane, M. F.-O'Creevy and P. Willman, 'Personality and domain-specific risk taking,' *Journal of Risk Research* 8:2 (2005).

Another RTQ tactic is to ask about hypotheticals like, "What would you do in the event of a 20% market correction?" in the hope that this hypothetical would have some predictive power in a period of actual market turbulence. Once again, science gives a cold shower: "Moreover, there has been little direct evidence of correlation between hypothetical financial decisions made on paper versus real financial decisions involving live market transactions."[86]

A number of studies have shown that risk-taking behavior is tightly linked to the emotional state of the subject and the emotion-producing properties of the task. For instance, people take more risk when a task is framed negatively ("This is what you might lose") versus positively ("This is what you might gain"). Mood is also closely correlated with risk-taking and those who have positive mood induced show distortions in their perceptions of risk. Andrew Lo and colleagues make the case that risk-taking behavior is heavily influenced by situational variables as they interact with the emotional lability of the investor:

> "These limitations suggest that risk-taking may be context-dependent, and that characterizing the context along some standardized dimensions may be a more productive line of inquiry. We propose that the emotional or affective state of the decision-maker and certain affective properties of the environment are plausible candidates for such a characterization."[87]

Whereas most RTQs measure sterile, cerebral notions of risk, the messy lived experience of risk-taking occurs at the intersection of personal neuroticism and the fear-inducing nature of a given situation. Inasmuch as most RTQs fail to measure context or emotional reactivity, they are of limited utility. Perhaps this is why Jason Zweig reports that the test-retest reliability (i.e., the likelihood that the same person will get similar results on subsequent iterations of an assessment) of RTQs is "a coin flip." Heraclitus' idea that, "No man ever steps in the same river twice, for it's not the same river and he's not the same man" is highly applicable to risk management.

---

[86] A. W. Lo, D. V. Repin and B. N. Steenbarger, 'Fear and Greed in Financial Markets: A Clinical Study of Day-Traders,' MIT Sloan Working Paper No. 4534–05 (March 2005).
[87] Lo, Repin and Steenbarger, 'Fear and Greed in Financial Markets.'

Remove the fear of loss

In the throes of the second worst financial crisis in United States history, auto manufacturer Hyundai introduced a program that shows a deep understanding of human psychology and might just have saved their company. With economic fears putting off large purchases and the fear of unemployment a reality for people of all economic strata, Hyundai introduced the Assurance program, promising consumers that the company would buy back their car in the event that they lost their job. A mere 350 people ended up selling back their cars, but Hyundai's removal of the fear and anxiety surrounding the purchase led them to sell 435,000 vehicles in 2009, an 8% increase at a time when many automakers were approaching bankruptcy.[88]

Perhaps the dirtiest little secret of active investment management today is that many managers are so fearful for their jobs that much of what passes for active fund management is simply passive investment management with active fees. Tom Howard of AthenaInvest found in his exploration of closet indexing that, "For the typical fund, low-conviction positions outnumber high-conviction positions by three-to-one."[89]

In their 2009 paper, Martijn Cremers and Antti Petajisto introduced the concept of "active share," or how greatly a portfolio differed from the benchmark against which it was compared. They found that truly active managers (those with 60% or greater differentiation from their index) had outperformed historically and that greater differentiation tended to lead to greater outperformance.

In his 2013 update, Petajisto found that high active share portfolios outperformed dramatically from 1990 to 2009 and that these active funds had tended to hold up well during periods of crisis. As he notes, "I found that the most active stock pickers have been able to add value to their investors, beating their benchmark indices by about 1.26% per year after all fees and expenses."

---

[88] R. Schmidt, 'Frozen: Using behavioral design to overcome decision-making paralysis,' *Deloitte Insights* (October 7, 2016).
[89] T. Howard, *Behavioral Portfolio Management* (Harriman House, 2014), p. 95.

Cohen, Polk and Silhi (2010) found that a fund's best idea (as determined by position size) generated average annualized outperformance of 6% per year. Even more importantly, they found that performance decreased in a stepwise fashion as position size decreased! Much of the conversation around active managers' historical underperformance has drawn the erroneous conclusion that these managers do not have stock picking skill. To the contrary, it would seem that much of what besets active managers is not the ability to successfully pick stocks, but the courage to pick them in concentrated enough doses that they lead to successful outperformance.

Those who employ professional must take a lesson from Hyundai and remove the fear and anxiety associated with tracking error and career risk. Behavioral investors should be rewarded for their innovation, diligence, honesty and most of all adherence to a thoughtful process, rather than fearing for their jobs. Only as career incentives align with best practices and a deep understanding of human behavior will we get the kind of active asset managers that we truly deserve.

Procrastinate (a little bit)

One of the most surprising cures for excessive conservatism is something you may already be doing at work: procrastinating. Research conducted at the Tilburg Institute for Behavioral Economics Research found that subjects chose the default option 82% of the time when asked to decide in an instant, but only 56% of time after being given a short delay. Speed tends to be the enemy of good decision-making and immediacy nudges us to rely on biased thinking and over rely on the status quo.[90] So, when tasked with making an important investing decision, take time to reconsider your immediate choice and see if you still think the same after more thought.

Mitigate disaster

Peters and Slovic parse the psychological elements of risk into two camps – dread and risk of the unknown. Dread is their shorthand for

[90]   B. Frick, 'How to beat our status-quo bias,' Kiplinger (December 2, 2010).

catastrophic loss of capital and the unknown is the risk of unforeseen calamities.

Academics differentiate between risk and uncertainty with the distinction that the former has known probabilities and the latter entails ambiguous gambles. Playing blackjack with a single deck of cards is risky, whereas investing in capital markets is somewhere more middling along the risk-uncertainty continuum. And while this may seem like semantic trifling at first, neuroimaging studies demonstrate that risk and uncertainty actually activate different areas of the brain. Using fMRI, researchers have found that ambiguity, but not risk, causes an activation of the frontal insula and amygdala. Similarly, they found that brain-damaged participants showed no difference in brain activation between risky and uncertain conditions, ironically leading them to act more rationally than their neurotypical peers.

Risky situations, where probabilities are understood, lend themselves to logical and statistical thinking. Uncertain situations like capital markets, where "unknown unknowns" run rampant, require looser controls in the form of rules of thumb. Investing capital comes with a host of unknowns, but uncertain outcomes make the need for certain processes that much more important. As behavioral investors tilt probability in their favor over extended periods of time, they reduce uncertainty and improve the probability of getting the right result for the right reasons.

As much as we dislike uncertainty, our world would be mind numbingly dull without it. Stocks would cease to be profitable, sporting events would be dull, comedy would lose its bite. Consider the person who remains unattached to avoid risking heartache and finds loneliness in the process. Or the would-be entrepreneur who never makes the leap of faith and wastes a career working at a job he hates. The irony of obsessive loss aversion is that our worst fears become realized in our attempts to manage them. Behavioral investors take a clear-eyed view of risk and uncertainty in a world that distorts them out of fear, and their lives are richer for it.

No regrets

So much of conservatism boils down to regret aversion – we would rather lose with inaction than have the possibility of winning by taking action. Once again, a rules-based system is the best way to avoid the paralysis brought about by regret aversion. Buy, sell and hold decisions are made in an emotionally cool state in a manner that is informed by research. This rules-based approach takes discretion out of the picture entirely and allows the fund manager a psychic scapegoat. If things go wrong, blaming the model feels better than kicking yourself.

Prepare for the worst

Why is it that the residents of Pompeii watched Vesuvius erupt for hours without evacuating? Why did tens of thousands fail to evacuated New Orleans as Hurricane Katrina approached? Why did passengers on the Titanic ignore orders to disembark even as the luxury liner approached the iceberg that would end their lives?

Each of the aforementioned moments of paralysis in the face of disaster are part of a failure of imagination known as the *normalcy bias*. Simply put, the normalcy bias is the belief that "all that has been is all that will ever be." Pompeii had seen earthquakes before and New Orleans had seen torrential rains, the citizens of each city imagining that this time would be like the last, until it wasn't. Estimated to impact as much as 70% of us, normalcy bias leads us to believe that we have is experienced is all we can ever experience.[91]

A 2001 study by sociologist Thomas Drabek found that when people were ordered to leave to escape a natural disaster, the average evacuee checked with four different sources before deciding how to act.[92] Journalist Amanda Ripley, author of *The Unthinkable: Who Survives When Disaster Strikes*, suggests that a decision to act in the face of a crisis consists of three parts; denial, deliberation and decisive movement. Although created for coping with natural disasters, Ripley's framework can be valuable to investors who find themselves in the throes of a potential financial crisis as well.

The behavioral investor takes denial off of the table from the outset, understanding that financial tumult is a natural part of every investor's

[91]   E. Inglis-Arkell, 'The frozen calm of normalcy bias,' Gizmodo (May 2, 2013).
[92]   A. Ripley, 'How to get out alive,' *Time Magazine* (April 25, 2005).

lifetime and that corrections happen every year on average and that full blown bear markets occur every 3.5 years on average. Understanding and accepting a high level of volatility from the outset is a prerequisite to sound investing: if you've seen it before you will see it again and you've not experienced it just wait a little longer.

Deliberation and decisive movement can be problematic because we tend to be psychologically at our worst at the very moment when we most need to be in charge of all of our faculties. As I cited in *The Laws of Wealth*, the average investor loses 13% of their IQ in a time of financial duress. The best antidote against bad behavior in a moment of potential threat is an investing system for managing risk that is adhered to in all weather. The specific type of system, whether a simple process of broad diversification or a more complex tactical system, is far less more important than the discipline to define rules in peacetime and adhere to them in wartime.

A behaviorally-informed investment paradigm should be robust to periods of mania and panic even greater than those observed historically. It is worth repeating that every developed country in the world has suffered equity market losses of at least 75%, so at least that level of disaster is possible in your lifetime. But the behavioral investor prepares for what could be and not just what has been. After all, there is no assurance that the Great Depression will be the Greatest Depression when considered on a long enough timeline. The behavioral investor's most difficult job is to set in place a system that recognizes the reality that most market volatility is a short-term blip while still humbly respecting the rare capability of financial markets to destroy capital at a clip that is nearly unrecoverable.

Flip the script

Charlie Munger, Warren Buffett's right-hand-man, is most commonly known for admonition to "invert, always invert." Although Munger popularized the phrase, the original idea belongs to esteemed mathematician Carl Jacobi who was espousing the benefits of considering, "Why might I be wrong?" or "What is another way of viewing this situation?" Nick Bostrom, known primarily for his doomsday musings on artificial intelligence, has proposed a more elaborate theorem in this same vein that he refers to as the "reversal test." Bostrom says:

> "When a proposal to change a certain parameter is thought to have bad overall consequences, consider a change to the same parameter in the opposite direction. If this is also thought to have bad overall consequences, then the onus is on those who reach these conclusions to explain why our position cannot be improved through changes to this parameter. If they are unable to do so, then we have reason to suspect that they suffer from status quo bias."[93]

To make these ideas a little more intuitive, consider your morning cup of coffee. Let's say you have taken the advice of many a personal finance guru to question every expense and have been confronted with your daily Starbucks addiction. But applying the reversal test, rather than asking yourself whether to spend five dollars on coffee, you instead ask, "Would I take a payment of five dollars NOT to drink coffee that day?" If the answer is yes, you should abstain. Munger and Jacobi's ideas around inversion and Bostrom's suggestion to reverse both offer simple but powerful ways to reframe our thinking in a manner that moves us away from tradition and toward more lucid ways of thinking.

* * *

Conservatism risk is a by-product of our asymmetrical preference for gain relative to loss, and for the status quo relative to change. We like winning much more than losing and the old way much better than the new way, all of which contorts our ability to see the world clearly. This conservatism effect can be observed in our resistance to new ways of being (status quo bias), our preference for no risk at all relative to large incremental decreases in risk (zero risk bias), and an aptness to privilege our current self over the needs of our future self (hyperbolic discounting).

A preference for the familiar may be understandable, but it can also rob us of the opportunity to meet new people, explore new ways of

---

[93]   N. Bostrom and T. Ord, 'The reversal test: Eliminating status quo bias in applied ethics,' *Ethics* 116 (July 2006), pp. 656–679.

being and properly allocate our wealth. Embracing the unfamiliar is a commitment that enriches a life as surely as it improves investing.

Crafting conservatism resistant portfolios

- **Fact**: The perceived riskiness of an asset class often has more to do with its short-term than long-term performance. **So what?** Behavioral investors load up on assets, like stocks, that are perceived as more risky than is accurate.

- **Fact**: Risk taking is more situationally than personally determined. **So what?** Avoid fear-inducing situations and ensure that portfolio management processes are rules-based rather than discretionary.

- **Fact**: Bubbles are a natural, recurring feature of capital markets. **So what?** Have a rules-based system for avoiding catastrophic loss that is infrequently (i.e., every few years) activated.

Chapter 10.
The Behavioral Investor Hones Attention

"It is a very sad thing that nowadays there is so little useless information."

— OSCAR WILDE

THE SALEM WITCH trials, conducted in colonial Massachusetts between 1692 and 1693, resulted in the deaths of over 20 women. The fear of witches in the New World was a holdover from Europe, where tens of thousands of women feared to be in league with the Devil were executed between the 1300s to the end of the 1600s. In the late 1600s, a war between France and England, King William's War, was playing out on colonial American soil and led to the displacement of hundreds of refugees, many of whom fled to Salem. This influx of refugees placed a strain on an already struggling community and led to conditions perfect for hysteria. In January of 1692, the daughter of a local clergyman and two of her friends started to exhibit strange symptoms: unintelligible utterances, physical contortions, and fits of rage.

As a father of three small children, this sounds like any given Tuesday at the Crosby household, but I digress. Spurred on by a local doctor who attributed their symptoms to the supernatural, the girls accused three women of having hexed them: an elderly woman, a homeless woman, and a Caribbean slave. The former two denied the accusations vehemently but the slave, named Tituba, fessed up to being in league with the powers of darkness. With this admission, the fuse was lit and the dormant witch hysteria began to run amok in the colonies.

Ostensibly being good Christian people of law and order, the colonists could not simply burn a witch without proof. Witch hunting "experts" set forth a number of theories for how to divine whether or not someone was indeed a witch, including eyewitness accounts and "spectral evidence" such as having dreamt of being cursed by the accused. But the most famous test involved water. The accused was thrown in the water, where buoyancy was seen as evidence of guilt and drowning was evidence of a false accusation (small consolation to the now-deceased innocent party). The accusers had set up a kangaroo court that operated by a set of rules incapable of gathering relevant data. The obvious catch-22 of the water trial was that you were guilty or dead, hardly the dispassionate weighing of evidence that we would hope for when making a high-stakes decision.

Attention risk is born of our disposition to evaluate information in relative terms and let salience trump probability when making investment decisions. *Salience* is the psychological term for prominence, meaning that our attention can be hijacked by low-probability-high-scariness things like shark attacks while ignoring high-probability-low-scariness dangers like taking a selfie near a busy street (Yes, far more people have died in the last year from selfies than shark attacks.) It's what led the New Englanders to ignore the unwinnable nature of the witch trials and ignited a moral panic spurred on by stories that were vivid, if nonsensical.

It also leads us to rate the unfamiliar as more risky and show a preference for domestic stocks (home bias) and familiar names (mere exposure effect), regardless of their fundamental qualities. In a world in which attention is a valuable resource we must be vigilant against noise-peddlers of all sorts. To do so requires a system for distinguishing meaningful information from cacophony, which is where we journey next. The following three-part test will help you to recognize *probably* when you see it.

Three tests of an investable idea

The first hurdle an idea must clear to be considered worthy of a behavioral investor is that it has a rich history of empirical support. The data must support your assertion, period.

But if theory without data gives us witch trials, it must also be noted that data without theory can be just as dangerous. I noted earlier the 95% covariance between Bangladeshi butter production and S&P 500 moves. The data exists but the theory does not – why on earth should those two things be correlated? A similarly spurious correlation is the Super Bowl Indicator, which states that if a team from the American Football Conference (AFC) wins the Super Bowl, we will experience a bear market, and that a win from the National Football Conference (NFC) augurs a bull market. The indicator was first "discovered" by Leonard Koppett in the 1970s when he realized that it had never been wrong until that point. As of 2017, the Super Bowl Indicator still enjoys an 80% success rate.

Just as theory with no data leads to witch trials, data with no theory can lead us to chase shadows of truth. If there is no good reason for a data point to correlate with outsized returns, it probably doesn't. Thus, sound theory is the second hurdle.

In most truth-seeking pursuits, it is enough to look for empirical evidence that is supported by a cogent theoretical framework. But financial markets offer a bit of a special case inasmuch as theoretically sound, empirically supported anomalies are prone to get arbitraged away as quickly as they are discovered. Smart people discover truths about the market, share them with the world, and return-hungry arbitrageurs ensure that those truths don't stay true for long.

Take, for instance, *calendar effects*, the market anomaly that suggests that certain days of the week or month offer the potential for outsized returns because of fund flows and other variables. Calendar effects were discovered by examining the data and thus pass our empirical hurdle. There is also a rational reason why they existed; events like paying taxes, receiving paychecks and rebalancing portfolios happen with some regularity with respect to timing and that regularity presented real opportunity, so the theory test is met.

But what calendar effects, and many other market anomalies, lack is the third and final trait that behavioral investors require: it must owe to an enduring psychological tendency. There is no psychic pain in arbitraging calendar effects. It is not behaviorally more difficult to buy on one day of the month versus another and so the effect vanished nearly as quickly as it was discovered. For a factor to be worthwhile to a behavioral investor it must be empirically supported, theoretically sound *and* behaviorally intransigent.

When it comes to determining whether or not a variable meets this third and most difficult-to-determine hurdle, one great guide is time. Named for a deli in New York, the Lindy Effect is the idea that the life expectancy of an idea is proportional to its current age. In a nutshell, ideas that have stood the test of time are likely to continue to stand the test of time. People have read the work of Homer for thousands of years and we can anticipate that middle school children will still be reading *The Odyssey* 500 years from now. Kim Kardashian's book of selfies, *Selfish*, recently landed on the *New York Times* bestseller list and is currently outselling *The Odyssey*. However, the Lindy Effect tells us that despite the intensity of its immediate reception, *Selfish* is not as likely to endure as *The Odyssey* precisely because it has not yet stood the test of time.

Calendar effects were discovered, got a handful of professors tenure, and were quickly arbitraged away. Conversely, factors like value and momentum have endured over time and can be said to be robust to the Lindy Effect. They have endured and are therefore likely to continue enduring. While quality, originality and import may be some of the markers of Lindy endurance in literature, psychology seems to play that role when it comes to capital markets.

Value investing is psychologically difficult, something that will be discussed in great detail later in this book, and therefore endures in spite of the fact that we know it to be profitable. You can read every academic journal article and biography of Warren Buffett ever written and still find it stomach churningly difficult to buy the sort of unloved stocks that are the hallmark of the style. Value investing is empirically supported, theoretically sound and behaviorally rooted, and therefore meets all three criteria for investment.

Counterintuitively, results are a surprisingly poor predictor of how sound a strategy is. A market beating three-year track record (the minimum hurdle for most institutional investors) still has a 12.5% chance of being total luck. It takes nearly 25 years of track record to separate luck from skill, meaning that you can only know via results that a manager was good as she is nearing retirement. The deceptive nature of results makes our focus on theory, data and psychology all the more relevant.

My father, a deeply principled man and Rotarian, keeps a plaque with Rotary's four-way test on his desk. The four parts of the test are:

1. Is it the truth?

2. Is it fair to all concerned?

3. Will it build good will and better friendships?

4. Will it be beneficial to all concerned?

These four simple steps offer a guiding framework that my father uses to evaluate the quality of various actions he is considering. In much the same manner, the behavioral investor can use the three conditions of an investable idea to evaluate the soundness of both existing research and the new anomalies that will inevitable arise. Truth in capital markets emerges in ways that are evident to the senses and pleasing to the mind, but it endures by virtue of its roots in human psychology.

The three-part test of an investable idea isn't your only defense against financial noise. Read on for more practical ways to discern the things that matter from those that don't.

Tools for combatting attention bias

Play the odds, ditch the story

Jeff Foxworthy, that loveable avatar of all things backwoods, used to host a TV show called, *Are You Smarter Than a Fifth Grader?* It asked grade school questions of adults who had long since forgotten their lessons. Today, I will be your host on a game show that I call, *Are You Smarter Than a Rat?* Rather than quizzing you on the War of 1812 or long division, you'll be presented with two lights – green and red – that will flash randomly. Your task will be to determine whether the next flash will be green or red. To make your job that much simpler, I'll even tell you the odds! The green light will flash 80% of the time and the red light will flash 20% of the time. The rat you are competing against can't speak of course, so the green light will provide food while the red light will provide a small electric shock.

Consider your strategy for a moment: How would you best determine the color of the next flash with a known 80/20 distribution pattern? Most humans begin the task and immediately begin to look for noise in the chaos: they try to discern a pattern. Which makes sense if you think back to the opening chapter of this book and recall that organizing functional fictions into powerful social structures is what separates us from animals. By seeking to create signal in what is truly noise, human participants in this test are able to identify the red or green signal 68% of the time. The rats, on the other hand, have no need (or ability) for higher order thinking and quickly learn to just play the odds. Quickly ascertaining that food comes about four times more often than shocks, they learn to guess green every time and end up with an 80% hit rate. The rats have no need to beat the system or craft an elegant story and the simplicity of their approach allows them to outwit an ostensibly smarter opponent.

The market analogue of this is evident every time you turn on a financial news channel. Some Ivy League educated market wizard in a $3,000 suit is expounding a complicated macro thesis that interweaves everything from geopolitical threats to potential Fed moves to soybean production. Listening to such a story is hypnotic and rightly impressive; the human ability for higher order thinking and pattern recognition is on full display. But all too often our market wizard is like the human subject in our game show who has overcomplicated the task. The elegance of the story has overtaken the likelihood of its occurrence.

The behavioral investor thinks like a rat, caring only for probability in a world that craves sophisticated nonsense. When asked to weave a story on a prominent financial news network, a behavioral investor will have no grand thesis, no series of dominoes waiting to fall. Accordingly, she will never be invited back. Instead, she will pursue a process-driven path of tilting probability in her favor at every turn, secure in the knowledge that "probably" is a powerful word in investing.

Rely on averages

To examine the presence of the attention bias in your own thinking, please consider the following question:

> A police force uses breathalyzers that display false drunkenness in 5% of cases but are 100% accurate in detecting cases of true inebriation. On average, 1 in 1000 drivers is drunk. Suppose that a police officers stops a random car at a checkpoint and forces the driver to take a breathalyzer test that comes back positive. What are the true odds of this individual being drunk?

The most common response, drawing on the 5% false positive mentioned above, is that there is a 95% chance that the person stopped is drunk. Is that what you guessed? In reality, the odds are much lower and show how we tend to ignore base rates (low attentional salience) in favor of a specific observation (high attentional salience). Thinking fast leads us to believe with 95% certainty that the person stopped is a drunk driver but a slower, more contemplative consideration of the facts tells a much different story.

Consider that, on average, if our checkpoint stops 1000 drivers that one of them will be drunk and will be correctly identified as such. This means that 999 drivers will not be drunk but that a full 49.95 of them (5% of 999) will be identified as having broken the law. The true odds of being both drunk and identified as such in a random stop would be the base rate of one divided by the number of positive breathalyzer tests (49.95 false positives plus the one true positive, or 50.95, with 1/50.95 = 0.019627). Far from our attentionally salient guess of 95%, the true odds of being correctly identified by a random breathalyzer stop are really just south of 2%!

Don't feel bad if you missed this though; when similar problems were given to Harvard medical students, nearly half guessed 95%.[94] Hell, I just wrote this and worked out the math myself and there is still a nagging part of me that wants to believe the power of the observation over the logic of the story. Such is our all too human tendency to ignore averages.

The lesson here is that a consideration of averages can lead us to appropriately prepare for an uncertain future and manage risk. If 50% of people get divorced, you, on your wedding day (the happiest day of your life!), have a 50% chance of divorce too. A Longboard Asset Management study found that nearly 40% of stocks lose money over their lifetime, that 64% underperform a broad market index and that one-quarter of stocks account for basically all of the gains in the market over time. For active stock pickers, that means that the shares you have just spent months researching and believe in so fully have a one in four chance of being a real winner.

This dose of cold reality can seem depressing until you realize its potential for avoiding disaster. Imagine a world in which couples, before walking down the aisle, received appropriate pre-marital counselling and thought deeply about their decision to come together. Or an asset management industry market, not by bravado, but by a reverence for the task of managing other peoples' money and the attendant difficulties therein. It can be painful consider in the here and now that we are average, but it can prevent a lifetime of painful tomorrows.

Look for simple solutions

I grew up in Huntsville, Alabama, a town affectionately known as the Rocket City because of a proud heritage of contributions to the space industry. Home to Space Camp and the US Space and Rocket Center, the Huntsville skyline is dominated by a Saturn V rocket. While the Saturn V is undoubtedly the star of the show, my attention was drawn

---

[94] D. Greller, 'Jumping to conclusions – base rate neglect,' *Invisible Laws* (September 11, 2011).

to a space shuttle on the museum grounds on a recent visit to my hometown. While passing by the shuttle, I was keyed in on a detail that seemed out of place; the external fuel tank looked rough and rusty compared to the gleaming, white exterior of the rest of the shuttle. A little research unearths that the fuel tank's orange appearance is not the result of design negligence, but rather an example of the power of simple solutions to have enormous reach.

The space shuttle's first two voyages – STS-1 and STS-2 – featured an external fuel tank that was painted the same brilliant white as the solid rocket boosters and the orbiter itself. But after these early explorations, it become apparent that the shuttle would benefit from a bit of a diet; it needed to shed roughly 600 pounds to function at optimal capacity.[95] Undaunted by the task, rocket scientists set out to do what rocket scientists do. They experimented with space age materials and looked for aerodynamic efficiencies, all to no avail. At a point of particular frustration, a low-paid line worker became aware of these efforts and suggested quite simply, "Why don't you just stop painting the tank?" The paint required to paint the tank weighed right at 600 pounds and the rest is ugly orange history.

Odds are, you are reading this book looking for some sort of edge in financial markets. Insights that will help you wring a few extra basis points out of a market that can feel remarkably efficient at times. This is a worthwhile cause, but in these efforts you must be sure not to overlook the simple and effective solutions that might be staring you in the face. Morningstar, keepers of the keys to a financial data goldmine, found that fees are the best predictor of fund performance. Not a rockstar manager, not an empirically valid process, not an informational edge, but fees.[96]

Further, a team at Fidelity set out to examine the behaviors of their best-performing retail accounts in an effort to isolate the behaviors of truly exceptional investors. When they contacted the owners of the best performing accounts, the common thread tended to be that they

[95]   T. Rogoway, 'This is why the space shuttle's external fuel tank stopped being painted white,' *Foxtrot Alpha* (October 16, 2015).
[96]   R. Kinnel, 'How fund fees are the best predictor of returns,' Morningstar (October 4, 2016).

had forgotten about the account altogether or had died. So much for isolating the complex behavioral traits of skilled investors!

Attentional bias leads us to have what behavioral finance expert Brian Portnoy refers to as "a fetish for complexity" that can lead us to ignore important tools at our disposal on a snipe hunt for something grander.

Avoid being too smart by half

Alexander Pope is generally credited with coining the idea that "a little knowledge is a dangerous thing," a sentiment excerpted from his 1709, 'An Essay on Criticism', where he opined:

> "A little learning is a dangerous thing; drink deep, or taste not the Pierian spring: there shallow draughts intoxicate the brain, and drinking largely sobers us again."

However, Pope's warning about cursory knowledge is actually predated by a similar expression penned by an anonymous author, going only by the initials AB, who wrote in 'The Mystery of Phanaticism':

> "...a little knowledge is apt to puff up, and make men giddy, but a greater share of it will set them right, and bring them to low and humble thoughts of themselves."

Original credit aside, this idea absolutely holds sway in the study of behavioral finance and is a useful caveat for those seeking to root out error in their decision-making process. Becoming knowledgeable about oneself and the machinations of human thought can be a giddy, dizzying affair that excites us to the point that we are eager to apply our knowledge. But if this knowledge is applied too superficially, it can exacerbate our existing decisional errors as a result of having learned more! Our knowledge of psychological bias can become just another cog in the machine of our bad reasoning.

Consider Taber and Lodge's work in 'Motivated Skepticism in the Evaluation of Political Beliefs'.[97] They found a handful of different ways in which our pre-existing beliefs about the world impact our

---

[97] C. S. Taber and M. Lodge, 'Motivated skepticism in the evaluation of political beliefs,' *American Journal of Political Science* 50:3 (July 2006), pp. 755–769.

thinking, some of which are actually worsened by further education. Two examples include:

1. **Attitude polarization** – Exposing subjects to a balanced set of pro and con considerations actually strengthened their initial position.

2. **Sophistication effect** – Knowledgeable subjects actually showed a greater tendency to engage in confirmation bias, disconfirmation bias, and prior attitude effect (evaluating supportive arguments more favorably than counter arguments).

Knowledge of behavioral tendencies can be used as a bright light of introspection about our motives, but it can also be used as a cudgel to hit dissenters with as we carry on defending the status quo. To avoid this misuse of knowledge, the behavioral investor should be sure to apply extra scrutiny to matters that are personally meaningful to us or that we wish deeply to be true or false. We must also consistently seek feedback from those with diverse viewpoints, track our own decisional efficacy and examine the deepest motivations behind our thoughts and actions. It is only in so doing that we are able to combat the real human tendency to hold information that we cherish to a laxer standard than that we disdain.

Size matters

Warren Buffett states that the combination of likelihood and impact are at the heart of everything Berkshire Hathaway does: "Take the probability of loss times the amount of possible loss from the probability of gain times the amount of possible gain. That is what we're trying to do. It's imperfect, but that's what it's all about." Put more concretely, a low likelihood event with great upside or downside may be well worth attending to. Conversely, a likely event with limited scope may just as well be worth ignoring.

Given both the psychological (we hate losses 2.5 times as much as gains) and mathematical (it takes a 100% gain to erase a 50% loss) realities of negative events, they warrant special consideration by behavioral investors.

Nassim Taleb gives a wonderful example of this in his book, *Fooled by Randomness*. He relates the story of meeting with fellow traders and sharing with them his belief that the market would likely rise in the following week. Realizing that he had a short position on, the traders were confused. Why be short a market you think is likely to rise? To explain, Taleb showed them the following chart.

Event	Probability	Outcome	Expected Value
Market Goes Up	70%	+1%	+0.7
Market Goes Down	30%	−10%	−3.0
Total	100%		−2.3

Taleb believed there to be an asymmetry between the size of losses and gains that might occur. Although there was a greater likelihood that the market would rise (as is almost always the case), the repercussions of a falling market, however unlikely, were much more dramatic. Thus, he operated from his best estimate of expected value and not just simple probability.

Probability confirms that optimism ought to be the de facto position of the well-informed investor: markets usually go up. But there are two things that begin to give investors pause and would warrant taking a more defensive position. The first is flagging momentum, which increases the probability that the market will fall in value. The second is steep valuations, which increase the intensity of the potential crash. The further disconnected the market becomes from its long-term averages, the more violently it crashes back to earth at such time as it does revert.

Thus, the behavioral investor has the default position of being aggressively invested until such time as momentum begins to slacken (probability) and valuations are extreme (intensity). Such an approach honors both the value of probability and the potential intensity of a low probability occurrence. The behavioral investor learns to ask both, "How likely is it?" and "How big is it?"

Give it time

One of the most frustrating aspects of probabilistic investing is that sometimes doing the right thing does not guarantee a good result.

You are sometimes left with the worst of both worlds – the lack of a comforting narrative and a poor result. It frankly stinks, and the knowledge that you played by the rules is small comfort. It is precisely for this reason that probabilistically informed investing gets abandoned with regularity. It is only with time and multiple iterations that probability evinces its true value.

As Cullen Roche points out on his blog, Pragmatic Capitalism, the market is essentially random when viewed on a daily basis.[98] An investor following a rules-based behavioral approach is not much more likely than a monkey throwing darts to get a good result. Daily fluctuations average a gain of 0.03%.

Considered on a monthly basis, returns begin to take some shape but there is still a great deal of noise. Accordingly, there is very little guarantee of getting the right result for taking the right action.

But as we back out even further, real patterns begin to emerge. The annualized return of the market is nearly 13% from 1950 to present and a clear, positive trend now emerges. The longer your horizon, the more likely you are to get the right result for the right reason. Behavioral investing must be long-term to be effective.

Creating a behaviorally informed portfolio is like running an insurance company in microcosm. First, you protect yourself against negative externalities by screening out the infirm. The ethics of this are questionable, but insurance companies charge smokers, the obese and those with pre-existing conditions a premium precisely because they are likely to be expensive to insure. Likewise, a behavioral investor begins by *doing no harm* and screening out any stocks that appear to be fraudulent, at risk for bankruptcy, or otherwise sick.

Second, the insurance company and shrewd investor both diversify. Just as the healthiest triathlete can die in a freak accident, even inexpensive, high quality stocks with a catalyst have an uncertain fate. By bundling risk (i.e., diversifying), the likelihood increases that doing the right thing for the right reasons will pay off.

[98]   C. Roche, 'Great investors think in terms of probabilities,' Pragmatic Capitalism (November 10, 2014).

Finally, be patient. The long-term prognosis for any individual human is, well, not great. No amount of good diet and exercise keeps us from the inevitability of illness and death, and yet, insurance companies do just fine (too fine, frankly, but that's another book), because most people are healthy most of the time. Similarly, the long-term prognosis for most stocks is shockingly bad. Longboard Asset Management's, 'The Capitalism Distribution' paints the picture:

- 39% of stocks were unprofitable.

- 18.5% of stocks suffered catastrophic losses of at least 75%.

- 64% of stocks underperformed the Russell 3000.

- 25% of stocks account for almost all performance.

Just as insurance companies profitably cover humans prone to disease and death, behavioral investors can reap tremendous financial rewards from a system in which a great many stocks underperform or flat out collapse. Doing so requires persistence in the face of short-term failure and adherence to a set of time-tested principles. But most of all it takes patience.

Like many of the tendencies we have discussed herein, attention bias is the by-product of a strained system looking for practical shortcuts. While this system of bringing the scariest and loudest information to the fore works nicely in some contexts, it can be the undoing of an investor looking to act sensibly in a world of breathless pundits and panicked counterparties. By taking a step back and applying some of the exercises mentioned above, the behavioral investor is able to keep her head when all around are losing theirs.

Creating attention proof portfolios

- **Fact**: "Probably" is a powerful word in investing. **So what?** Complicated macro narratives should be scrupulously ignored.

- **Fact**: The likelihood of an event and the intensity of its impact are both important considerations. **So what?** The default state of a strategy should be bullishness, but ought to include a contingency for low-likelihood-high-intensity events.

- **Fact**: Data without theory and theory without data both produce spurious results. **So what?** An investable factor must be empirically evident, theoretically sound and have roots in behavior.

Chapter 11.
The Behavioral Investor Manages Emotion

"I don't want to be at the mercy of my emotions. I want to use them, to enjoy them, and to dominate them."

– OSCAR WILDE, *THE PICTURE OF DORIAN GRAY*

DR. MARTIN LUTHER King, Jr. arrived in Washington on the evening of August 26 without any prepared remarks for his address to the hundreds of thousands of supporters that would gather in front of Lincoln Memorial the next day. Whereas his fellow speakers that day had meticulously prepared and had handed out advance copies of their remarks, Dr. King had hung back, hoping to imbue his speech with an authenticity and urgency of which over-preparation can be the enemy. That night, the great man first set pen to paper, not finalizing his remarks until well after midnight. As he set down his pen and retired to bed, there was no mention of "I have a dream" anywhere in his prepared remarks.

King approached the podium, prepared to give a speech about racial harmony, albeit devoid of what we now know to be his signature oratorical turn of phrase. Just before commencing, Mahalia Jackson, a gospel singer in the audience, shouted "Tell 'em about the dream" referencing his mention of a dream of racial unity mentioned five years earlier in Detroit. Setting aside his notes and speaking from the heart, King then launched into what may well be the most powerful speech in American history. Dr. King's extemporaneous approach gave full expression to the emotion he felt as part of the civil rights movement and has inspired generations of Americans to be wary of the bigotry of the past. By harnessing the power of emotion that day, King secured his legacy and changed the fate of a nation.

Emotion served Dr. King well because he was tasked with changing the minds, but more importantly the hearts, of an American people mired in the legacy of slavery and Jim Crow. But as we have learned in previous chapters, behavioral adaptions that are rational and even recommended in one context can prove ill-suited for the often unorthodox demands made upon us as investors. In *The Laws of Wealth*, I highlight a number of discrepancies between the realities of our lived everyday and what I call, Wall Street Bizarro World. To name just a few, on Wall Street the future is more certain than the present, the crowd is less intelligent than an individual, and doing less is better than more. We could easily add to that list the reality that emotion, a trait that evolved to help us make faster and better decisions in our daily lives, can lead us seriously astray when making investment decisions.

Emotion risk stems from the fact that our perceptions of danger are colored by both our transitory emotional states and our individual propensity toward positivity or negativity. Emotion leads most of us to underrate the possibility of bad things happening to us (optimism bias), to avoid even thinking about what might go wrong (ostrich effect) and to ignore the important role emotion plays in our decisions (empathy gap). When fear does break through, it can become so powerful that we can be immobilized by trying to avoid pain (negativity bias). But for all the havoc emotion can wreak on a rational investment process, many investors also speak to an intuitive sixth sense that informs decision-making. Is reducing the emotional aspects of investing possible or even desirable, or are we leaving a valuable form of advantage on the table?

Our understanding of emotion is expanding and, with it, so are the number of emotions themselves. Rene Descartes believed in just six core emotions and no less an authority than Pixar's *Inside Out* speaks to five, but modern researchers paint a far more nuanced picture that is highly culture dependent. As Dr. Tiffany Watt Smith says:

> "Fear might seem like an irreducible emotion of our most animal selves. But the Pintupi, whose home is in the deserts of western Australia, speak of as many of as 15 distinct sorts of fear, for instance the fright that makes you jump up and look around you (*nginyiwarrarringu*); the creeping dread that a rival is seeking revenge (*ngulu*); and the terror felt when malevolent spirits are around (*kanarunvtju*)."

A second complicating factor in the delineation of emotion is that some feelings are experienced very much as a combination of other emotions. Consider nostalgia, which is equal parts sadness, longing, fondness, and joy. Dr. Watt Smith, who has herself compiled an *Encyclopedia of Feeling*, has named and described over 150 different types of emotion, a giant leap from Descartes' idea of scarcely a handful.

While a definitive taxonomy of emotion may not be forthcoming, the point remains that emotion is powerful, pervasive and impacts every choice we make and every minute of each day. Emotion can assist our decisions or destroy them, but it is only as we became aware of its power and ubiquity that we are effectively able to make it serve our ends. To begin this effort, please consider the following.

Tools for overcoming emotion

Don't beat it, join it

Many martial arts rely on what is referred to as the Circular Theory of Self Defense, meaning that the momentum and exertion of an attacker can actually be used to your advantage. Imagine being rushed by a would-be assailant who speeds toward you with arms extended. Rather than meeting the full force of his momentum head on, you might side step this rush, deflecting the outstretched arm, leading him to rush past, now vulnerable to counter attack. This approach of working *with* a powerful force and not *against* a powerful force is instructive to investors seeking to manage emotion en route to making wise investment decisions. It can be tempting to want to stop emotion in its tracks, but, oftentimes, the more adaptive approach is to repurpose it for more favorable outcomes.

Behavioral finance is sometimes mistakenly seen as a vehicle for ridding investors of their pesky emotions and irrational quirks en route to them becoming something like the *Homo Economicus* that economists long imagined them to be. If we could just rid ourselves of irrationality, the thought goes, we would make perfect financial decisions. The only problem is, sometimes behavior that is irrational in the strictest sense of the word can greatly aid our quest to reach our financial goals. Being a behavioral investor is less about adhering to some textbook notion of rationality and more about understanding and bending the idiosyncrasies of human nature to our advantage.

Consider the work of Nobel Prize winner Richard Thaler who first discovered and named what we now refer to as "mental accounting," the tendency to separate money into different buckets and spend or save it differently depending on how it is labeled. Studies have shown that people are apt to save money labeled as a rebate but to spend money labeled as a bonus. Barack Obama and his advisors, Richard Thaler among them, used framing to position the stimulus given out after the Great Recession as a bonus to incent recipients to buy big screen TVs rather than hoard it.

This simple notion is the basis for goals-based investing or *personal benchmarking*, the process of intentionally dividing money into safety, income and growth buckets and investing it accordingly. It seems incredible that something as simple as labeling money can induce us to save and invest differently, but as George Loewenstein says, "While it seems like an inconsequential process, earmarking can have a dramatic effect on retirement savings. Cheema and Soman (2009) found that earmarking savings in an envelope labeled with a picture of a couple's children nearly doubled the savings rate of very low income parents."

Is it rational that we save twice as much money when someone plays on our feelings of love for our children? Absolutely not. Can we understand this about ourselves and use it to our advantage? Absolutely.

What Richard Thaler was cleverly able to do was demonstrate that behavioral traits largely deemed harmful can actually be used for good. Take for example the status quo bias, which is the tendency toward inaction. Thaler, understanding that people tended to make a decision once and not question it again, determined to use this to the benefit of the woefully unprepared American pre-retiree. He developed a program titled Save More Tomorrow that allowed savers to make a decision once to automate their savings behavior and auto-escalate the amount withdrawn when their pay increased.[99] Thaler understood that asking people to make the right decision month after month was much more difficult than simply setting it and forgetting it. Once again, it is patently irrational that we should be so susceptible to the status quo bias that we can lock in a behavior once and effectively forget about it for life. But by some estimates this simple idea has contributed more than 29 billion dollars to the accounts of American savers.[100]

Rational? Maybe not, but I'll take it. Just as Thaler and his colleagues discovered, some of our psychological peccadillos can be understood and repurposed for our own benefit. It is entirely possible to take your laziness, aversion to change and excessive emotionality and make them work for your own benefit.

Meditate (yes, seriously)

Meditation and mindfulness have been discussed with a sort of breathless reverence for the past few years that has led cynical skeptics like myself to want to run fast in the other direction. After all, things positioned as too good to be true often are, in both capital markets and life more generally. But in the case of meditation, a deeper dive into the research gave me a greater sense of what the fuss was all about and convinced me that perhaps thousands of years of spiritual practice was better informed than my naïve skepticism. If it's good enough for Ray Dalio, Paul Tudor Jones, BlackRock, Goldman Sachs (all of whom have

---

[99] R. Thaler and C. Sunstein, *Nudge: Improving Decisions About Health, Wealth, and Happiness* (Penguin, 2009).

[100] A. Kings 'Important money lessons from Nobel Prize in Economics winner Richard Thaler,' Born2Invest (October 11, 2017).

meditation programs in place for employees) and literally billions of practitioners worldwide, maybe it's worth considering.[101]

One of the central themes of this book is that working to slow down our reflexive thinking when making important financial decisions can lead to improved outcomes. To use Daniel Kahneman's parlance, "thinking fast" leads us to rely on heuristics, biases and shortcuts, whereas the more effortful "thinking slow" leads us to consider decisions in their full contextual splendor. In one study, participants who took part in a mindfulness exercise and then were asked about their implicit associations with respect to age and race showed less reliance on bias than a control group who had not completed the mindfulness exercise.[102] The simple act of slowing down and heightening awareness reduced reliance on well-worn biases and allowed participants to judge people of different ages and races on their individual merits and not as an overgeneralized whole. The positive potential for applying such nuanced thinking to investment decision-making can hardly be overstated.

Although it is a gross simplification, emotion in and around financial markets is often lumped into one of two categories: fear or greed. Meditation, it would seem, is well positioned to tame both. A meta-analysis of 47 trials and 3515 participants found that meditation decreased anxiety, lessened depression and decreased pain. Weaker, but still positive, evidence was found for reducing stress levels and improving overall quality of life.[103] For those on the *fear* end of the fear and greed continuum, meditation is powerful medicine.

It is perhaps no surprise to learn that meditation can reduce anxiety, but the literature suggests that it can also rewire the way that we think about and anticipate rewards. Seeking out rewards is a universal human behavior, but taken to the extreme, greed can be becoming all

---

[101] J. Voss, 'Meditation for investment professionals,' *Enterprising Investor* – CFA Institute (February 29, 2016).

[102] A. Lueke and B. Gibson, 'Mindfulness meditation reduces implicit age and race bias,' *Social Psychological and Personality Science* (November 24, 2014).

[103] M. Goyal, S. Singh and E. M. S. Sibinga, 'Meditation programs for psychological stress and well-being,' *JAMA Internal Medicine* 174:3 (2014), pp. 357–368.

consuming, leading to everything from lower ratings of subjective well-being to Ponzi schemes of the Madoff variety. A study by Kirk, Brown and Downar that matched 34 meditators with 44 matched controls found that those who meditated showed lower neural activations in the caudate nucleus and ventromedial prefrontal cortex during reward anticipation when compared to their less enlightened peers. What does this all mean in plain English? The parts of the brain associated with greed – expecting and anticipating reward – are actually less active in the minds of those who meditate. Fear and greed, responsible for calamitous financial decisions as diverse as bank runs, investment bubbles, and affinity fraud, both show evidence of being tamed by the simple act of mindfulness meditation.

Most impressive of all is the growing body of evidence that meditation seems to be able to physically restructure our bodies in certain ways, a reality that almost sounds like science fiction. Telomeres are pieces of DNA that cap our chromosomes and work to fight chromosomal deterioration. Although they are not thought to cause a particular disease per se, they do tend to shorten with age and are present in those with a variety of conditions including diabetes, heart disease, cancer and mental illness. Dr. Linda E. Carlson compares them to the plastic cap on a shoelace which, if intact, keeps the larger lace from fraying and becoming worn.

To study the impact of meditation on our physical health, Dr. Carlson assigned breast cancer survivors into three groups. The first group was randomly assigned to a two-month meditation and yoga course; the second to a longer group therapy treatment protocol and the control group received six hours of stress management training. When the blood of the 88 participants was analyzed, the telomere length of those in the meditation and therapy treatments were significantly longer than those in the stress management training. Amazingly, meditation and therapy seem just as adept at preserving our physical health as they are at preserving our sanity.[104]

Don't be fooled by the monastic trappings of meditation; one needn't shave their head or wear orange robes to benefit from this time-

[104] B. Stetka, 'Changing our DNA through mind control?' *Scientific American* (December 16, 2014).

tested strategy for managing emotion. At their core, mindfulness and meditation are all about focusing on present thoughts and actions in a non-judgmental way, a simple pursuit that is within reach of all of us. The CFA Society, led by Jason Voss, has developed a set of practical tools for novice meditators. myriad apps exist for mobile meditators, the internet is full of practical advice for getting started and books like *Meditation for Fidgety Skeptics* are emerging to help people like me to see the light.

An investor in touch with the present moment is one that is able to own, label and appreciate emotion without allowing it to unduly influence an important decision.

Managing strong emotion

Throughout this book, I have professed a number of my more controversial beliefs about how asset managers should go about their business. I believe that a systematic approach to investing is optimal and that manager discretion should be very limited.

For one, I believe that managers should be paid for the degree to which they adhere to a process and that performance should be ignored entirely. Ideally, investment managers would work somewhere between 4 and 12 days per year and spend the other 361 days a year in the pursuit of ideas that challenge their existing beliefs.

I don't imagine that anyone is going to take me up on my performance agnostic four-day work-year idea, so in lieu of that, I'll propose some tools below for managing the sort of strong emotions that can be the undoing of even the best system. After all, an empirically sound process that is overridden in a moment of panic (as all systems can be), is no better than no system at all.

At times when you feel like straying from your rules, it can be useful to consider Michele McDonald's R.A.I.N. model, a simple but powerful system for managing an episode of acute stress. The acronym is as follows:

- **Recognition** – Deliberately observe and name what is occurring in your body and mind. For instance, "I feel my heart and mind racing."

- **Acceptance** – Acknowledge and accept the presence of whatever you observed above. You don't have to love it, but fighting will make it worse.

- **Investigation** – Ask yourself what stories you are telling yourself and examine what thoughts are present.

- **Non-identification** – Now that you have recognized, accepted and investigated your stress, you must realize that you are more than your emotions. You can feel something without being defined by it.

Rational thinking can feel cold, sterile, and remote. Emotion on the other hand, feels pervasive, urgent and real. Because of its power to commandeer focus, emotion can lead us to conflate our emotional reality with external realities. By recognizing, accepting and investigating the antecedents of our emotional response, it can become another valuable piece of information as part of a larger tapestry of exploring the truth, and will cease to be mistaken for the truth itself.

Automate, automate, automate

This book could easily have been three words long: automate, automate, automate. It likely wouldn't have sold well, and you might have ignored the advice on account of it seeming too simple, but the fact is that many of the thornier elements of emotion can be done away with entirely by slavishly following a system of investment rules in all types of market weather. This concept is most vividly embodied in the story of Odysseus, the Greek king of Ithaca, from Homer's epic, *The Odyssey*. The king is best remembered for his decade long journey home after the Trojan War as well as the wooden horse he used to surreptitiously access enemy fortifications. But for our purposes here, we are less concerned about his skills as a warrior and more interested in what might be his most important action of all: an act of restraint.

In Greek folklore, sirens were the dangerous creatures whose songs and beauty lured sailors close only to dash their ships along a rocky shore. But the sirens weren't just thought to be lusty mermaids, as they are commonly depicted today. No, the sirens were reputed to have wellsprings of knowledge that could be whispered in the ear of a sailor, but ultimately served of little use since they were the last words that he would ever hear. The trick, heretofore unaccomplished by even the most skillful sailor, was to gain access to the sirens' knowledge without paying the ultimate price for that wisdom.

After consulting with Circes, Odysseus arrived at a workaround; he would have his crew fill their ears with beeswax while he would have himself lashed to the mast of the ship. In so doing, his shipmates would be invulnerable to the sirens' whiles and he would still be able to gain access to the depth of their learning. As expected, as Odysseus heard the song of the sirens, he flailed and begged to be unfettered, but his men remained true to their discipline and did not give in to the pleadings of their leader. Just as Odysseus was a man of strength and action, many investors have been successful based on lives of boldness and proactivity. But in Odysseus we find an exemplar of the ways in which sometimes the most prudent action is restraint.

Even the most educated professional investor suffers from what is commonly known as *restraint bias*, or the tendency to overestimate our ability to control impulsive behavior in the moment. If everyone in the world received comprehensive nutritional counseling, it would do nothing to change the fact that eating a donut in a period of stress is more satisfying than eating asparagus. Likewise, giving in to panic selling or buying glamour stocks of poor quality are done, not because of lack of knowledge, but rather due to lack of restraint. The behavioral investor must tread the path of Odysseus, seeking to glean the best possible outcomes all the while cognizant of our own susceptibility to the stressors of an emotional moment. The behavioral investor must never forget that they would eat the donut too.

Learn to recognize emotion

Set down your book for just a moment, take a deep breath and ask yourself, "What emotional state am I in right now?" It's harder than it sounds, isn't it? Left to our own devices, our emotional state becomes our truth. It just *is*. Emotion is so pervasive and helpful that asking a human to describe what he feels like in a given moment can be a bit akin to asking a fish what it feels like to be wet. And yet, learning to recognize and label emotion is crucial for the behavioral investor because emotions so dramatically impact the way that we evaluate risk, think about money and experience time tradeoffs.

For instance, a Harvard study found that sad people would accept 34% less money just to get paid – now. It has been said that sadness is the inability to construct a future and this experiment certainly bears this out.[105] But sadness isn't the only emotion wont to truncate timelines. Anger has also been shown to make us impatient and it seems that **any** strong emotion has the impact of shortening time horizons and increasing impatience, two of the worst things an evidence-based investor could ever hope to do.[106] Feelings of fear lead us to experience uncertainty, while anger instills a sense of confidence. As you might expect, people who are angry tend to take bigger risks and minimize the potential danger involved.

It is not desirable or even possible to rid your investment decisions of emotion, but it is possible to increase your awareness of your emotional state, and understand how it impacts your appraisal of risk and opportunity. This is a real skill that must be honed over years of conscious practice, in good times and bad, if it is to pay true dividends in a time of crisis. To the novice, the very state you find yourself in can serve to blind you to an elevation of emotion. Feelings of anger or euphoria do not feel elevated in an angry or euphoric moment; they feel justified.

The 12-step addiction literature teaches those in recovery an acronym – H.A.L.T. – that would also serve investors very well. The acronym stands for *hungry, angry, lonely, tired* and is a reminder to abstain from making important decisions in any of these emotional states.

Emotion enriches our lives and streamlines our decision-making, but in the extreme it can blind us to solutions that would otherwise seem obvious.

---

[105] J. S. Lerner, Ye Li and E. U. Weber, 'The financial cost of sadness,' *Psychological Science* (2012).
[106] H. Aarts, K. I. Ruys, H. Veling, R. A. Renes, J. H. B. de Groot, A. M. van Nunen and S. Geertjes 'The art of anger,' *Psychological Science* (September 20, 2010).

Crafting emotion resistant portfolios

- **Fact**: Intuition exists but only in areas that provide quick, reliable feedback. **So what?** Listen to your gut is profoundly dumb advice for investors.

- **Fact**: Our body experiences urges to act that are only later interpreted mentally. **So what?** Build a model and follow it slavishly.

- **Fact**: Situational variables are more predictive of behavior than individual variables. **So what?** Avoid emotion-inducing situations like watching financial news and frequently checking account balances.

- **Fact**: Our willpower is quickly exhausted. **So what?** Have I mentioned that you should build a model and follow it slavishly?

PART FOUR.
BUILDING
BEHAVIORAL
PORTFOLIOS

THIS BOOK BEGAN with a look at the sociological difficulties surrounding investment decision-making, in specific that you are a member of a species that values social cohesion over rationality when making decisions. We next examined how the brain and body, marvels of evolution and design elsewhere, are poorly matched to the specific task of compounding wealth. Finally, we investigated the four behavioral tendencies that emerge as a result of both place and person.

The point in all of this has never been knowledge-for-knowledge's-sake, but rather to provide a rich education about the contextual ground on which investment decision-making takes place, with an eye to developing investment systems robust to human error. The goal is to teach correct principles and allow you to build something special. And while there is no one "right answer" with respect to how to manage a behavioral portfolio, the weight of evidence points to a few common themes:

- Systems trump discretion.

- Diversification and conviction can coexist.

- Prepare for bursting bubbles without being too fine-tuned to them.

- Less is more when it comes to information.

- Look for evidence, theory and roots in behavior.

Many of the truths about behavioral finance outlined in this book are now more or less accepted by the broader world of finance, which represents significant progress in a relatively short amount of time. However, there remains a gaping chasm between theory and application when it comes to investment management. It is one thing to accept that humans are fallible and that markets are inefficient, but it is quite another to embrace the sometimes-radical reinvention of our processes

177

required by a deep understanding of the trust of behavioral science. In this fourth part of the book, we take a step in that direction by offering up some concrete steps toward constructing behaviorally-informed equity portfolios.

Chapter 12.
Investing a Third Way

IN RECENT YEARS, a rather vitriolic debate has emerged around the "passive versus active" investing debate. This debate, like all discussions that become heated, is becoming less and less about the facts at hand and is increasingly seeing participants decamp into tribes who are more concerned about pointing fingers than assessing facts. The behavioral investor is first and foremost an evidence-based investor who looks for truth in the shades of grey so often ignored by less psychologically attuned herds. To that end, we will now examine some of the strengths and weaknesses of these two investment approaches and suggest a third way, that I refer to as rules-based behavioral investing, or RBI.

Rule-based behavioral investing

	RBI	Passive	Active
Low fee	✓	✓	
Diversified	✓	✓	✓
Potential outperformance	✓		✓
Low turnover	✓	✓	
Manages bias	✓		

Passive investing: what gets measured gets dumb

"What could be more advantageous in an intellectual contest – whether it be chess, bridge, or stock selection than to have opponents who have been taught that thinking is a waste of energy."

— WARREN BUFFETT

The colonial French regime in Hanoi, Vietnam had a problem: rats. The French, not exactly known for their ruggedness, were upset by the number of rats in Vietnam and set forth what seemed like a sensible plan to eradicate the pests. For each rat killed by a Vietnamese citizen, the French would pay a small bounty. Not wishing to deal with dead rat bodies *in toto*, a tail of the deceased rat was deemed to be sufficient evidence. But it wasn't long after the program began that the ruling class began to notice something unexpected. Rattails were being turned in by the dozens, but the rats in the street didn't seem to be getting any less numerous. Instead, the clever Vietnamese were severing the tails, turning them in for the money, and releasing the rats back into the sewers to make more baby rats whose tails could eventually be lopped off. A similar incident was observed in India during the time of British colonial rule. A reward was set for every dead cobra and so enterprising Indians began to – you guessed it – raise cobras on snake farms. The Cobra Effect is now shorthand for what is officially referred to as Campbell's' Law, which states, "when a measure becomes a target, it ceases to be a good measure."

Campbell says of the tendency for measurement to corrupt efficacy, "The more any quantitative social indicator is used for social decision-making, the more subject it will be to corruption pressures and the more apt it will be to distort and corrupt the social processes it is intended to monitor." A recent example occurred in my adopted hometown of Atlanta, Georgia. In an effort to hold teachers accountable, the government passed laws around high-stakes testing, meaning that teacher raises and ongoing employment were contingent on students successfully passing competency tests. In what ended up being a messy criminal cover-up, elementary school teachers were altering test scores to ensure that they were able to keep their jobs. Less dramatic examples lead educators to "teach to the test," meaning that students learn the specific material necessary to pass the test without necessarily achieving mastery of the subject more broadly.

Campbell says of this phenomenon, "achievement tests may well be valuable indicators of general school achievement under conditions of normal teaching aimed at general competence. But when test scores become the goal of the teaching process, they both lose their value as indicators of educational status and distort the educational process in undesirable ways." The very process of trying to define a gold standard can result in its bastardization. It has been said that "what gets measured gets done," but it is equally true that "what gets measured gets dumb."

Passive management, which makes the yardstick the investment vehicle, falls prey to some of the shortcomings of the Cobra Effect as a result. But before I render a nuanced behavioral critique of passive investing (and anger an army of Bogleheads with pitchforks), let me speak to some of its considerable strengths.

To be as direct as possible, passive investing should be the de facto choice of those uninterested in the art and science of investment management. By buying a diversified basket of index funds that covers a variety of asset classes, *know nothing* investors (who often know a great deal) are likely to beat more than 90% of active managers and have time to focus on pursuits more meaningful than compounding wealth. Since passive management eschews costly research and rock star managers, passive vehicles tend to be far less expensive than their active brethren; a huge win for investors. All else being equal, investors should always choose the least expensive fund as fees cut directly into performance and can dramatically reduce wealth over a lifetime of investing.

But passive funds are not just inexpensive – they have consistently spanked active funds over just about any timeframe you'd care to consider. Just look at the results of the SPIVA Scorecard, a comparison of how active managers have done relative to their passive counterparts. Over five and ten-year periods, respectively, 88.65% and 82.07% of large capitalization money mangers were beaten by passive approaches to investing (and that's before their fees!). The results for small capitalization stocks, often considered to be less efficiently priced and therefore more favorable to active management, are just as damning: 87.75% of small cap managers were bested by passive approaches over the past ten years.

I am writing this at a time when asset flows are moving 3-to-1 in favor of passive investment vehicles. Vanguard, arguably the face of index investing, is raising a billion dollars per day! Passive approaches have soundly and consistently beaten their active counterparts and have done so at a fraction of the cost.

But if there is one lesson to be learned from financial history, it is that universal consensus tends to portend bad news. As Aaron Task said in his thoughtful blog piece, 'Pride Cometh Before the Fall: Indexing Edition': "when 'everybody' knows something, it's usually a good time to head in the opposite direction. And what 'everybody' knows now is that the very best, smartest investment you can make is an index fund." Is it possible that indexing being the de facto right answer is somehow making it less right?

A victim of success

One Cobra Effect of indexing is that the very inclusion of a company in an index leads to an immediate increase in the price-to-earnings and price-to-book ratios of the stock. Being a part of an index means that millions of investors will buy the stock, not based on any fundamental belief in its goodness, but rather lockstep adherence. This causes valuations to rise, and expected forward returns to fall, on what can only be considered inconsequential information. The rise of passive investing also means that stocks included in large indices tend to be less informationally efficient than those not in such company. Michael Mauboussin and company report that, "in mid-2016, passive index funds and ETFs owned 10 percent or more of 458 of the 500 companies in the S&P 500. In 2005, that was true for only 2 of the 500." Increasingly, large swaths of a corporation are being bought and sold out of habit and not conviction, meaning that prices are less and less reflective of true value.

Speaking to this phenomenon Jesse Felder has said, "'passive investing' will ultimately become a victim of its own success. The massive shift to index funds over the past 15 years or so drove the valuations of the largest index components to levels which guarantee poor returns going forward. Poor returns, in turn, will guarantee these inflows will turn to outflows and the virtuous cycle will become a vicious one." Or as Nassim Taleb says, "We have been fragilizing the economy, our health, political life, education, almost everything… by suppressing randomness and volatility… This is the tragedy of modernity: as with neurotically overprotective parents, those trying to help are often hurting us the most."[107] In capital markets, the right thing to do ceases to be the right thing to do when everyone does it.

Of crowded bars and crowded trades

The El Farol bar problem is a game theoretic conundrum that speaks nicely to some of the problems around active and passive investing. The problem, based on a bar in Santa Fe, is as follows. There is a small town in New Mexico with a finite population of people and every Thursday night, all of them want to go downtown to the El Farol bar. The problem is that the bar is small and if it becomes too crowded, it's no fun for anyone. In specific:

- If less than 60% of the population go to the bar, they'll all have a *better* time than if they stayed at home.

- If more than 60% of the population go to the bar, they'll all have a *worse* time than if they stayed at home.

Unfortunately, everyone must decide at the same time, without any foreknowledge of how busy the bar will be. Clearly, if everyone uses the same strategy for determining whether or not to attend the bar, the problem will never be solved. The parallels to investing are obvious and nicely laid out in the Credit Suisse report, 'Looking for Easy Games':

> "This leads to a paradox: the more individuals who are informed, the more efficient prices become, and the less value there is in being informed. Efficient prices lead investors to move from active to passive, which may create inefficiencies from which active managers can profit. So if everybody invests actively, you want to be passive."

---

[107] N. N. Taleb, *Antifragile: Things That Gain from Disorder* (Random House, 2014), p. 5.

In both bars and markets, it takes a diversity of opinions for everyone to have a good time.

The *tragedy of the commons* is a system where individuals acting in their own self-interest harm the common good by spoiling a resource through their collective action. The most frequently cited example is allowing the cattle of individual farmers to graze on common ground owned by the government. Considered individually, it is in the best interest of every farmer to allow his cattle to graze on land that is kept up by the township. Considered collectively, the very act of so much cattle on so little common ground almost ensures that it will become overgrazed and useless to all parties. In the cattle example, people taking rational individual action inadvertently undermine the broader system.

A similar dynamic seems present when considering indexing. Passive investing makes a great deal of sense when considered individually; it offers attractive fees, broad exposure and acceptable historical returns. But this can create a dangerous crowded bar problem in markets, as Blake LeBaron notes:

> "During the run-up to a crash, population diversity falls. Agents begin to use very similar trading strategies as their common good performance begins to self-reinforce. This makes the population very brittle, in that a small reduction in the demand for shares could have a strong destabilizing impact on the market. The economic mechanism here is clear. Traders have a hard time finding anyone to sell to in a falling market since everyone else is following very similar strategies. In the Walrasian setup used here, this forces the price to drop by a large magnitude to clear the market. The population homogeneity translates into a reduction in market liquidity."[108]

Like a Vietnamese entrepreneur with a cleaver, we distort the efficiency of markets by our very attempts to codify and control them. The behavioral investor understands and seeks to mimic the best parts of passive investing – low turnover, rock bottom fees and appropriate diversification – without succumbing to absentminded buying and selling.

---

[108] B. Carlson 'How market crashes happen,' A Wealth of Common Sense (January 8, 2017).

Active investing: where are the customers' yachts?

Active portfolio management plays an important role in maintaining the health of capital markets, and while it has historically been disadvantageous to a slight majority of investors net of fees, it is also absolutely necessary if markets are to function. The aims of active management – to outperform a passive benchmark on a risk adjusted if not absolute basis – are universally appealing. Sadly, delivery against these stated aims has not been as uniform.

One of the ostensible benefits of active management is that it should save us from behavioral errors, but the research suggests that professionals are just as prone to making boneheaded mistakes as you or I. Charles Ellis points out in *The Elements of Investing*, "professionally managed funds tend to have their lowest cash positions at market tops and highest cash positions at market bottoms." Just like us, they greedily load up when stocks are expensive and sell in panic when stocks become attractively priced.

The primary assumed benefit of active management is, of course, performance, but active managers must deliver said performance after accounting for fees and trading costs. As cited in *The Fundamental Index*, the impact of these two obstacles is dramatic, accounting for between 0.5% and 2% annual underperformance for active managers. Active managers have of late been quick to scapegoat the broader environment – accommodative Fed policies, recovering from the throes of a deep recession – but the fact is that the trends discussed above are pervasive and long-standing. As Jason Zweig of the *Wall Street Journal* says:

> "Despite what you've heard and what many of you fervently believe, underperformance is not merely a temporary by-product of the narrow market of the past few years. Over the decade ended in mid-1974, 89% of all money managers lagged the S&P 500. Over the 20 years ended in 1964, the average fund underperformed by roughly 110 basis points. Even from 1929 through 1950, not a single major mutual fund beat the S&P. Take any period you like; the results are invariably discouraging."

Inasmuch as time is money in the world of active management (Ivy League math geniuses don't work for free!), it is essential that all investment-related due diligence must be more additive than it is expensive. For every 99 cents you spend on thinking about how to pick stocks, you must deliver no less than $1 of value. But a Vanguard study of how investment committees spend their time casts serious doubt on how well investors' fund fees are being put to use. They found that investment committees allocate their time thusly:

- **40%** – looking at past performance; not predictive of future performance by their own admission.

- **10%** – manager selection; Dr. Brian Portnoy cites evidence that only 5% of professional fund of fund managers show discernible skill at vetting managers.

- **11%** – non-investment issues; making coffee and "How was your weekend?"

- **13%** – "other"; not overwhelmed by the value added here.

- **25%** – strategy decisions; finally, some value!

Suppose that you are undeterred by some of the bad press around active investing and want to try and select one of the unicorns that outperforms with regularity. One of the difficulties in selecting an active manager, as set forth in *Conviction in Equity Investing,* is that, "active portfolio management is nearly unique in the world of commerce, in the inability of the consumer to identify true value before – and often after – buying the product." A car has aesthetic and objective appeal that can be readily apprehended. You can sit in the seat and see how it looks and check the window sticker for miles per gallon. Funds have metrics too, but as the fine print is always quick to disclose, past performance is not predictive of future results. In fact, mean reversion being what it is, past performance is often inversely proportional to future success! It's the equivalent of sitting in a Mercedes on the dealership lot only to have it turn into a Yugo once you drive it home. Nothing that is commonly included in due diligence – not past results, not historical standard deviation – gives you a clear sense of how an actively managed fund will perform in the future.

How investment committees spend their time

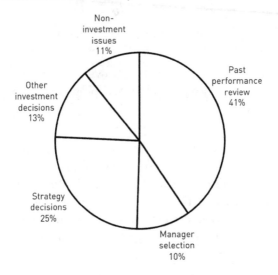

Source: 'Conviction in Equity Investing,' Hewitt EnnisKnupp (2012)

The lion's share of time and money spent by investment committees is in pursuit of activities that add significantly to fees but little to performance. The inability of managers to discretionarily predict investment talent, the vagaries of the market itself and the unreliability of past performance all point to one variable as being the most important part of due diligence – process.

Manager selection is a snipe hunt. Past performance is ephemeral. A disciplined process with behavioral guardrails is the best predictor of future success and yet most (expensive!) resources are aimed at efforts that have a high appearance of validity and little to no actual worth. Active management has the potential to benefit both individual investors and the capital markets in which they invest, but all too often it fails to realize the full measure of its potential through a combination of greed, hubris and a misunderstanding of human behavior.

Strengths and weaknesses of active investing

- **Strengths** – Potential for outperformance, potential for risk management, price discovery works for the greater good

- **Weaknesses** – high fees, low conviction, poor historical performance, behavioral risks not appropriately managed

Understanding the weaknesses of both active and passive approaches to investing is a discomfiting but necessary place to start. Passive management succeeds because it is automated, low fee, and diversified; traits that are laudable but easily replicated. Its weaknesses are that it can lock in bad behavioral tendencies (e.g., buying large, expensive stocks) and lead to an overall "fragilization" of markets through an unthinking approach.

Active management works, when it works, because it can protect investors from behavioral errors, respond to changing market conditions, take advantage of the cognitive errors of others and work for the greater good by virtue of its heterogenous decisional style. Sadly, most of the potential benefits of active management are never realized as a result of managers' failures to constrain their own behavioral shortcomings, a lack of conviction and excessively steep fees.

If all of this deconstruction has you wondering if there's a better way, I believe that there is. The behavioral investor, having critically examined the strengths and weaknesses of both approaches, can create a system that draws on the best parts of both. Such an approach would include:

- Appropriate fees.

- *Goldilocks* diversification.

- Responsiveness to market conditions.

- Basis in research.

- Low turnover.

- Systematic to avoid bias.

We can call this approach, rules-based behavioral investing or RBI.

Chapter 13.
Behavioral Investing is Rules-Based

R IGHT THIS MOMENT, you are missing most of what is going on around you. By focusing your attention on the words on this page, you are ignoring a far greater amount of data in your immediate surroundings: the faint humming of a fluorescent light, the slight tension in your body required to sit up, the sensation of your tongue touching your teeth and the roof of your mouth, the whir of a distant lawnmower.

The capacity of the entire processing system – conscious and unconscious – is enormous, about 11,200,000 bits. But Dr. Bob Nease suggests that of the millions of bits of information our brains process each second, a mere 50 bits are allotted to conscious thought! As Ap Dijksterhuis says, "…the unconscious does not have a capacity problem. If the unconscious is a modern computer, consciousness is nothing more than an old abacus." He goes on to say, "The low capacity of consciousness suggests that it may not be up to the task of making complex decisions… the consequence being that consciousness will only deal with a subset of information. This may come at expense of the final decision." If the bulk of our processing power is intuitive and not deliberative, it seems reasonable to suggest that our financial decisions will improve as we are better able to tap into that wealth of subconscious wisdom: an idea with strong support in arts and letters.

We are a society in love with the idea of intuition. In an age when computers are able to think and learn and jobs are increasingly becoming automated, it is comforting to think that there is something unique and almost ineffable about the abilities of the human family. If you find yourself in the camp that romanticizes unconscious reasoning, it must be said that you are in good company. Steve Jobs' work was powerfully impacted by his study of non-Western views of rationality and he was particularly moved by what he observed in India. Jobs said:

> "The people in the Indian countryside don't use their intellect like we do, they use their intuition instead, and the intuition is far more developed than in the rest of the world… Intuition is a very powerful thing, more powerful than intellect, in my opinion. That's had a big impact on my work. Western rational thought is not an innate human characteristic, it is learned and it is the great achievement of Western civilization. In the villages of India, they never learned it. They learned something else, which is in some ways just as valuable but in other ways is not. That's the power of intuition and experiential wisdom."

Author and activist Anne Lamott has this to say about the rationality versus intuition dialectic:

> "The rational mind doesn't nourish you. You assume that it gives you the truth, because the rational mind is the golden calf that this culture worships, but this is not true. Rationality squeezes out much that is rich and juicy and fascinating."

Finally, French philosopher Henri Bergman:

> "We see that the intellect, so skillful in dealing with the inert, is awkward the moment it touches the living. Whether it wants to treat the life of the body or the life of the mind, it proceeds with the rigor, the stiffness and the brutality of an instrument not designed for such use. *The intellect is characterized by a natural inability to comprehend life.* Instinct, on the contrary, is molded on the very form of life. While intelligence treats everything mechanically, instinct proceeds, so to speak, organically. If the consciousness that slumbers in it should awake, if it were wound up into knowledge instead of being wound off into action, if we could ask and it could reply, it would give up to us the most intimate secrets of life."

You would be hard pressed to find a book or movie that celebrated the sterility of rational decision-making over following the heart, but the behavioral investor demands statistics and not sonnets. As we examine the research around decision-making via intuition, a complex picture emerges that gives greater color to how and when individual discretion can be used and where it must be scrupulously avoided.

The evidence for intuition

The research on intuition is fascinating in part because some of the results seem downright metaphysical. One Cornell study tested intuition and precognition by asking participants to select between two "curtains" on a computer, one of which contained an erotic image. The slides were randomized, totally obscured by the digital curtain and yet, across all 100 sessions, participants showed an increased ability to correctly identify erotic slides than non-erotic slides! More incredible still, the subjects physiological responses tended to predict the correct curtain even a few seconds before the computer had created the image.

Another test of intuition presented participants with two decks of cards from which to draw with the aim being to make as much money as possible. One deck was constructed to give big wins followed by big losses, whereas the other deck was set to give small gains and almost no losses. Participants were told to look for a pattern and asked to articulate the rigging of the two different decks once they had figured it out. Participants were able to vocalize a hunch at about 50 cards and were able to speak definitively to the pattern at 80 cards, but registered an intuitive, physiological response much earlier. As early as ten cards in, participants' sweat glands on the palm opened slightly when reaching for a card from the more volatile deck. The subconscious knew what the conscious mind took much longer to articulate.

Ap Dijksterhuis has done pioneering work on the outcomes of intuitive versus deliberative decision-making that has resulted in some fascinating findings. Unsurprisingly, he finds that "consciousness has a low capacity, causing choosers to take into account only a subset of the relevant information when they decide." He also finds that conscious reflection can lead to inappropriately weighting data, leading to poor decisions that eventually lead to regret. For instance, participants who chose their favorite poster among a set of five after thinking deeply about the choice showed less post-decision satisfaction than participants who only looked at them briefly.

This deliberation-without-attention hypothesis makes the controversial claim that conscious thought, limited as it is in capacity, is best suited to making simple decisions, whereas unconscious thought should remain the purview of complex choices. If you need to choose an oven mitt, think deliberatively, but if you want to buy a house, tap intuition. To test this notion, researchers asked people to look at four cars that were objectively better or worse (the best car had 75% positive characteristics versus just 25% positive characteristics for the worst car). This was repeated across simple (four variable) and complex (12 variable) scenarios, with participants being asked to either deliberate on their decision for four minutes or by distracting them with anagrams before making a choice. Consistent with the deliberation-without-attention hypothesis, conscious decisions led to better choices in the four variable condition, but worsened in the 12 variable condition.

As complexity increases, deliberate thinking begins to fold in on itself and it becomes difficult to know how the various facets of a decision ought to be weighted. After all, how should one best compare a car with good gas mileage but limited visibility to another with good horsepower but mediocre aesthetic appeal? This effect doesn't seem limited to cars, either. Wilson and Schooler (1991) asked participants to evaluate different college courses and make decisions accordingly. In one condition, participants were asked to make a near-immediate decision about which course to take after only a cursory examination of the facts. In a second condition, participants were asked to carefully analyze the pros and cons of the various courses and write down their reasoning. As with the cars, those who deliberated more fully made worse decisions and focused on a more limited set of criteria. As complexity proliferates, decision-making ability disintegrates. More interesting still is that unconscious decisions seem to lead to better subjective appraisals post-choice. People tend to be happier with their choices when they don't give them much thought.

It's settled then! All we have to do to become stock picking experts is shut off our brains, rely on intuition and let the metaphysical magic of the subconscious take over. Well… not so fast. Because, for all of the wonderful evidence in favor of intuition, there is a great deal that speaks against it, especially when it comes to the specific task of making investment decisions. A 1968 study by Lewis Goldberg analyzed the performance of a model-based approach to assessing mental illness versus the clinical judgment of trained doctors. Not only did the simple model outperform the psychologists' intuition head-to-head, but it also bested psychologists who were given access to the model.[109]

Models have also been shown to outperform human intuition in predicting the outcomes of Supreme Court decisions,[110] Presidential elections (Nate Silver), movie preferences, prison recidivism, wine quality, marital satisfaction and military success, to name just a few of the over 45 domains in which they have demonstrated their superiority.[111] A meta-analysis performed by William Grove, David Zald, Boyd Lebow, Beth Snitz and Chad Nelson found that models equal or beat expert decision-making a whopping 94.12% of the time, meaning that they are only defeated by human discretion 5.88% of the time.[112] Moreover, many of the domains in which algorithms greatly outperformed had human behavior as a central component (as do financial markets). Job turnover, suicide attempts, juvenile delinquency, college academic performance, length of psychiatric hospitalization, and occupational choice all showed more than a 17-point effect size in favor of the algorithms.

Shanteau (1992) shows evidence that discretionary expertise and intuition are evident in livestock judges, astronomers, test pilots, soil judges, chess masters, physicists, mathematicians, accountants, grain inspectors, photo interpreters, and insurance analysts. Professions that showed poor evidence of discretionary expertise and intuition include stockbrokers,

---

[109]   W. Gray and T Carlisle, *Quantitative Value: A Practitioner's Guide to Automating Intelligent Investment and Eliminating Behavioral Errors* (Wiley, 2012), p. 27.

[110]   Gray and Carlisle, *Quantitative Value*, p. 27.

[111]   B. Carlson, *A Wealth of Common Sense* (Bloomberg, 2015), p. 93.

[112]   W. Gray, J. Vogel and D. Foulke, *DIY Financial Advisor: A Simple Solution to Build and Protect Your Wealth* (Wiley, 2015), p. 23.

clinical psychologists, psychiatrists, college admissions counsellors, judges, human resources professionals and intelligence analysts.

Noticing a trend? The more central humans are to the discipline in question, the less intuition and human judgment work. You can make great discretionary choices about wind sheer, soil density or a profit and loss statement, but introducing the peccadillos of humankind makes it an altogether different conversation. Sure enough, Shanteau lists the following as the criteria for making good discretionary decisions: predictable outcomes, static stimuli and the availability of good feedback. Capital markets, in which human behavior is absolutely central, meet none of these conditions.

Forecasting guru Philip Tetlock says emphatically what the meta-analysis says statistically: "It is impossible to find any domain in which humans clearly outperformed crude extrapolation algorithms, less still sophisticated statistical ones." The research is unequivocal – if you are using human judgment instead of a process to make investment decisions, you are doing more work for a diminished result.

Cultivating intuition

One spring day, Pablo Picasso was sitting in a park, sketching, when he was approached by a fan of his work who recognized the great man. Ecstatic, she begged the artist to draw a quick portrait of her. Picasso humored his fan and spent a few brief moments drawing before handing the woman the portrait. The woman began exclaiming about how perfect the drawing was, how artfully it captured her essence and how it was certain to be treasured by generations to come. When she asked Picasso how much she owed him, he replied, "$5,000, madam." Aghast at such an exorbitant fee for just a few minutes work, the woman protested, reminding Picasso that the entirety of the work only took him five minutes. Looking her squarely in the eye, the artist offered this rejoinder: "No, madam, it took me my whole life."

Intuition is the silent coming together of a lifetime of learning and must be cultivated if it is to be useful. Crandall and Getchell-Reiter (1993) relate the story of nurses in neonatal intensive care units (NICU) who learned to detect sepsis in infants even before it would be flagged by medical tests. When asked how they had developed this remarkable ability, the nurses had no answer. They just could. When researchers began to study this gift, they found that many of the nurses' correct intuitions ran contrary to common best practices and that almost none of them had appeared in the medical literature. The nurses had nurtured intuitive expertise through the simple, unglamorous process of long hours of hard work accompanied by immediate feedback. Like Picasso, their genius was born of the mundane and not the miraculous.

Simon (1992) offers a definition of intuition that squares with both my knowledge of the literature and my anecdotal experience: "The situation has provided a cue: This cue has given the expert access to information stored in memory, and the information provides the answer. Intuition is nothing more and nothing less than recognition." All too often, investment coaches position "listening to your gut" as some sort of unequivocal good. In truth, that advice is only as good as the degree to which the decision lends itself to intuitive judgment and level at which your gut has been educated.

But even the best-informed intuition is only as good as the milieu in which it finds itself and environmental cues remain the best predictor of whether or not intuition can be trusted. In the absence of a certain level of predictability and rapid feedback, neither of which are present in financial markets, intuition lacks soil fertile enough to take root. We have reason to trust the intuition of a NICU nurse, a physicist or a mathematician, but very little reason believe the instincts of a therapist or stock picker (sadly, I am both). Such intuitive shortcomings are not the fault of the experts in question, but rather the discipline in which they ply their trade. As Murray Gell-Mann correctly noted, "Imagine how hard physics would be if electrons could think."

Intuition is powerful in many domains but ill suited to the vagaries of allocating capital. Understanding this to be the case, some investors learn all that they can about markets and seek to deploy that knowledge in good times and bad through the exercise of free will, our next area of consideration.

Free will

Did you choose to read this book?

The question seems so obvious as to be absurd, "Of course I chose to read this book," you think, "and I'm going to choose to quit reading it if you keep asking me stupid questions." A subjective experience of free will is at the heart of the human experience; it feels like we are living our lives deliberately and that our minds are heading up that effort. As William James observed more artfully, "the whole sting and excitement of our voluntary life… depends on our sense that in it things are really being decided from one moment to another, and that it is not the dull rattling off of a chain that was forged innumerable ages ago."

But James himself, the grandfather of modern psychology, was among the first to posit that free will may well flow from the body to the brain and not the other way around as it is more commonly perceived. According to James, the brain might become aware of a physical impulse like increased heart rate so quickly that its impact on cognition would be imperceptible. Although the body was truly driving the brain, our perception would be the exact inverse. Controversial at the time, James' ideas have become increasingly mainstream as our ability to study sensation and perception has increased.

Solomon Asch, a pioneering gestalt psychologist, conducted studies of group conformity that are still widely discussed today. Asch's conformity study was conducted with groups of eight individuals, seven of whom were "confederates" of the study, which is to say, in on the joke. The participants were asked to look at a series of lines and determine which line on the right was the same length as the line on the left. The stimulus was similar to the one you see pictured below.

During the first two administrations of the test (there were 18 total), the confederates were instructed to give the appropriate answer. But starting with the third iteration, the seven confederates gave the same incorrect answer and the researchers noted the responses of the one respondent unaware of what was going on. Clearly, the point was to determine to what degree the clueless volunteer succumbed to conformity versus giving what was plainly the correct answer. In the first two iterations, the oblivious participant gave the correct answer over 99% of the time.

When the effects of conformity began to take hold, they gave the correct answer just 67% of the time. The problem itself could be no simpler – the correct line is evident to even my grade school children – but the effects of conformity proved irresistible for a large subset of the experimental population.

Asch line drawings

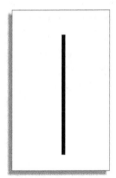 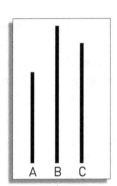

In a stroke of good fortune, modern science has given us access to technology that Solomon Asch could only have dreamed of in his day – functional magnetic resonance imaging (fMRI). This technology allows us to monitor the brain activity of volunteers in a modern-day version of Asch's experiment and gives greater context as to how these decisions are made. Neural images of those who conformed showed limited activity in the forebrain, the part of the mind associated with critical judgment.

Instead, they evinced activity in the posterior brain, an area associated with vision and perception. Rather than simply doubting their choices or making a choice to follow the crowd, the brain scans suggest that those who were swayed by conformity may have capitulated because the opinions of the crowd actually changed the physical means by which they apprehended the size and shape of the lines! Peer pressure had not simply shaped opinions, it had morphed reality. Study leader Gregory Berns said it well: "We like to think that seeing is believing" but the study suggest that, "seeing is believing what the group tells you to believe."

EEG research backs up the findings of the Asch Experiment 2.0 and provides further evidence that the body first registers what the mind only later becomes aware of. The exact moment that we become aware of our intention to act in a certain way trails the initial wave of brain activity by 300 milliseconds, a small but important gap. What's more, our ability to act on that behavior lags our awareness by another 200 milliseconds at a minimum, meaning that we experience a desire before we can even articulate or act on that desire. Because this all operates beneath our consciousness, our lived experience is of free will when in fact, "both the sensation of intention and the overt action are caused by prior events which are inaccessible to consciousness." Our experience of thinking and then acting on that thought misses the crucial first step by which an impulse imprints on us physically, catalyzing the whole chain reaction.

Even if we suppose that free will exists at some level (for what it's worth I believe that it does), there is an enormous body of evidence supporting the idea of automated financial decision-making.

Willpower

The tedium of lengthy road trips provides opportunities for conversations – both trivial and thought provoking – that might otherwise never occur. On one such trip with my wife, having exhausted all of our "would you rather" scenarios (e.g., Would you rather no one attend your wedding or your funeral?), the conversation turned to weightier matters. When asked, my wife noted that she would have liked to be born in America in the 1960s if given the option of any time and any place. My immediate follow up question was, "If you had been alive then, do you think you would have been a vocal proponent of racial equality and civil rights?" This led to related questions such as, "Would you have stood against the oppression of your Jewish neighbors?" if you had lived in 1940s Europe. In a cold state and with the benefit of history, it is easy to imagine oneself as a moral crusader, but the research on behavior and willpower tells a more complicated story.

Stanley Milgram, a Yale psychologist, studied our willpower in the face of authority. Milgram's study, conducted less than 20 years after the conclusion of World War II, set out to answer the question, "Were the Nazi rank and file culpable accomplices or just regular men following orders?" To test this, Milgram recruited psychologically healthy men to take part in a study that purported to study the relationship between punishment and learning. Participants would teach a "learner" on the other side of a brick wall a series of exercises. Then the teacher would gauge learning by asking a question of the learner. If they gave the correct answer, they would proceed to the next question. An incorrect response would lead the teacher to administer a punishment (electric shock) of ascending intensity with each subsequent missed question. The deception involved in the study was that in place of a learner, there were actually only tape-recorded screams that led the teacher to believe that he (all participants were male) was harming his pupil.

To simulate the effects of authority, a "doctor" in a grey lab coat sat inside the room where the test was being administered and gently prodded the participant to "please continue with the experiment" in the event that he became unsettled with harming the learner. Before conducting the experiment, Milgram asked his students, other professionals and even Holocaust historians what percentage of respondents would shock a stranger with a near-lethal (so they thought) level of voltage for missing a few silly problems on an exam. Across the board, estimates were in the low single digits. In reality, nearly two-thirds of participants shocked the learner all the way to the maximum level!

In a twist on the study, Milgram denigrated the character of the learner before beginning the experiment by telling the teacher that they had been "acting like an animal" before being situated across the wall. When the authority figure besmirched the good name of the learner, the willingness to shock all the way to 450 volts rose to over 90%. In a follow-on study, Milgram interviewed those who had shocked the learner to the maximum level and all agreed, in direct contradiction to the data, that they would be unwilling to do harm to a stranger if so instructed by an authority figure. Milgram's primary finding was, "often it is not so much the kind of person a man is as the kind of situation in which he finds himself that determines how he will act." Willpower, it seems, has more to do with circumstance than personal fortitude, a realization that can pain a human family longing to feel in control.

Evidence from the world of marketing shows us just how contextual our behaviors really are. Martin Lindstrom reports that, "when classical music was piped over loudspeakers in the London Underground, robberies dropped by 33%, assaults on staff by 25%, and vandalism of trains and stations by 37%."[113]

He goes on to relate that environment can determine whether we choose to buy a bottle of French Chardonnay or German Riesling. Says Lindstrom, "Over a two-week period, two researchers at the University of Leicester played either accordion heavy, recognizably French music or a German bierkeller brass band over the speakers of the wine section inside a large supermarket. On French music days, 77% of consumers brought French wine, whereas on bierkeller music days, the vast majority of consumers made a beeline for the German section of the store."

Opportunity, not personal ethics or religious affiliation, is also the best predictor of marital infidelity and studies show that wealthy, good looking people who travel frequently are the most likely to stray. One survey of marital infidelity found that Audi drivers were the most likely to cheat, followed by BMW and Mercedes. Why no Kia? Well, it's not because Kia drivers are morally superior to people who drive Bimmers and Benzes, it's because nobody wants to sleep with someone who drives a Kia! It's easy for us to sit in judgment of people like Tiger Woods who cheat on their spouse, but his actions would invariably be repeated by many of his accusers who found themselves in a position of similar opportunity.

If something as simple as music can impact everything from vandalism to vino to va-va-vooming outside of marriage, imagine how dramatically our behavior is shaped by the bombardment of financial news and opinions we receive during a time of financial tumult. An investor may know in her heart that she ought to be greedy when others are fearful, but she is also receiving powerful contextual cues in the form of CNBC commentators telling her that the sky is falling, to say nothing of the fear she feels when opening her quarterly portfolio statements. As much

[113] M. Lindstrom, *Buyology: Truth and Lies About Why We Buy* (Crown Business, 2010), p. 158.

as we may hate to admit it, research shows that you are about as weak or strong, good or evil, as the situations in which you find yourself.

And if willpower being so contextually determined wasn't bad enough, even when we do exert self-control, research suggests that our limited reserves are quickly used up. In one study, students were asked to memorize and recall either seven or two digits, at which time they would be rewarded with their choice of either fruit or cake. A majority (59%) of those with the easy task chose the healthy option, while almost two-thirds (63%) of those who memorized the longer string of numbers went with the cake. Similar studies have shown that dieters who pass on a basket of snacks offered early in the day eat more ice cream as part of a taste test later in the day. When our limited reserves of restraint are depleted in one area, they seem to give way elsewhere.

One common critique of lab studies is that they lack real-life applicability because of their low stakes. "Fruit and cake are one thing, but people act differently when real dollars are on the line," they say. But willpower fatigue was very much on display in an actual study of car buyers and the results cost them thousands of dollars. Buyers customizing their cars were studied as they chose between, among others things, four styles of gearshift, 13 varieties of rims, 25 engine configurations and fully 56 different interior colors. Early in the process, customers carefully thought through and rationally weighed each decision, but as the process wore on the willpower wore out. Decisions made later in the process were far less vetted and customers were much more likely to settle for the dealer's chosen default. As dealers began to understand this tendency, they reoriented the presentation of options with high dollar options coming last, and ended up charging the buyers about $2,000 more than when the big ticket items had been positioned earlier in the sequence. Even when the stakes are high, there is just so much restraint that we are able to muster.

Baumeister, whose work around emotion, willpower and decision-making is enormously applicable to investors, concludes his 2003 paper with a summary of the findings on the subject. They include:

- Emotional distress (the kind caused by market volatility) leads to a failure to consider all options and shifts people in favor of high-risk, high-reward payoffs, even if they are objectively poor choices.

- When self-esteem is threatened (I'm looking at you struggling hedge fund manager), people lose their ability to self-regulate. Arrogant people in particular (did I mention hedge fund managers?) rush to prove their critics wrong, even if it means taking big risks.

- The need to belong is a central feature of human motivation and when this need is thwarted (as it must necessarily be in patient, contrarian investing) irrational and self-defeating acts become more commonplace.

When asked how he survived the horrors of the Holocaust, renowned Austrian psychiatrist (and my personal hero) Viktor Frankl said, "Between stimulus and response there is a space. In that space is our power to choose our response. In that response lies our growth and freedom." The experience of Frankl, who lost everything and everyone he loved in the concentration camps, seems to speak against the more deterministic stance I have just taken with respect to free will. Frankl had every excuse to return hate with hate and yet he survived and thrived through force of will and a focus on personal meaning that he shared with the world in *Man's Search for Meaning*, perhaps the greatest book ever written.

But as important as Frankl's story is, it is revered in large part because it is so improbable. Faced with similar odds, few of us would show Frankl's level of resilience. The larger conversation about whether free will exists is beyond both the scope of this book and my mental capacity. But the particular point, that investing behavior is dramatically impacted by externalities, is one that all who put money to work should grasp. The behavioral investor understands the true freedom that exists in understanding freedom's limits.

Chapter 14.
Behavioral Investing is Risk First Investing

"The best plan is... to profit by the folly of others."

— PLINY THE ELDER

AT THE HEIGHT of the dot.com boom, the stock of the stodgy Computer Literacy Inc. rose by 33% in a single day simply by changing their name to fatbrain.com. Funnier still is the tale of Mannatech Inc., whose shares shot up 368% in the first two days following the initial public offering. Tech-crazed investors (ahem, speculators) were keen to invest in anything to do with the internet and a company called Mannatech certainly sounded like it fit the bill. The only problem was that Mannatech makes laxatives.

These two stories may sound like aberrations cherry-picked to prove a point, but in the run up to the NASDAQ crash, companies that changed their name to include some mention of the internet outperformed their peers by 63%! In theory, a stock is as valuable as its discounted future profits. In reality, something as silly as a name change can have a dramatic impact.

It is in the best interest of the behavioral investor that errors like this exist; they are the source of potential outperformance. However, the very same human frailties that give life to behavioral arbitrage give birth to the wealth destroying realities of bubbles, panics and crashes. In a phrase, it is the task of the behavioral investor to "exploit error and avoid terror."

Toil and trouble

It is a tribute to the enduring nature of human irrationality in markets that bubbles have existed since before the development of organized stock exchanges. In 15th century Germany, fractional interest in silver mines, called *kuxe*, were traded and even purchased on credit. As described on the website ValueWalk:

> "Transactions were settled at financial fairs during which share prices could fluctuate dramatically. These were famously condemned by Martin Luther in 1554: 'Ich will kein kuks haben! Es ist spiegelt, und es will nicht wudeln [gedeihen] dasselbige gelt.'
>
> 'I will have nothing to do with kuxen. They are play money and will not generate hard cash.' "

One generation after the *kuxe* bubble, the Dutch Golden Age gave rise to the Tulip Bubble, where a single bulb traded for as much as a townhome. But living through a bubble seems to do very little to inoculate the coming generation against similar folly. The International Monetary Fund reports that bubbles are now regarded as a "recurrent feature of modern economic history" and cites 23 instances of stock market bubbles in just the US and UK between 1800 and 1940. Bubbles have been and always will be with us and the investor that ignores these dramatic dislocations from fundamental value does so at her own peril.

It makes sense that bubbles occur in financial markets fraught with uncertainty, but Vernon Smith and his co-authors actually found that bubbles seem to occur naturally, even in markets with well-defined prices and a finite time horizon. Smith and company gave subjects some

List of some notable manias, panics and crashes

Tulip mania (Netherlands) – 1637

South Sea Bubble (UK) – 1720

Bengal Bubble (UK) – 1769

Credit Crisis of 1772 (UK)

Financial Crisis of 1791 (US)

Panic of 1796–7 (US)

Panic of 1819 (US)

Panic of 1825 (UK)

Panic of 1837 (US)

Panic of 1847 (UK)

Panic of 1857 (US)

Panic of 1866 (UK)

Black Friday (US) – 1869

Paris Bourse crash of 1882 (France)

"Encilhamento" (Brazil) – 1890

Panic of 1893 (US)

Panic of 1896 (US)

Panic of 1901 (US)

Panic of 1907 (US)

Great Depression (US) – 1929

Recession of 1937–8 (US)

Brazilian Market Crash of 1971

British Market Crash of 1973–4

Souk Al-Manakh Crash (Kuwait) – 1982

Black Monday (US) – 1987

Rio de Janeiro Stock Exchange Crash – 1989

Japanese Asset Price Bubble – 1991

Black Wednesday (UK) – 1992

Asian Financial Crisis – 1997

Russian Financial Crisis – 1998

dot.com Bubble (US) – 2000

Chinese Stock Bubble – 2007

Great Recession of 2007–9 (US)

European Sovereign Debt Crisis (2010)

Flash Crash of 2010 (US)

money and let them trade a financial asset whose fundamental value was well known (i.e., equal to the expected dividends it paid) over a clearly defined period of time. Even in this controlled setting, prices rose well above true value, only to come crashing down near the end of the time horizon.

A great deal of work has gone into trying to replicate the results of Smith's study and to determine whether the findings are robust to various markets and market participants. "Experienced" traders (i.e., those who have played the game before) can learn to extinguish bubbles with repeated practice, but form the bubbles once again as soon as the valuation numbers change. The simulated market has been run allowing short selling, using different kinds of markets, with a variety of rules. In all conditions, bubbles occur.

A Harvard study sought to replicate Smith's work with one important departure: there was no ability to speculate and no "greater fool" to whom inflated assets could be passed on. Even in this kid-gloved simulation, you guessed it, bubbles and crashes occur. As this study reports, "the results suggest that the departures from fundamental values are not caused by the lack of common knowledge of rationality leading to speculation, but rather by behavior that itself exhibits elements of irrationality." Even in experimental markets artificially constrained in ways that real-world never will be, error and terror reign.

The shape of bubbles

While Shiller's effort to create diagnostic criteria for bubbles is laudable, the fact is that no two are exactly alike. Sure, they have common features like inflated asset values, but what happens next (which is all that matters) is far less predictable. In a path-breaking work on the nature of bubbles, Greenwood, Shleifer and You ('Bubbles for Fama') share some fascinating findings. Among the most compelling is that only a slight majority of bubbles actually burst. The researchers identify 40 bubbles (defined as a 100% run up in two years or less) from 1928 to present, but note that just over half crashed (defined as a 40% loss over two years or less). Among those bubbles that did eventually burst, the damage was swift and pervasive: "In 17 of the 21 episodes in which there is a crash, the industry experiences a single-month return of –20% or worse during the drawdown period."

Another interesting finding was that the size of the crash was largely commensurate with the size of the run up – dramatic increases in price tended to lead to more dramatic drawdowns. As Michael Batnick of Ritholtz Wealth Management writes in his summary of their research, "If shares in an industry increased by 50%, the probability of a crash over the next two years is just 20%. A 100% return increased the odds of a crash to 53%, and a 150% return increased the odds of a crash to 80%." The takeaway? Only about half of bubbles burst, but when they do – watch out.

Can you spot a bubble?

Dr. Robert Shiller, Nobel Laureate in Economics, suggests that bubbles can be diagnosed using a checklist in much the same manner that a psychologist would examine the mental health of a patient against the diagnostic criteria for a given mental illness. Dr. Shiller offers the following as a starting point for spotting bubbles:

- Have asset prices increased sharply?

- Is there public excitement about these price increases?

- Is there an accompanying media frenzy?

- Are there envy-inducing stories of common people striking it rich?

- Is there a growing interest in the asset class among the general public?

- Do "new era" theories seek to justify steep valuations?

- Have lending standards declined?

Tell me a story

As a child in Sunday School I was taught that the Devil was dangerous, not because he was conspicuously evil, but because he was a master of seductive half-truths. Likewise, it can be said that nearly every bubble begins with a grain of truth. It is only when that truth becomes distorted through human narrative that the danger is made manifest.

It is true that the internet changed our lives and revolutionized the way that the world does business. The untruth was that any company with a .com after their name would be a party to that revolution. Bubbles are born and die on fundamentals but are fueled by our need to create stories all along the way. The process typically looks something like this:

- Price gains occur for fundamental reasons.

- Increasing prices attract attention.

- Narratives emerge to explain price gains.

- The positive narrative begets a cascade of increased price and volume.

- Narrative is broken, causing a return to fundamentals.

Robert Shiller defines a bubble as "a social epidemic where price increases lead to further price increases" and stories are the means by which a spark of fundamental value becomes a raging fire of irrationality.

Teeter and Sandberg speak to the power of story to create and sustain bubbles in the aptly named, 'Cracking the Enigma of Asset Bubbles with Narratives' and cite three specific reasons why narrative is so powerful. First, asset bubbles typically form around new ideas or innovations for which there is limited historical precedent. This being the case, historical measures of fair value are either non-existent or seen as not being directly applicable. In the absence of historical data, story rules. Second, bubbles tend to occur during periods of loose regulation and easy credit, and the euphoria of such environments privileges story over analysis. Finally, in a high-speed world with a glut of investment opportunities, our ability to process each possible offering is diminished by the sheer complexity, number and speed of what is on offer. In this noisy environment, story offers a welcome respite from the more tedious and cognitively taxing labors of quantitative due diligence. Stories help us make sense in the absence of data and provide quick and dirty approximations of value, but what happens when the story changes?

In my second TEDx talk, 'Sex, Funds and Rock N' Roll', I speak to some of the ways in which decision-making with respect to romantic love has a great deal in common with financial decision-making in times of mania. In short, being in love with a person or a stock tends to lead us to believe in a *happily ever after* and ignore data points more germane to making a good choice.

Arthur Schopenhauer commented on the power of sexual desire to cloud decision-making, saying: "We should not be surprised by marriages between people who would have never been friends... Love... casts itself on people who, apart from sex, would be hateful, contemptible, and even abhorrent to us... Directly after copulation the devil's laughter is heard." The Japanese actually have a word for the period of post-coital lucidity – *kenjataimu* – which translates to "the time of the wise man."

Freed from sexual desire, we begin to evaluate our decisions on a more rational plane and may regret choices made the night before or question our choice of partner. Similarly, investors have a moment of *kenjataimu* when the stories that have propped up the self-reinforcing effects of a bubble give way to the dispassionate return to market fundamentals. In love and money, stories only last so long, and eventually give way to harsher realities. To torture this metaphor just a little more, a behavioral investor must learn to enjoy the benefits of flirtation while being sure not to marry someone regrettable.

Trust but verify

In a very real sense, it is a scary proposition to entrust your hard-earned wealth to a market insane enough to drive a laxative company into the stratosphere simply for having "tech" in its name. Likewise, understanding the frequency and severity of bubbles, panics and crashes can make even the steeliest investor want to hide his money in the backyard. But just as surely as knowledge of error and terror are a prerequisite to successful investment management, they cannot be allowed to become all consuming distractions that lead investors to become overly bearish. The market has long punished pessimism and it is a truism that just because the market is crazy does not make you a shrink.

As William N. Goetzmann of Yale points out: "Placing a large weight on avoiding a bubble, or misunderstanding the frequency of a crash following a boom, is dangerous for the long-term investor." Ben Carlson makes similar points about the asymmetry of fear in his article, 'Crash Rules Everything Around Me':

- US stocks rose 400% in the 1980s, but all we can talk about is the 1987 crash.

- Bonds gave investors a total return of over 100% in the 1990s, but we focus on the interest rate spike of 1994.

- Emerging market stocks rose 185% in the 1990s, but we live in fear of the 1997 emerging market currency crisis.

Being a behavioral investor means being respectful and aware of bubbles and crashes without becoming paralyzed by that knowledge. The only insanity greater than not insulating yourself against wealth destroying crashes is becoming so fearful of them that you miss out on all of the good that markets do.

Maintaining this balance requires a system for becoming conservative that is rules-based, infrequent and accounts for both our short-term tendency to be raptured by stories and the longer-term tendency of the market to revert to fundamentals. Rather than being a slave to one intellectual camp or another, a behavioral investor must learn to use both value and momentum approaches for the time and season to which they are best suited.

Avoiding terror

On August 29, 2005, the 50 levees designed to protect the citizens of New Orleans, Louisiana failed, flooding over 100,000 homes and filling the city with tens of billions of gallons of water. The scope of the tragedy is hard to fully grasp. Over 1,800 lives were lost, one million people were displaced and $108 billion in damages occurred in what the Federal Emergency Management Agency (FEMA) calls, "the single most catastrophic disaster in US history."

Most of the damage done during Hurricane Katrina was attributable to Acts of God, but mankind had its share of blame as well. The levees, thought to be a nearly impenetrable last defense against flooding, were a downright failure. The reasons for this are myriad: a miscalculation of soil density, the incompleteness of as many as one-third of the levees, the use of improper materials, and the fact that many of the levees were considerably too short, which lead to "overtopping." In many places, the levees reached a height of only ten feet and were helpless against the 24-foot waves wrought by the storm. The problem with the levees was one that is often observed in finance: they were designed to manage the greatest storm that had ever been and not the greatest storm that could ever be.

The process of stress testing used by banks and risk managers looks to the past for information on the duration, strength and severity of market drawdowns and tries to ensure that processes are in place that are historically robust. The problem with this, of course, is that *The Greatest Crash of All Time* only retains that crown until it doesn't. There is no guarantee, and even very little reason to believe, that all that has been is all that will ever be. Nassim Taleb refers to this ruinous thinking as "the Lucretius Problem," named for the Latin poetic philosopher who opined that the fool believes that the tallest mountain in the world will be equal to the tallest one he has observed. A related problem is the "turkey problem," named for the foolish fowl enjoyed at Thanksgiving. If the turkey simply appeals to historical truths he will be greatly misled about the true nature of risk. The farmer appears every day bearing gifts of water and grain, that is, until the one day that he arrives wielding an ax. While there may be no historical precedent for such behavior, it sure matters to the turkey once it appears.

Like a mostly-benevolent-but-sometimes-homicidal farmer, the market mostly giveth but can certainly take away in dramatic fashion. As a result, the thing to do is usually nothing at all. Buy and hold proponents Vanguard examined the performance of accounts that made no changes versus those who had made tweaks and found that the "no change" condition handily outperformed the tinkerers. Meir Statman cites research from Sweden showing that the heaviest traders lose 4% of their account value each year to trading costs and poor timing, and these results are consistent across the globe. Across 19 major stock exchanges, investors who made frequent changes trailed buy and hold investors by 1.5 percentage points per year. Jason Zweig pithily sums up the futility of excessive activity in his *Devils Financial Dictionary* definition of Day Trader: "n. See also IDIOT."

But for all of the evidence that market timing is foolish, there is equally compelling evidence that a buy and hold approach can yield unsatisfactory results for even the most patient investor. Michael Batnick published the table below, which provides a sobering look at how poor real returns can be over even long periods of time and how regular such occurrences truly are.

Real growth of one dollar

1929–1943	$1.08
1944–1964	$10.83
1965–1981	$0.94
1982–1999	$11.90
2000–present	$1.35

Urban Carmel, who writes at The Fat Pitch, shared some fascinating insights in his post, 'When Buy and Hold Works and When It Doesn't.' He found that the S&P 500 was below its real (i.e., inflation adjusted) value 30 years later a surprising 15% of the time. In fact, in real dollars the S&P was below its 1929 peak in 1985 – 56 years later! Of course, this means that very long-term inflation-adjusted returns were positive 85% of the time, but this is small consolation if your entire investment lifetime is a period of low to negative growth.

Using a metric called Tobin's Q (much like the price-to-earnings ratio but with a more stable balance sheet calculation instead of earnings), Carmel illustrates (unsurprisingly) that long periods of underperformance are preceded by steep valuations. Twenty-year periods of paltry to negative performance have been preceded by Q values greater than 1, a level attained in 1929 (1.07), during the Tech Bubble (1.64) and at the time of writing (1.15).

Revisiting Batnick's periods of low real returns using Shiller CAPE, we also observe that long periods of poor performance often begin with overvaluation that is worked off over time. The Shiller CAPE levels of the broad market on January 1 of each the years cited above were as follows:

- 1929 – 27.06

- 1944 – 11.05

- 1965 – 23.27

- 2000 – 43.77

- Today – 28.80

- Mean – 16.67

Over the past 100 years, the ability of the global economy to create and compound wealth has staggered the mind and stymied the permanently pessimistic. But the blossoming of global prosperity has not occurred without significant stretches of scorched-earth volatility. Indeed, as Meb Faber points out, "all of the G-7 countries have experienced at least one period where stocks lost 75% of their value. The unfortunate mathematics of a 75% decline require an investor to realize a 300% gain just to get back to even." He goes on to say:

> "Individuals invested in US stocks in the late 1920s and early 1930s, German asset classes in the 1910s and 1940s, Russian stocks in 1927, Chinese stocks in 1949, US real estate in the mid-1950s, Japanese stocks in the 1980s, emerging markets and commodities in the late 1990s, and nearly everything in 2008, would reason that holding these assets was a decidedly unwise course of action. Most individuals do not have a sufficiently long time frame to recover from large drawdowns from risky asset classes."

Buy and hold makes sense for most people most of the time, but this is no guarantee that your timeline or context will make it sound advice for you in particular.

Of rules and their exceptions

Thus, the student of market psychology finds himself at an awkward crossroads. He understands that market timing is typically ineffectual, but is also aware of times in history when broad market levels have become obviously and grossly disconnected from any measure of fundamental value. From the Roaring 20s and the Nifty Fifty to the Tech Bubble and the Housing Crisis, periods of mania have been relatively frequent, easy to spot with typical valuation metrics and have had dramatic wealth-destroying effects.

If the rule is "don't time the market," is it possible that there are ever exceptions to the rule? I believe that there are and that consistent with our behavioral emphasis on contrarianism, they are infrequent, painful to implement and will run directly contrary to what feels right. As Howard Marks says, the perversity of risk is that it is most present when it is least felt.

It is therefore incumbent upon the behavioral investor to create a system that allows him to get most of the grain while scrupulously avoiding beheading. Most of the time this means staying invested because what the market does most of the time is go up. Between 1872 and 2003, the S&P 500 was up 63% of years and down 37% of years. But research by First Trust drives home the necessity of a behavioral parachute in times of trouble. Although the average bull market is much longer than the average bear market (8.9 versus 1.3 years), the average cumulative loss in bear markets is 41%. In addition to the obvious financial carnage wrought by such a loss, the behavioral damage may be even greater. Very few people can see their wealth diminish by 41% and maintain the appropriate appetite for risk.

Much like an earthquake, no one knows when the next market crash is coming, but that doesn't mean we can't create a system that becomes more conservative when the ground starts to shake. As Nassim Taleb says, "Not seeing a tsunami or an economic event coming is excusable; building something fragile to them is not." All of this of course begs the question, "What might such a system look like?"

Seeking to create systems to thwart the catastrophic losses just mentioned, some investors have turned to momentum-based models.

The most commonly used of these is some variant of a 200-day moving average, where an asset class is held as long as it is above the 200-day average of its price and sold when it dips below. Much like momentum in physics, the theory with price momentum is that both strength and weakness will persist. Jeremy Siegel applied this approach to both the Dow Jones Industrial Average (DJIA) and NASDAQ in his classic, *Stocks for the Long Run*. Siegel's test bought the index when it closed at least 1% above the 200-day moving average and moved to Treasury bills when it closed at least 1% below. Using this simple, mechanical strategy, Siegel notes modest outperformance when applied to the DJIA and a healthy 4% per annum outperformance when tested on the NASDAQ from 1972 to 2006.

Taking a similar approach, Meb Faber tested a ten-month moving average (ten-month SMA) approach in his 'A Quantitative Approach to Tactical Asset Allocation,' now the second most downloaded paper on The Social Science Research Network. Faber measured the ten-month average at the end of the last trading day of each month and bought when the monthly price was above the ten-month SMA and sold and moved to cash when the monthly price was below that level. The simplicity of Faber's approaches belies its power to decrease volatility and compound returns – the results were dramatic. From 1901 to 2012, the timing model returned 10.18% per year as opposed to 9.32% for the S&P 500. More impressive still, it decreased volatility sizably, from 17.87% to 11.97%, and amplified returns accordingly. While $100 invested in the index became $2,163,361, the timing model yielded a final value of $5,205,587.

Many investors, steeped in the buy and hold tradition, will find it irksome that I am suggesting that there are instances, however rare, when investors should seek safety and time the market. Many will point to the example of Warren Buffett who has said repeatedly that his favorite holding period is forever, as someone assiduously averse to any form of market timing. However, Buffett's words are a classic case of "do as I say not as I do." As Jesse Felder reported in 2017, at that moment Berkshire Hathaway was sitting on its largest pile of cash ever (over $50 billion) at a time when equity valuations were rivaled only by their Tech Wreck, Great Recession and Great Depression levels. As

David Rolfe says of the Oracle of Omaha, "The guy's just not going to spend the cash to spend it. (He's) the best market timer I ever saw."

Speaking of Buffett, a less pithy but more pertinent quote can be found in his 1992 Berkshire Hathaway Chairman's Letter: "The investment shown by the discounted-flows-of-cash calculation to be the cheapest is the one that the investor should purchase... Moreover, though the value equation has usually shown equities to be cheaper than bonds, that results is not inevitable: When bonds are calculated to be the more attractive investment, they should be bought."

The Oracle is not an "all stocks all the time" investor, but rather a thoughtful allocator who, let's face it, times the market. Buffett market-timed the internet bubble and he is doing so again today, not out of recklessness but out of an understanding of probability. High prices paired with slack momentum and negative sentiment has always presaged poor returns. This time could be different but I'm not counting on that and neither is Buffett.

Peter Lynch correctly quipped that, "far more money has been lost by investors preparing for corrections or trying to anticipate corrections, than has been lost in corrections themselves." But as Jesse Felder points out in his *Felder Report*, it should be noted that Lynch's milieu must be taken into account when assessing his record and advice. Lynch's career, spanning from 1977 to 1990, included a time period during which equities hovered right at one standard deviation below their average valuation (as measured by market cap to GDP). By comparison, we currently find ourselves more than two standard deviations *above* the average by that very same measure. In fact, the most richly valued month in Lynch's career (September, 1987) is directly comparable to the absolute nadir of the last 15 years (March, 2009). Periods of cheap valuation like the markets Lynch lived through lead to positive forward returns and make buy and hold approaches very attractive. Just as a six foot tall man can drown in a river that is three feet deep on average, investors can drown in equity markets that average 10% a year returns over long periods of time.

Rule-based behavioral approaches like ours seek first and foremost to tilt probability in favor of the investor, which means that the default behavior for market participants should be patience, calm and inactivity.

Likewise, any rules aimed at timing market participation should lead to infrequent action and look for every excuse to stay invested.

The Philosophical Economics blog suggests an interesting twist on market timing – specifically, looking at market timing in much the same way that we consider asset allocation. An investor with a long-term 40/60 allocation to stocks and cash would have little hope of an impressive return, tilted as they are toward safety. Likewise, any system that keeps investors on the sidelines 60% of the time will harm their performance dramatically. However, just as a prudent investor might keep a small portion of her wealth in low-risk assets for protection of principal and sanity, a behavioral investor can follow a systematic process for infrequently taking risk off of the table when the market is poised to do its worst. Indiscriminate, gut-level, frequent activity is a sin, no doubt, but I echo Cliff Asness in saying that, "Market timing is an investment sin, and for once I recommend that you sin a little."

Chapter 15.
Behavioral Investing has No Masters of the Universe

IT GOES WITHOUT saying that most asset managers are tasked with generating large returns, but imagine for a moment that you were given just the opposite task; to create a portfolio designed to do as poorly as possible. Where might you begin to assemble such a monstrosity?

You might begin by violating some of the foundational assumptions of good investing by having an undiversified portfolio of, say, just five stocks. You might further throw a wrench in the works by purchasing stocks with high valuations (shown in the research to do poorly over time), or that are thinly traded. But despite your best efforts to create a stinker of a portfolio, it is entirely possible that this dumpster fire would in fact perform very well!

Sure, holding just a few stocks increases your chances of underperformance, but it simultaneously increases your chances of outperforming a benchmark. Buying expensive (high valuation) stocks has tended to be a poor decision over long periods of time, but in the short run it is indicative of high hopes for the future. Try as you might, it is entirely possible that even the most haphazardly slapped together group of holdings could in fact perform very admirably.

Now daydream with me that you are charged with performing as poorly as possible in a game of chess. Not so hard is it? In fact, if you're like me, getting destroyed at chess is the easy part and performing well would be the difficult task. When considering whether a task is one of primarily luck or skill, Michael Mauboussin suggests that we do the very thing we just attempted: we try to fail on purpose. Games of skill are hard to fail on purpose – you could win at roulette despite your best efforts to the contrary – but winning a game of skill is much easier to throw intentionally. All of this begs the question, is investing primarily a game of luck or skill, and what are the implications for how we make investment decisions?

Professor Aswath Damodaran adds two additional conditions to Mauboussin's test of luck versus skill. For Damodaran, success requires both clear definitions and measurement over a robust number of trials. In skill-heavy games like basketball or chess, you win or lose. In golf, you are under or over par; success is clearly defined. Investing is a much different story. Consider a fund manager who was down just 10% in 2008. By relative measures this is an enormous success, he beat the benchmark by an incredible 2800 basis points! But in more practical terms this could still be construed as a failure. After all, you cannot buy a house or food with relative returns and even a small loss in relative terms can be quite dramatic in absolute terms. Should this sort of performance be considered success?

Turning our attention to the number of trials question, consider trying to judge the talent of a basketball player based on a single three point shot. Most anyone with sufficient arm strength will make a lucky three pointer from time to time, but the strength or weakness of any individual player becomes apparent only as they take hundreds of shots. Asset managers, whose careers typically last between 20 and 30 years, take a very limited number of shots if we consider one year to be the shortest length of time against which performance is considered. There are currently around 7,000 mutual funds and a roughly equivalent number of hedge funds. If we assume that these managers have a 50/50 chance of being above or below the benchmark on any given year, we could assume that there would be 420 managers who could be expected to outperform the benchmark for five years in a row, even if the whole affair was left entirely up to chance! Fourteen fund managers would be expected to beat the benchmark a full decade in a row, a feat that has rarely been achieved in practice.

Apologists who point to a few handfuls of successful investors over time, the "What about Buffett?!" argument, would do well to remember just how frequently even a totally skill-less endeavor would be expected to produce consistent winners. If anything, the evidence points to successful processes (e.g., value, momentum) as being the secret sauce of sustained success more than the innate gifts of a given individual. By all three measures, investing skews toward luck: success can be achieved by accident, performance measurements are hazy, and iterations are limited.

The last .400 hitter?

Marked by significant rule changes, baseball's modern era began in 1903. Over the 38 years that followed, seven different players batted .400 for a total of 12 instances (Rogers Hornsby, Ty Cobb and George Sisler all had multiple .400+ seasons). The last big leaguer to hit over .400 was Ted Williams in 1941. In the more than 70 seasons that have followed, no player in either league has hit over .400 and Rogers Hornsby's modern era record of .424 is expected by many never to be broken.

The reasons for this untouchable record have nothing to do with the absolute skill of the players involved. If anything, turning the Albert Pujols or Mike Trouts of the world loose on the pitchers of yesteryear would be a bloodbath; they are almost certainly better in absolute terms. The difference is rather that the rising tide of improved nutrition, better training, and sturdier equipment has raised all boats. As Larry Swedroe says, "In many forms of competition, such as chess, poker or investing, it's the *relative* level of skill that plays the more important role in determining outcomes, not the *absolute* level. The 'paradox of skill' means that even as skill level rises, luck can become more important in determining outcomes if the level of competition is also rising."[114] Hitters have improved, sure, but their improvements have slipped relative to the competition – namely, pitchers and fielders – and a similar trend seems to be afoot in investment management.

Just as the fame, notoriety and money involved in baseball have given rise to greater talent, the investment management industry has long

[114]   L. Swedroe, 'Why alpha's getting more elusive,' ETF.com (November 21, 2014).

robbed more consequential industries (like medicine) of great young minds precisely because of the financial rewards involved. Charlie Ellis noted in the *Financial Analysts Journal* that, "Over the past 50 years, increasing numbers of highly talented young investment professionals have entered the competition. ... They have more-advanced training than their predecessors, better analytical tools, and faster access to more information." The unsurprising result he says is that "the increasing efficiency of modern stock markets makes it harder to match them and much harder to beat them, particularly after covering costs and fees." Is it possible that Warren Buffett and Peter Lynch are to investing what Ted Williams and Ty Cobb are to baseball – the last .400 hitters?

The paradox of skill that some have posited theoretically, others have examined empirically and the results aren't pretty. In 'Luck Versus Skill in the Cross-Section of Mutual Fund Returns,' Eugene Fama and Kenneth French purport that there is only skill in the top two percentiles of managers they examined. Sebastian and Attaluri in their, 'Conviction in Equity Investing,' find that the percentage of managers delivering skill beyond fees and expenses has fallen from about 20% two decades ago to just 1.6% by 2011. Asked to summarize his work, Sebastian says that more than 98 of 100 institutionally-oriented equity investment products of all styles spanning the globe have failed to add true value above fees and costs.

Luck in skill's clothing

The decline in fund managers that show skill is not entirely attributable to the influx of talented young Ivy Leaguers vying for Bentleys and yachts. Sadly, much of what is labelled skill-based active management today is not active at all. Closet indexing, as passive-in-active-clothing is called, leaves investors with the worst of all possible worlds – high fees without meaningful differentiation – and the problem is more widespread than most imagine. Tom Howard of AthenaInvest found in his exploration of closet indexing that, "For the typical fund, low-conviction positions outnumber high-conviction positions by three-to-one."[115] Dr. Wesley Gray of Alpha Architect found that just 8% of ETFs

---

[115]   T. Howard, *Behavioral Portfolio Management* (Harriman House, 2014).

and 23% of mutual funds differed meaningfully from their benchmarks. What's more, Gray found that the more active a fund was, the more expensive it tended to be, with truly actively managed funds clocking in at an average of 128 basis points. The research is clear that the vast majority of actively managed funds do not differ meaningfully from their benchmarks, giving no possibility to exhibit skill, and those that do make investors pay handsomely for this. This combination of high fees and/or low conviction almost ensures that a fund will look skill-less, even if there are skilled people on the team.

Although there is more than a little luck involved in investing, research suggests that skill does exist, but can only be showcased when the manager has the guts to be different. In their 2009 paper, Martijn Cremers and Antti Petajisto introduced the concept of *active share*, or how greatly a portfolio differed from the benchmark against which it was compared. They found that truly active managers (those with 60% or greater differentiation from their index) had outperformed historically and that greater differentiation tended to lead to greater outperformance.

In his 2013 update, Petajisto found that high active share portfolios outperformed dramatically from 1990 to 2009 and that these active funds had tended to hold up well during periods of crisis. As he notes, "I found that the most active stock pickers have been able to add value to their investors, beating their benchmark indices by about 1.26% per year after all fees and expenses."

We will begin to see more skill as we start to see more guts.

Luck and its implications

Rounders is a 1998 movie starring John Malkovich, Edward Norton, Gretchen Mol and Matt Damon, which tells the story of a reformed gambler who must return to the world of high stakes poker to relieve a friend of a debt (spoiler alert: lest John Malkovich relieve the friend of his life). In one of my favorite scenes in the movie, Mike McDermott (Damon) is trying to convince his partner (Mol) that poker is in fact a game of skill. In a heated moment he shouts, "Why do you think the same five guys make it to the final table of the World Series of

Poker every year? What, are they the luckiest guys in Las Vegas? It's a skill game, Jo." We understand intuitively that there is an element of luck to poker and yet, Mike does have a point. If the whole thing is all about chance, how is that the same people have such regular success? The answer lies in understanding how best to prepare for games of luck versus games of chance.

Winning a skill-based game like chess or basketball requires the same thing that is needed to get to Carnegie Hall – practice. Tasks with a significant degree of luck require a different discipline altogether. They are won, over multiple iterations, by obedience to a set of rules. In a strange way, what matters in games with a strong element of chance is not the outcome of any particular event, but the quality of your decisions. You win at chess through repetition. You win at poker and investing through mental toughness. Poker theorist David Sklansky suggests that you should consider yourself the winner of a poker hand, not based on the eventual outcome, but by whether or not you had the highest probability of winning when all of the money went in the pot. The same goes in investing. Learning to score your investment wins and losses based on the quality of your decisions and not on the quality of the outcome is the key to managing your emotions, appropriately measuring your own performance and living to fight another day.

In his superb, *The Superinvestors of Graham-and-Doddsville*, Warren Buffett takes to task those who believe that the market is efficiently priced and that success within owes to sheer luck. He begins his discussion with a conversation about orangutans flipping coins. He concedes that if 225 million orangutans had engaged in a coin flipping exercise, 215 of them would be predicted to "call" 20 flips in a row correctly. But, he goes on:

> "If you found that 40 came from a particular zoo in Omaha, you would be pretty sure that you were on to something. So you would probably go out and ask the zookeeper about what he's feeding them, whether they had special exercises, what books they read, and who knows what else. That is, if you found any really extraordinary concentrations of success, you might want to see if you could

identify concentrations of unusual characteristics that might be causal factors."[116]

Buffett does not deny that luck is a part of the investment process, but he acknowledges a larger truth: consistent success in luck-heavy environments is attributable to good rules. In Buffett's case, the rules in question are the "buy cheap" teachings of value guru Benjamin Graham.

The discussion of luck versus skill in investment management goes far beyond theoreticals and should directly inform the way that behavioral investors structure their portfolios. Understanding that markets are part luck and part skill informs us that we should emphasize rules over practice and that we should hold portfolios that are diverse enough to protect against bad luck but differentiated enough to benefit from tilting probability in our favor in a rule-based manner.

Acknowledging the place of luck should chasten our ego in good times and soften our fall in bad times. And while success through strict obedience to rules is not as sexy as practicing three pointers like an NBA star, it has the potential to be just as rewarding.

[116] W. Buffett, 'The Superinvestors of Graham-and-Doddsville,' Columbia Business School (May 17, 1984).

Chapter 16.
Sample Behavioral Investment Factors

THIS FINAL CHAPTER will apply previous lessons around testing investing methods to two of the most discussed ideas in asset management – value and momentum. Consistent with our three-part test, we will begin by looking for empirical evidence and then take a closer look at the theoretical underpinnings and behavioral roots of these ideas. Additionally, we will discuss their interplay in a behavioral process called reflexivity that provides a model for thinking about the boom-bust cycles that are the product of human misreaction.

The evidence for value

Codified by Benjamin Graham and popularized by Warren Buffett, value investing is the practice of buying stocks believed to be trading at less than their intrinsic value. Basically, it's bargain shopping. Turning to our three determinants of an enduring factor, theoretically, it makes sense that paying less is preferable to paying more. Empirically, there is now over a century's worth of evidence data that value investing works. Lakonishok, Vishny and Shleifer examined the effect of price-to-book values on returns in, 'Contrarian Investment, Extrapolation and Risk.' They found that low price-to-book stocks (that is, value stocks) outperformed the high price-to-book glamour stocks 73% of the time over one-year periods, 90% of the time over three-year periods and 100% of the time over five-year periods.

In 'Decile Portfolios of the NYSE, 1967–1985,' Yale Professor Roger Ibbotson ranked stocks by deciles according to price-to-earnings ratios and measured their performance from 1967 to 1985. Ibbotson found that the stocks in the cheapest decile outperformed those in the most expensive decile by over 600% and the "average" decile by over 200% over that time period. In a similar study, Eugene Fama and Kenneth French examined all non-financial stocks from 1963 to 1990 and divided them into deciles based on their price-to-book values. Over the period of their study, the least expensive stocks returned almost three times as much as the most expensive.

One of the most exhaustive examinations of the various value factors was conducted by James P. O'Shaughnessy in his excellent read, *What Works on Wall Street*. O'Shaughnessy used the now-familiar methodology of dividing stocks into deciles and observing returns from 1963 to the end of 2009. His results highlight the efficacy of value investing and the power of slightly improved annualized returns to greatly compound wealth. Looking at price-to-earnings (P/E) ratios, he found that the cheapest decile of stocks with respect to P/E ratios turned $10,000 into $10,202,345 for a compound rate of return of 16.25% per year. Compare that to the index return of 11.22% that would have turned that same $10,000 into a mere $1,329,513. Buying cheap stocks would have made you $9,000,000 dollars more and done so with less volatility, defying the efficient market notion that more risk is required for great returns.[117]

But what of the most expensive decile of stocks, the glamour names? The highest decile of P/E ratios turned $10,000 into $118,820 by 2009, over one million dollars less than the index and $10 million less than buying the despised value stocks. These numbers illustrate dramatically the words of Warren Buffett: "You pay a very high price in the stock market for a cheery consensus. Uncertainty is actually the friend of the buyer of long-term values."[118] I could go on, but I imagine my point has

---

[117]   J. P. O'Shaughnessy, *What Works on Wall Street* (McGraw-Hill, 2011), p. 85.
[118]   LouAnn Lofton, *Warren Buffett Invests Like a Girl: And Why You Should, Too* (HarperBusiness, 2012), p. 71.

been well and truly proven by now. Value stocks tend to provide greater returns with lower volatility and incredible consistency – what's not to like? A lot, as it turns out from a psychological perspective, which is why value investing has endured and is likely to continue to endure as an investable factor.

The psychology of value investing

To illustrate the behavioral roots of value investing, let us turn our attention to, of all places, the pineapple. As described in the School of Life's, 'Why We Hate Cheap Things' presentation, Christopher Columbus was the first European to taste the pineapple and he was immediately taken with its odd form and acidic sweetness. Columbus tried to transport some of these spiky treasures back to the Old World but they proved hard to ship, which made them exceedingly rare. Accordingly, in Columbus' time a single pineapple cost roughly $5,000! Rare and precious as they were, they began to be fetishized by royalty. Catherine the Great and Charles II were both noted pineapple boosters, but their enthusiasm was unrivaled by the Fourth Earl of Dunmore who had a temple constructed to honor the fruit. By the 19th century though, things were beginning to change. Large pineapple farms now existed on Hawaii and improvements in transportation technology now made it far easier to transport pineapples. As pineapples become more ubiquitous, they began to be ignored, and now sell for about $1.50. The pineapple, of course, is the same as it ever was, but our perception of its value and even quality are dramatically diminished by its decreased price. It seems unlikely that we savor our fruit salad today with a fraction of the intensity of, say, Catherine the Great.

The story of the pineapple demonstrates the close link between price and perceived worth, an idea that was proven artfully by the work of a "horizontal wine tasting" conducted by Stanford Professor Baba Shiv. Shiv had participants lie on their backs in an fMRI machine and gave them carefully titrated doses of wine, each with an accompanying price tag. He then measured the brain activity of the participants as they sipped each of the wines, looking for a relationship between price and cerebral processing. Specifically, Shiv wanted to examine the part of the brain, the ventral medial prefrontal cortex, that we know codes for pleasure.

Sure enough, participants showed more activity in the pleasure centers of the brain when they thought they were drinking $90 wine versus $10 wine. The only problem was that it was all $10 wine! The participants were given the same wine in each condition, meaning the differences in pleasurable brain activity were attributable directly to perceived differences in price rather than the quality of the wine itself. All else being equal, we look to price as the foremost determinant of quality.

For much of our pre-industrial past conflating price and value made perfect sense. Artisans crafted goods by hand and the more care that was put into the creation, the better it tended to be. Today, in a period of automation and cheap access to natural resources, the relationship between cost and value is more tenuous than ever and in capital markets it can be accurately said to be inverse. The more you pay, the less you get. Behavioral investors must create processes that allow them to decouple the spurious mental correlation between price and value and think like a child. A child, who, knowing nothing of the price or provenance of a toy, sets it to the side to engage with the truly interesting part of the gift: the box.

A second psychological root of the enduring efficacy of value investing is what Daniel Kahneman refers to as What You See Is All There Is, which he (mercifully) shortens to WYSIATI. This idea suggests that there are two parts to evaluating any message – the story and the source of the story. The story itself triggers the automatic thinking ("System 1 thinking") and is the easiest and most immediate means by which we make a decision. Evaluating the source of the story requires a great deal more time, attention and intellectual horsepower, and therefore may not receive adequate attention. As Kahneman suggests, we tend to react to the content of a message reflexively without stopping to determine whether the source of the story was water cooler gossip or the *New York Times*. As Kahneman says in *Thinking, Fast and Slow*, "System 1 is radically insensitive to both the quality and the quantity of the information that gives rise to impressions and intuitions."[119]

What You See Is All There Is applies to value investing inasmuch as the stock price is the story and the fundamentals that underlie that price are the source of the story. Most investors, reflexive and cognitively lazy

[119]   D. Kahneman, *Thinking, Fast and Slow*, p. 86.

as they are, react solely to the story without ever pausing to consider the veracity of its origins. Barberis, Mukherjee and Wang demonstrate this very thing in their paper, 'Prospect Theory and Stock Returns: An Empirical Test.' The researchers show that, "For many investors, their mental representation of a stock is given by the distribution of the stock's past returns. The most obvious reason why people might adopt this representation is because they believe the past return distribution to be a good and easily accessible proxy for the object they are truly interested in, namely the distribution of the stock's future returns." Barberis and team go on to demonstrate that this leads investors to load up on lottery like stocks with dramatic past returns; findings that held across 46 countries from 1926 to 2010.

Our minds are primed to think that all we see is all that will ever be. And so much of the difficulty of investing stems from the fact that "what you see is exactly the opposite of what you get." Stocks that have done well in the past three to five years tend to do poorly for the next few years. Those who make many trades tend to be outperformed by those who make few trades. This tendency for black to be white and up to be down is what I have often referred to as "Wall Street Bizarro World" and it accounts for the staying power of value strategies.

But value investing isn't just counterintuitive, it actually causes us physical pain. Eisenberger and Lieberman set out to test the hypothesis that social isolation can cause real pain by asking participants to play a computer game. In the game, players think that they are playing with two other players, who will all throw a ball back and forth to one another. In reality, the other two players are computer controlled and are designed to isolate the participant after a period of including them in the ball throwing activity. The researchers found that this social exclusion generated brain activity in the anterior cingulate cortex and the insula, the same parts of the brain activated by real physical pain. Value strategies are the investment equivalent of not getting the ball thrown to you and by definition require you to zig when others are zagging.

It's no wonder then that growth funds outnumber value funds by fully 70%. Value investing is sensible, empirically robust and has behavioral roots that make it psychologically and physically hard to execute, passing all three hurdles of a sound behavioral investment idea. It's worth it, but nobody ever said it would be easy.

The evidence for momentum

Momentum is a financial extrapolation of Newton's first law of motion: every object in a state of uniform motion tends to remain in that state of motion.[120] As Corey Hoffstein of Newfound Research puts it, "Momentum is a system of investing that buys and sells based upon recent returns. Momentum investors buy outperforming securities and avoid – or sell short – underperforming ones... They assume outperforming securities will continue to perform in absence of significant headwinds."[121]

Digging a little deeper, there are actually two types of momentum: absolute and relative. Absolute momentum compares a stock's recent performance to its own historical performance, whereas relative momentum examines the moves of a security relative to other securities. Both rely on a similar maxim: strength and weakness persist over the short-term.

I will provide a truncated history of momentum research below; those interested in a more comprehensive take should read the work of Gary Antonacci (*Dual Momentum Investing*) and Corey Hoffstein ('Two Centuries of Momentum' white paper). Although viewed by some value investing purists as voodoo, momentum actually has a two-century-long history of empirical support.

As early as 1838, James Grant published a volume that examined the wildly successful trading strategy of English economist David Ricardo. Grant says of Ricardo's success:

> "As I have mentioned the name of Mr. Ricardo, I may observe that he amassed his immense fortune by a scrupulous attention to what he called his own three golden rules, the observance of which he used to press on his private friends. These were, 'Never refuse an

---

[120] G. Antonacci, *Dual Momentum Investing: An Innovative Strategy for Higher Returns with Lower Risk* (McGraw-Hill, 2014), p. 13.
[121] C. Hoffstein, 'Two Centuries of Momentum,' Newfound Research.

option when you can get it,'—'Cut short your losses,'—'Let your profits run on.' By cutting short one's losses, Mr. Ricardo meant that when a member had made a purchase of stock, and prices were falling, he ought to resell immediately. And by letting one's profits run on he meant, that when a member possessed stock, and prices were raising, he ought not to sell until prices had reached their highest, and were beginning again to fall. These are, indeed, golden rules, and may be applied with advantage to innumerable other transactions than those connected with the Stock Exchange."[122]

Although it had been practiced ad hoc for years, the first rigorous empirical examination of momentum was produced by Herbert Jones and Alfred Cowles III in 1937. Jones and Cowles found that from 1920 to 1935, "taking one year as the unit of measurement… the tendency is very pronounced for stocks which have exceeded the median in one year to exceed it also in the year following."[123]

By the 1950s, investment newsletter author George Chestnutt had this to say of momentum strategies:

"Which is the best policy? To buy a strong stock that is leading the advance, or to shop around for a sleeper or behind-the-market stock in the hope that it will catch up? On the basis of statistics covering thousands of individual examples, the answer is very clear as to where the best probabilities lie. Many more times than not, it is better to buy the leaders and leave the laggards alone. In the market, as in many other phases of life, the strong get stronger, and the weak get weaker."[124]

A contemporary of Chestnutt, Nicholas Darvas introduced "BOX theory," wherein he bought stocks reaching new highs (i.e., having broken out of their old box) and hedged his bets with tight stop losses. Said Darvas of his methods, "I keep out in a bear market and leave such exceptional stocks to those who don't mind risking their money against the market trend."[125] Robert Levy introduced the concept of relative

[122] Hoffstein, 'Two Centuries of Momentum.'
[123] Antonacci, *Dual Momentum Investing*, p. 15.
[124] Antonacci, *Dual Momentum Investing*, p. 16.
[125] Hoffstein, 'Two Centuries of Momentum.'

strength in the late 1960s, but following his efforts momentum went largely ignored for nearly three decades.

As the fundamental investing approach of Benjamin Graham (and later Warren Buffett) began to take hold, momentum was increasingly seen as a form of near-charlatanism. Buffett himself minces no words when discussing his distaste for price momentum: "I always find it extraordinary that so many studies are made of price and volume behavior, the stuff of chartists. Can you imagine buying an entire business simply because the price of the business had been marked up substantially last week and the week before?"[126]

In more recent years, momentum has seen an increase in acceptance among theorists, because whatever mortal quirks may drive its presence, its persistence and pervasiveness are undeniable. In 'Returns to Buying Winners and Selling Losers: Implications for Stock Market Efficiency' by Jegadeesh and Titman, we see that from 1965 through 1989, winning stocks continued to outperform losing stocks on average over the next six to 12 months. And the size of the outperformance was sizeable – 1% per month, even after adjusting for return differences owing to other risk factors.[127]

Indeed, the effects of momentum tend to be pervasive and not limited with respect to market, place or time. Chris Geczy and Mikhail Samonov conducted what is affectionately referred to as the "world's longest backtest" and found that momentum effects have persisted in the US since 1801![128] Momentum signals have worked well in the UK since the Victorian Age (Chabot, Ghysels and Jagannathan, 2009) and have proven their power and persistence across 40 countries and more than a dozen asset classes.[129] So deep-seated are our psychological tendencies toward momentum that, "the momentum premium has

---

[126] Buffett, 'The Superinvestors of Graham-and-Doddsville.'

[127] N. Jegadeesh and S. Titman, 'Returns to buying winners and selling losers: Implications for stock market efficiency,' *The Journal of Finance* 48:1 (March 1993), pp. 65–91.

[128] C. Geczy and M. Samonov, 'Two centuries of price return momentum,' *Financial Analysts Journal* 72:5 (September/October 2016).

[129] C. S. Asness, A. Frazzini, R. Israel and T. J. Moskowitz, 'Fact, fiction and momentum investing,' *Journal of Portfolio Management* (Fall 2014).

been a part of markets since their very existence, well before researchers studied them as a science." To put it mildly, it seems as though the empirical proof condition of the three-part test is met. Next, let's examine the reasons why momentum exists and whether or not those reasons are behavioral at heart.

The psychology of momentum

It is innate tendency of humankind to project the present state of things into the future indefinitely. In so doing, we create one of the most important and exploitable market anomalies – momentum.

Most academic theories posit a direct, linear relationship between risk and reward: Want a bigger return? Take a riskier bet. But both Jegadeesh and Titman (1993) and Fama and French (through their three-factor model) found no evidence of a risk-based explanation of the momentum effect. Essentially, momentum defied the laws of financial physics and offered greater reward with no additional risk. In the absence of risk-based explanations for its outperformance, researchers have turned to behavior as the best possible descriptor of why momentum effects occur.

Daniel, Hirshleifer and Subrahmanyam propose two behavioral patterns – self-attribution and overconfidence – as the likely genesis of momentum effects. Overconfidence is intuitive enough, but to understand self-attribution, think of being in traffic. If you accidentally cut someone else off during your morning commute, you're likely to ascribe that behavior to an honest mistake or not being fully caffeinated yet. However, when you are cut off by someone else it's unlikely that you are so gracious and contextual in your assumptions about their behavior. We tend to ascribe our own successes and blame our failings on externalities, whereas we are quick to ascribe others' failings to permanent personal characteristics. I cut you off because I haven't had my coffee, you cut me off because you're a bad person.

Investors are generally overconfident about their skill and sources of information and when, for reasons of luck or skill, their bets pay off in the form of rising prices, that overconfidence is further bolstered. This overconfidence becomes paired with self-attribution in the sense that investors attribute the rising prices to their own stock picking genius and not some combination of luck and skill, which is more likely the truth.

This cycle of overconfidence and self-congratulations leads rising prices to keep rising. Markets that move against the investor's initial thesis are of course dismissed as so much bad luck, leaving the ego and tendency to self-congratulate very much intact for the next bit of good luck.

Other theorists propose different reasons for momentum effects, but still put behavior in the driver's seat. Edwards (1968) as well as Tversky and Kahneman (1974) suggest that the responsible behaviors are anchoring and insufficient adjustment. Anchoring can best be understood by contemplating the words of the dandruff commercial that, "You never get a second chance to make a first impression." When you meet someone new you begin forming opinions of them within seconds. These first impressions, or anchors, then set the guardrails within which future impressions tend to fall. If you meet someone and find them affable and kind, affability and kindness will be what you will assume from them in the future. Likewise, investors anchor on the current price and trajectory of a stock and project a similar trajectory into the future without end. Rooted as we are in these first impressions, we are slow to update our beliefs about the changing fortunes of a company, even in the presence of new and compelling data.

In a related vein, Wason (1960) suggests that momentum effects are the product of confirmation bias and representativeness. People make a purchase believing what they believe ("This stock is good!"), do not want to be disabused of those notions (confirmation bias) and look at recent price moves as being indicative of future moves (representativeness).

One final behavioral explanation for momentum has to do with investor reaction to information, with both overreaction and underreaction pointed to as possible reasons for the persistence of momentum. The idea of overreaction is that investors are greedy, return chasing fools who drive prices ever higher. Underreaction is the thesis that information is only slowly incorporated into prices for reasons ranging from inattention, to liquidity constraints, to the tendency toward conservatism mentioned throughout this book.

Although I've tried to present each of the various behavioral explanations for momentum in this section, I must admit I really don't care which is the "right" answer. Because whatever the specific reasons why momentum exists, the evidence seems clear that the reasons are behavioral, and that's good enough for me. Momentum has existed for hundreds of years and has persisted for two decades post-discovery. This sort of staying power in capital markets full of hungry arbitrageurs is always the mark of human psychology.

Many experts consider momentum to be not just a factor but *the* factor. Fama and French don't mince words: "The premier market anomaly is momentum. Stocks with low returns over the past year tend to have low returns for the next few months, and stocks with high past returns tend to have high future returns." As James O'Shaughnessy says, "of all the beliefs on Wall Street, price momentum makes efficient market theorists howl the loudest." In a perfect world, there would be no good reason to pay more for a business today than yesterday simply because of positive price action. But this isn't a perfect world, it's a world ruled by human behavior and thus exhibits all of the attendant quirks.

Annualized premia for value, size, beta and momentum, 1927–2014

Value	5.0%
Size	3.4%
Beta	8.4%
Momentum	9.5%

Source: B. Carlson, 'Why Momentum Investing Works,' July 7, 2015

Reflexivity: the dance of value and momentum

"Why, then, 'tis none to you, for there is nothing either good or bad, but thinking makes it so."

— WILLIAM SHAKESPEARE, *HAMLET*

Like peanut butter and chocolate, momentum and value are wonderful on their own, but even better together. Cliff Asness says it best in his piece, 'A New Core Equity Paradigm':

> "Value and momentum remain the two strongest findings of academic and practitioner research of the last 30 years. While academics continually identify new market anomalies, which purport to offer significant risk-adjusted excess returns, and the Street routinely spins new stories to sell them, value and momentum stand head-and-shoulders above the rest – no other styles have performed so well, for so long, and in so many places. Both value and momentum have long histories of providing attractive returns, have performed well across markets and across asset classes, and have persisted for decades after their discoveries. Importantly, the two strategies perform even better when combined."

Value and momentum work, independently and in concert, precisely because they exhibit the three hallmarks of an investable factor: empirical evidence, theoretical soundness and a behavioral foundation. One of the most infamous psychological studies ever conducted, commonly cited to demonstrate the corruptive influence of power, also serves as a powerful tutorial on the human tendency to reify the present and project it into the future indefinitely.

Any Psych 100 course is likely to feature discussion about the Stanford prison experiment – a mock prison set up in the basement of the psychology department to study the impact of the power differential between prisoners and their guards. Twenty-four men, mostly white, mostly middle class, were recruited for the study and were arbitrarily assigned to either a "guard" or "prisoner" condition. Guards underwent a brief training in which they were instructed not to physically harm or withhold food from the prisoners. The prisoners were "arrested" in their homes by the actual Palo Alto police, who subjected them to a booking process identical to that experienced by real criminals. Although the roles were randomly assigned, the participants almost immediately began taking on either the ruthlessness or the helplessness of the group that they were assigned to represent.

Originally slated for two weeks, the study was called off after only six days owing to the inhumane treatment of prisoners by the guards. Day one passed uneventfully, but as early as day two the prisoners had begun to revolt, barricading themselves in a room by using their mattresses as a shield. Upset with this small uprising, the guards retaliated, placing offending prisoners in solitary confinement and denying them food and water. The guards eventually subjected some prisoners to searing verbal taunts, instructed compliant prisoners to harass and belittle the noncompliant, and forced them to urinate and defecate in small buckets that they would not allow to be emptied. Philip Zimbardo, the psychologist overseeing the study, became so enthralled by the interactions that he was impervious to the ill treatment the prisoners were receiving. It was only when his then-girlfriend (now wife) Christina Maslach came by to interview some of the subjects that she pointed out the horrors being perpetrated and encouraged Zimbardo to shut down the experiment.

The positive feedback loop that Zimbardo experienced behaviorally occurs everywhere – from financial markets to marriages to nature – and can be defined as an event that is amplified by the very event that gave rise to it. Chemical reactions cause heat that catalyzes further reactions. One cow moving causes three cows to move which causes a stampede. Ponzi schemes are better able to attract new victims as they grow and have an increased ability to make false payments.

Zimbardo set the loop in motion by assigning status to the guards and prisoners, who then began to engage in guard-like and prisoner-like behavior, which further enhanced the reality of the whole enterprise. It is by virtue of just such a feedback loop that a Stanford freshman could be turned into a profane, screaming guard forcing a classmate to sleep near his own feces in just under a week.

But nothing lasts forever and even the most virulent feedback loop eventually folds in on itself. Donella Meadows says it best: "Positive feedback loops are sources of growth, explosion, erosion, and collapse in systems. A system with an unchecked positive loop ultimately will destroy itself. That's why there are so few of them. Usually a negative loop will kick in sooner or later." Eventually, the excesses of a feedback loop become its very undoing and the whole process begins again in reverse. Capital markets, driven by the same human actors that arbitrarily dehumanize their peers, are nothing more than a series of positive and negative feedback loops careening toward and away from the mythical notion of fair value. This circular relationship between cause and effect is known as *reflexivity*.

George Soros, who has written most lucidly about this concept, states that two conditions must be present for reflexive markets to exist: 1. Thinking participants whose view of the world is partial and distorted 2. These distorted views can become self-reinforcing. We have discussed at length the sociological, physiological, neurological and psychological distortions to which market participants are prone and our discussions of momentum and WYSIATI give ample evidence that belief can be self-reinforcing. Both conditions are abundantly met, resulting in a market that is episodically inefficient with an overarching pull towards efficiency. The market is both never fully efficient and always crashing toward efficiency. The misunderstanding of this notion is the root cause of most disagreements among the various schools of thought and the source of bad policy around money management.

Hardcore passive management enthusiasts overemphasize the overarching pull toward efficiency and mistake the general trend for the Gospel Truth. In so doing, they overlook valuable opportunities for return enhancement that are available to behavioral investors. Advocates for traditional active management are quick to point out the behavioral anomalies present in the market but mistake the occasional presence of inefficiencies with the ability to spot and appropriately act on them in real time. The two conditions of market efficiency – the price is always right and no free lunch – don't hang together as some active managers would like to believe. Markets can fluctuate wildly from true value, but it can still be very difficult to beat the market. A true understanding of the reflexive nature of markets requires a healthy respect for their overall bent towards efficiency with a rules-based system for capitalizing on hints of inefficiency. Nothing else will do.

Returning to our two conditions of reflexivity (imperfect views that are self-reinforcing), it becomes easy to see how a feedback loop is set in motion. To catalyze the whole process we need some bit of news or information to which people can react. The Fed, which releases 45,000 pieces of economic data each month, and the 24/7 financial news outlets, are happy to oblige here. That information is taken in by market participants, each with their own subjective experience borne of cultural, psychological and experiential differences. The sense that is made of this information as it passes through our subjective meat grinder is necessarily partial and imperfect, nicely fulfilling the first of Soros' conditions. This information, having now been processed, is acted upon in ways that can often become self-reinforcing.

Take Amazon (AMZN) for example. Amazon had its initial public offering (IPO) in 1997, billed as "the world's biggest bookstore." The nascent company offered the prospect of disrupting a stodgy old industry and received an avalanche of great press as a result. That good press has resulted in attractive gains for the stock that has gone from $18/share to over $1000/share in just about 20 years. Along the way, the soaring market cap, bolstered by positive beliefs, has provided a number of real benefits. Amazon's success has allowed them to fund further growth at remarkably low financing costs. Their reputation has allowed them to recruit some of the best talent in the tech industry as well as hide costs by including stock options as a large part of employee compensation packages. This is not to suggest that Amazon, who I truly believe to be a once-in-a-generation brand, is all hype. Rather, it is to demonstrate how early positive or negative beliefs about a company can produce economic realities that bring about the very thing imagined. Amazon's success is absolutely a result of hard work, great talent, and product innovation, but that process has been greatly abetted by the subjective belief that it was bound to happen.

A similar feedback loop can be initiated, often more violently, when news is bad. The 1973 oil crisis resulted in rumors that toilet paper would be in short supply. These rumors led to subsequent runs on the grocery story where fearful citizens stocked up. This led to, you guessed it, an actual shortage of toilet paper that was wholly a consequence of perception.

More consequentially, this was evident in the housing crisis of the late 2000s. As housing prices began their precipitous decline, more and more homeowners found themselves *underwater*, meaning that the market value of the home was less than the mortgage. This provides ample reason for the homeowner to walk away from the home, declare bankruptcy and be free of the whole affair. Walking away means that homes are not taken care of and causes a glut of supply, both of which decrease prices and cause further walking away. Banks, on whose balance sheets the mortgages reside, are then undercapitalized and unable to lend to stimulate further economic growth. This lack of capital influx causes higher unemployment, which leads to an ability to meet a mortgage note, and the whole mess starts anew.

Reflexivity in nature

Feedback loops occur in nature and provide a useful means for thinking about the give and take of financial markets. Consider the "evolutionary arms race" between nectarivorous birds and the plants that support them. The birds, like hummingbirds, evolve long beaks to gain access to the life giving nectar in flowers. The flowers, for their part, evolve longer and longer trumpet-like shapes to prevent the birds from accessing the nectar. The bird in turn develops a longer beak and the cycle continues. This dynamism is also present in financial markets that resist cheap characterizations of being either totally efficient or grossly inefficient.

Reflexive processes begin with a kernel of truth (e.g., Amazon is going to change the way that books are sold) that is filtered through a subjective lens that leads to self-reinforcing feedback loops. These loops persist for a season, until a new bit of subjectively interpreted information sends them off, often in the other direction.

While efficient market theorists, convinced that the price is as right as it will ever be, suggest buying the whole market, and efficient market critics seek to purchase stocks that have become disconnected from fair value, behavioral investors take a middle path, understanding that the question is not "Is the price right?" but "Where is the price headed?"

When considered from a behavioral perspective, the price is never right but is often not wrong enough to be predictable. By combining value, momentum and an understanding of reflexive processes, the behavioral investor seeks to invest in a basket of stocks that imperfect subjective appraisal has unfairly punished, but that a positive feedback loop will soon reward with a push toward fair value. Imagining a reflexive process as a trip, value is the distance to be traveled and momentum is the speed at which the journey will take place. Combining value and momentum is the investment equivalent of a cross-country bullet train that covers a great deal of ground in the shortest amount of time possible.

Financial markets are forever headed toward true value without ever quite arriving. Money management approaches that doggedly insist on adherence to bottom-up fundamentals will be undone by long periods during which emotion trumps logic. Conversely, those who emphasize market aberrations fail to realize that the market is mostly right most of the time. A behaviorally-informed approach embraces the reflexive reality of markets by emphasizing fundamentals and trends in tandem.

Epilogue. Endure to the End

"I have heard of people who amuse themselves conducting imaginary operations in the stock market to prove with imaginary dollars how right they are. Sometimes these ghost gamblers make millions. It is very easy to be a plunger that way. It is like the old story of the man who was going to fight a duel the next day.

His second asked him, 'Are you a good shot?'

'Well,' said the duelist, 'I can snap the stem of a wineglass at twenty paces,' and he looked modest.

'That's all very well,' said the unimpressed second. 'But can you snap the stem of the wineglass while the wineglass is pointing a loaded pistol straight at your heart?'"

— EDWIN LEFÈVRE, *REMINISCENCES OF A STOCK OPERATOR*

IT CAN NOW be said that you are among the best-educated people in the world with respect to the ins and outs of behavioral investing. But the most important part of being a well-educated behavioral investor is understanding just how little education matters. The world is full of well-educated people who have made stupid choices, a phenomenon referred to by scientists as "dysrationalia." A survey of Canadian Mensa

Club members, whose membership is limited to those in the top two percentiles of IQ, demonstrates this nicely. Among those surveyed, 44% believed in astrology, 51% bought into biorhythms and 56% believed that Earth has been visited by aliens.

Martin Heidegger, a well-respected philosopher, used his keen mind in support of the Nazi party, using spurious arguments to defend reprehensible behavior. William Crookes, who discovered the element thallium, was repeatedly swindled by spiritual mediums but could never be persuaded to give up his spiritualist beliefs. And Isaac Newton, a scientist without equal, lost his fortune in the South Sea Bubble through a fundamental misunderstanding of the nature of markets and human behavior. Smarts, it would seem, are no guarantee of being a rational actor.

Yes, the lessons you have just learned will be least available to your mind when they are most needed. Studies suggest that we lose roughly 13% of our cognitive capacity under stress, lending credence to Nassim Taleb's advice: "Even once we are aware of our biases, we must recognize that knowledge does not equal behavior. The solution lies in designing and adopting an investment process that is at least partially robust to behavioral decision-making errors." In a very real sense, whatever success you achieve as a result of having read this book will come, not as a result of personal genius, but through acceptance of personal mediocrity.

When it comes to investing, you're not that great – sociology, physiology and neurology have seen to that – but that doesn't mean that there is no greatness within you. Becoming a behavioral investor is fundamentally about scraping away all of the bad lessons and fallacious visions that you've been sold and realizing that doing less gets you more. It is understanding that the less you need to be special, the more special you'll become. Most of all, it's about realizing that knowing yourself and building your wealth are parallel pursuits that can only be achieved as you have the personal courage to admit that you're pretty average, and in so doing, put yourself on the path to becoming so much more. Greatness is your birthright, specialness is your equilibrium, now just stop trying so hard and go and get it.

Index

CPSIA information can be obtained
at www.ICGtesting.com
Printed in the USA
BVHW081923190419
545943BV00004B/7/P